GUIDANCE AND COUNSELING

FOR CATHOLIC SCHOOLS

GUIDANCE

AND COUNSELING

FOR

CATHOLIC

SCHOOLS

LAWRENCE J. SAALFELD
Central Catholic High School
Portland, Oregon

LOYOLA UNIVERSITY PRESS
Chicago

Saalfeld, Lawrence J

    Guidance and counseling for Catholic schools. Chicago, Loyola University Press, 1958.

    264 p.   illus.   24 cm.

    Includes bibliography.

    1. Personnel services in education.   2. Catholic Church—Education. 1. Title.

LC485.S2   371.42   58—14343 ‡

Library of Congress

Nihil obstat

Martinus Thielen

Censor Delegatus

Imprimatur

✠ Eduardus D. Howard

Archiepiscopus Portlandensis in Oregon

Portlandiae

In festo Annunciationis Beatae Mariae Virginis

die 25a martii, 1958

LC
485
.S2

PREFACE

The nature of boys and girls, the needs that result from their very nature as human beings, and the problems that they experience do not differ radically whether these boys and girls are in public schools or in Catholic schools. The attitude that is taken toward their nature and needs and the methods used in the attempt to help solve their problems, however, will necessarily be quite different. A Catholic school must attach the greatest importance to the fact that these young people were born for heaven, that they have an obligation of accepting a body of revealed truth, that they owe obedience to the law of God and to the Church of God, and that dependence should be placed upon grace and the means of acquiring grace rather than on purely natural methods of solving problems. Moreover, Catholic schools often do not have the ample resources to provide the personnel or extensive services suggested in the many excellent books on guidance for the needs of public schools.

GUIDANCE AND COUNSELING FOR CATHOLIC SCHOOLS seeks to outline a practical method proper to the problems and needs of Catholic students. The principal aims are to set forth in an orderly fashion the duties of personnel, to recommend procedures for initiating a program, and to offer means of implementing a guidance and counseling program guaranteed to be *distinctly Christian*. The book is not designed as an extensive technical work, but as a "how-to-do-it" manual for principals and personnel. Much of it is applicable to the elementary school.

Chapters 1-11 deal with the organization, integration, and operation of the many phases of Christian guidance and counseling. Chapter 12 offers specimen forms and other materials that may be adapted to meet the needs of the individual school. Material which might perhaps have formed part of this book but which has been published separately under the title of *Group Guidance Units for Catholic High Schools* provides the busy teacher with a series of day-by-day units designed to assist in the formation of a Christian character and personality in boys and girls.

The author wishes to express his gratitude to all those whose encouragement brought these books to completion. Special appreciation is due to the Most Reverend Edward D. Howard, D.D., archbishop of Portland in Oregon, to the Reverend Willis L. Whalen, principal of Central Catholic High School, and to the many priests and sisters there for the years of cooperation that resulted in a working system of Christian guidance. The author also acknowledges the valuable assistance of the sisters of Marylhurst College, of his own sister, and of all who gave their prayers and enthusiasm.

A book suggesting methods of guidance of youth could not be written without revealing the careful and loving guidance which the author received from others in his own formative years. To the most dear and influential of all, my mother, this work is dedicated in affection and tribute.

May everyone concerned with the growth of the adolescent to Christian maturity find this book a helpful tool. May the Holy Spirit pour forth His light and aid upon all who cooperate in His work of building the kingdom of God upon earth.

L. J. S.

FEAST OF MARY THE QUEEN
MAY 31, 1958

CONTENTS

CHAPTER ONE

THE NATURE AND NECESSITY

OF GUIDANCE

Fifty years ago very little was being said or written about the obligation of the school to provide guidance services for its pupils. Zealous teachers were interested then, as they are interested today and as they have always been interested, in the general welfare and all-round development of the children committed to their care; but they did not look upon guidance as an activity requiring special training and the use of special techniques. The situation is quite different today. There is no teacher who does not know that guidance is a very important function of the school. There is no large school system that does not have some organized plan for rendering guidance. Almost innumerable books have been written on the subject, and we have educational magazines that are devoted to the task of supplying material on the subject of guidance.

THE NATURE OF GUIDANCE

Despite the fact that so much is being done in the field of guidance, there is still a certain obscurity as to the precise meaning of the term. Crow and Crow speak of the "considerable confusion concerning terminology" and of the attempts at clarification being made by the National Association of Guidance and Personnel Associations, the National Vocational Guidance Association, and the Federal Office of Education.[1] Because such confusion does exist, it is desirable that the meaning of the term as it is used in this book should be clearly explained.

In a broad sense anything that society does to educate its children may be considered guidance. Children of the Naskapi Indians were taught to catch caribou in pens, to hunt for small game, to fish, to gather berries for food, to weave from rabbitskins, to make birch canoes, and to construct conical shelters covered with bark or skin. They had their tribal customs and their religious rites. Children living in this culture were so guided by their parents and those with whom they associated that they accepted the culture and helped to perpetuate it. When in our elementary schools of today we teach children reading, writing, arithmetic, and the social studies we are purposefully endeavoring to prepare them to become useful and contented members of our own culture. Whatever the school does, then, can in some sense be said to be an attempt at guidance.

So great is the power of the curriculum and of life within the school to guide that Cardinal Newman refused to consider any other form of guidance necessary. He did not think that the principal of a secondary school need do anything special to make a boy a good citizen. If the school were well conducted and if teachers were efficient, the very process of receiving an education would make every boy as good a citizen as it was possible for him to become. Some have felt that Cardinal Newman's position on this point was extreme, but it is nevertheless true that the school does exercise some guidance in everything that it does. We are guiding a child in a certain direction when we insist that he must take at least one course in algebra or when we require him to study a modern language for two or more years.

By universal consent, however, the teaching of subjects is not looked upon as being a guidance activity. By guidance we understand all the measures that are undertaken, either in groups or individually, for the purpose of assisting individuals to make prudent

---

[1] Lester D. Crow and Alice Crow, *An Introduction to Guidance,* p. 50. New York: American Book Company, 1951.

decisions concerning their choices or their conduct. Before we can assist individuals in making decisions, we need to know something about the abilities and social background of these individuals. For this reason the gathering of data concerning individuals is looked upon as part of the guidance activity of a school. Guidance includes the giving of helpful information concerning steps to be taken or things to be done. Guidance includes answering questions prompted by the desire of individuals to know what they had best do. Guidance may be given to groups or it may be given to individuals. The attempt to help a single individual is often called counseling as opposed to guidance, and this book will consistently speak of guidance when there is question of work with groups and of counseling when there is question of work with individuals. As a matter of fact, the two words can be used almost interchangeably. If we counsel an individual, we are giving him guidance. If we address an entire group and discuss with them what should be done, we are counseling the group. By rather common agreement, however, counseling is looked upon as one of the forms that guidance takes and is restricted to work with individuals rather than with groups.

Certain subjects of the curriculum, especially courses on religion, citizenship, and family life, provide numerous occasions for referring to choices that should be made and conduct that should be pursued. We would not consider as a guidance activity the teaching of these subjects as such, but a teacher can, and oftentimes does, use such subjects as a means of giving guidance. There can be guidance in the classroom as well as in the homeroom. A great deal of guidance is also rendered in the club program, in the activities of the student council, and in the work of student government.

THE NEED OF YOUTH FOR GUIDANCE

Society cannot safely permit the youth of today to attempt to shape their lives without guidance. The youth of yesterday, in comparison with youth of the atomic age, encountered simple hazards and elementary obstacles in growth to maturity. Adults today know that the complexity of our modern environment gives birth to grave problems and that the broader experiences possible for the young can easily cause the propensity to sin to outweigh the attraction of sanctity. Keeping pace with the speed of American life throws youth into situations which often confuse even the mature and bewilder the strong. The ease of communication and the rapidity of transportation quickly carry the adolescent away from the protection of the home and school into a sweeping range of influences difficult to control. Even his more extensive education, which exposes him to more knowledge and information, conspires to give him less training of the will or too little practice in Christian action. All in all, mid-twentieth-century life demands of youth knowledge, habits, and virtues far beyond the simple requirements of previous periods of history.

Obviously, youth should not be expected to face the new world alone. The adolescent should not be left without adequate preparation to meet and master the elements threatening his successful future with its multiplied needs and adjustments. Depth of soul life, stronger character, a more enlightened mind, and a strengthened will are among the essential qualities to be developed if a young person is to be truly prepared "for what he must be and for what he must do here below, in order to attain the sublime end for which he was created."[2]

Parents today humbly and willingly recognize an inability so to prepare the child in all the necessary areas. Moreover, the school also acknowledges the insufficiency of its classroom instruction in traditional subject matter alone to educate the total individual for the exigencies of life. As a result both home and school have adopted a wider vista of education and have continually searched for additional means of equipping the whole child for his mission in life. Guidance and counseling services have taken root and have been accepted as playing a vital role in the guaranteeing of a well-rounded education.

Pope Pius XI justified the place of guidance in the school when he wrote: "Christian education takes in the whole aggregate of human life, physical and spiritual, intellectual and moral, individual, domestic and social, not with a view of reducing it in any way, but

[2] Pius XI, *Christian Education of Youth*, p. 3. New York: The America Press, 1936.

in order to elevate, regulate and perfect it, in accordance with the example and teaching of Christ."[3] This statement gives us the goals for which guidance must strive: the wholesome adjustment of the child, his development to his greatest excellence as a Christian, and his growth to competency in the society of the mystical body.

In the schools of today, then, guidance will have to devise the Christian method of satisfying the needs and aiding the adjustment of the student in every phase of life; counseling will have to lead the student individually to responsible self-direction in solving the problems accompanying growth to Christian maturity. The evolution of an organized plan for Christianizing these services which are truly works of mercy will be the hopeful objective of parents and educators. The result should be a program of training for citizenship on earth that merits membership in the kingdom of heaven.

Since high-school students are in the critical period of formation, greater emphasis has been placed upon the role of guidance and counseling at the secondary level. It is well known, however, that the attitudes and emotional patterns acquired in the early school years persist through high school and into adult life. If the student of a Catholic school is to develop the maximum personal responsibility and is to acquire the habit of prudent Christian action, guidance directed toward the achieving of these ends must begin at the elementary-school level. Perhaps the most fundamental task of the elementary school is to encourage the development of each child in terms of his capacity. His ability to make progress spiritually, intellectually, socially, emotionally, and physically depends upon the interaction of all phases of his life. A teacher who is familiar with typical developmental patterns should be able to deal successfully with individual growth patterns and to recognize serious deviations that call for expert diagnosis and assistance. When Thomas, whose intelligence and reading ability were above average, came to the sixth grade, he began to have serious difficulty with arithmetic. He showed very poor comprehension during classroom instruction based largely on material written on the blackboard. He seemed to have

[3] *Ibid.,* p. 32.

little difficulty with similar material when his teacher worked with him individually. There were no physical examinations in the school he was attending, and it was only at his teacher's suggestion that his eyes be examined that his progressive myopia was discovered. Susan, a normal and happy six-year-old, experienced unusual difficulty in first grade when required to learn the ordinary Catholic prayers. A study of home conditions revealed a serious deficiency in the practice of prayer and a lack of living faith in the members of the family. In such cases a referral to the priests of the parish may be necessary before a real solution can be effected for the child. Poor vision, unhappy family relationships, limited social experiences—these are just a few of the possible causes of arrested development or maladjustment. The teacher cannot be expected to be an expert in psychology, medicine, and sociology; but the teacher who is aware of individual needs will be alert to abnormalities and will refer the child to the proper agencies.

The elementary school has constantly to remind itself of the importance of individual needs no matter how insignificant they may appear to be. It has constantly to resist the pressure that larger classrooms put on the students and the teacher. The elementary school, even more than the secondary school, depends upon the efforts of each teacher to give needed guidance. Catholic insistence on the personal dignity of each child and on the importance of the religion class tends to facilitate guidance; but more explicit attention to the task of aiding students to meet their individual needs and of helping them avail themselves of the avenues of grace and of the services which the community offers is needed to reduce the confusion that our complex society is ever presenting to the young child.

Amid the conflicting standards and pressures of the modern world, the adolescent must solve complex problems of adjustment as well as form habits and make vocational decisions that influence his eternal destiny. A secondary school conscious of the serious obstacles to the Christian formation of students may not safely ignore the consideration of organized guidance services.

The Catholic school faithfully pursuing its Christian objectives has always had the essentials of a satisfactory guidance program in the devotion of teachers to the individual soul and in their constant encouragement of cooperation by students with divine grace. These things have served youth well in the past and should continue to be looked upon as essential means of forming "the supernatural man who thinks, judges and acts constantly and consistently in accordance with right reason."[4] In the past, schools either felt little need of organized guidance services or automatically provided a model program because the intimacy of the small school ensured teacher concern for individual needs.

Currently, however, Catholic schools must face, not only the new problems of the age, but also those resulting from the rapid growth of the school population. While preoccupied with securing a sufficient number of qualified teachers, the administrator may overlook the tendency to impersonal education that too often accompanies such growth. An impersonal type of education prevents the proper guidance of students and jeopardizes the thoroughly Catholic character of the school. Attention to the needs of the individual in soul and body, which should be distinctive of a Catholic school, ought not to be sacrificed in the attempt to educate the masses.

Carefully organized guidance and counseling services can do much to ward off the danger; and in fact such a program, operating efficiently, will capitalize on the advantages of growth in size and enrollment. The influence of more priests, brothers, sisters, and zealous lay teachers upon the individual, the diversified training of teachers, the expanded curriculum, the wider concept of education and its modern facilities, may be marshaled into a highly effective educational system. With these resources added to its traditional sources of strength, Christian education in our times will be assured and perfected. The only need may be a method or plan.

THE TWOFOLD PURPOSE OF GUIDANCE

Whatever may be said of the relationship between the individual and society, it is certain that the individual comes first in point of time. Societies begin to exist when individuals form themselves into

[4] *Ibid.*

groups. We will therefore consider guidance first as something that is needed by the individual and then as something necessary for the welfare of society.

Everyone needs guidance throughout his whole life. He needs the supernatural helps that come to him through the Church, and he needs the natural helps that come to him through association with other human beings. How often has not confidence in oneself and courage for action come through talking with another person! Adolescent boys and girls need these supernatural and natural guides in an urgent way because they are becoming aware of themselves as adults and of their possibilities and responsibilities. They are seriously thinking in terms of ideals and life goals. Their physical maturing is leading them to closer scrutiny of the code of moral and social behavior. They are more self-conscious and therefore sensitive to the least sign of nonacceptance. The school guidance program is concerned with supplying the basic and individual needs of each student so that he becomes able to meet the contingencies of his life now and in the future.

A student needs, not only intellectual training to satisfy his desire for knowledge, but also emotional security and certainty to live out that knowledge. What he learns, in fact, will be tempered by *how* he learns. A striking example of the effect of emotional insecurity is found in the case of a girl who had won a scholarship to an exclusive academy located in a wealthy suburb of Chicago. She came through the first half-year in the upper third of her class. She made friends easily and was well liked. Gradually, however, she became retiring and aloof; she dropped out of intramural sports and withdrew from social activities. Her grades for the year were far below what could have been expected of her. One teacher in talking with her uncovered the difficulty. As the girl had become more intimate with her schoolmates, whose fathers were professional or businessmen, she became more sensitive about her father's occupation, which was an exceedingly humble one. Unable to cope with her feelings of inferiority, she had shrunk from any kind of association with the other girls and had lost whatever interest in schoolwork she may once have possessed.

Every individual has certain basic needs that must be met. His happiness depends upon how he satisfies his needs. Some pupils may more readily apply what they know and thereby meet their own needs. The whole process—taking counsel with oneself, seeking the necessary information and knowledge, applying that knowledge to the particular circumstances of here and now—requires maturity and experience and must be learned. Growth in ability to meet one's individual needs in a wholesome, Christian way should be an outcome of a guidance program.

The welfare of society depends upon this, that each member should make good use of his gifts and talents. Many antisocial tendencies are due to needless frustrations or unhealthy ways of compensating for disappointment and discouragement. The delinquent teen-ager is contributing to the disruption of the social structure; but is not the inability of the docile child to achieve his potentiality also an injury to the community? A young member of a religious order once came in contact with an older man who was conducting some research on intelligence tests. To his own surprise, the young man when tested made a remarkable score, one certainly not indicated by his past accomplishment in his order. In a conference between the two, it turned out that the young man had entered in a class of exceptionally gifted men. Among them he felt overwhelmed and incapable of achieving notable success. Encouraged by the assurance that he was not intellectually inferior, he successfully undertook tasks that he had previously considered impossible. How can society gauge the loss when young people of high ability fail in high school or college because of unhealthy ideas that could have been corrected had guidance been available?

Society itself is a living, dynamic thing, and the Church of God is the mystical body of Christ. Zeal for the common welfare fulfills one of the man's deepest needs and he cannot respond to his strong urge to work in and for society without making his world a more Christian world in which to live. Nothing that a man may do is completely lacking in an effect on society. In particular, those who take upon themselves the responsibilities of family life are affecting the lives of many. "How can we estimate the loss when emotionally immature people marry and then find that marriage is no cure for immaturity? How do we compute the value of the lives that are ruined when a parent projects his own problems onto his children and keeps them from developing the abilities they have?"[5] The society that has happy, well-adjusted citizens will be the better society. The high-school student of today is the citizen of tomorrow, and planned guidance that will make of him a better citizen is now considered a necessity by all.

TYPES OF GUIDANCE SERVICE

There are five types of guidance that are needed both by the individual and by society. It would seem that any attempt at guidance, no matter what its nature may be, can be classified under one or another of these five types.

The first type is physical or health guidance. This is required because knowledge about the body and bodily needs, about food, rest, and wholesome exercise, helps the soul to function unimpeded by an unruly helpmate. Physical energies are to be directed and put into action by reason and will, but practical information about the needs of the body and how to satisfy them prudently will tend to relieve emotional tension and free the intellect for its proper work. Physical energies should be at the service of the higher powers of man and should not be a hindrance to him.

Basic concepts about the health of the body, normal exercise, and sports activities are good for all students. In some matters health guidance is frequently or inseparably connected with moral guidance. Intemperance, for example, is not only physically harmful, but is also immoral. The dignity of the human body as the temple of an immortal soul is a fundamental Catholic doctrine of inestimable value. Its absence in modern thought leaves a void that no amount of exhortation or threat can fill.

The second type is educational guidance. By this is understood guidance in regard to what to study and how to study. There is a

[5] Harry N. Rivlin, "The Role of Mental Health in Education"; in *The Fifty-fourth Yearbook of the National Society for the Study of Education,* Part 2, p. 13. Chicago: National Society for the Study of Education, 1955.

core of common knowledge and understanding that each student must penetrate according to his ability; there are other skills and sciences to which his unique talents and aspirations may direct him. Tests and records, autobiographical and objective, become effective tools in a guidance program for estimating capacities, recording past accomplishments, and tracing growth and progress. These data are then used in planning future tasks.

The benefits of this type of guidance are numerous. First of all, it concentrates on educating the individual and seeks to cultivate the intellectual powers of a unique human person. It fits him to become a communicative member of society. It opens up to him innumerable outlets, ways of expressing his creative talents and clarifying his ambitions and desires. Educational guidance, by directing the individual to activities for which he is fitted and to studies which will prepare him for his lifework, ensures the happiness of achieving something worthwhile. It harmonizes aspirations and achievement.

Closely allied to educational guidance is vocational guidance. Vocational education and guidance, in a large sense, has to do with life ideals and purposes. It is concerned with the spirit and attitude that a student takes to any occupation he decides is his way of being a responsible worker in this world in preparation for the next. It is concerned with the life ideals that a student feels can be motivating forces for him. The highest ideals are not always the strongest motives for action for an individual, since what is highest and most perfect does not appeal to all.

In the strictest sense of the term a vocation is a call to some one of the three great states of life—the priesthood or the religious life, marriage, or a dedicated life in the world. Vocational guidance is therefore concerned first of all with helping students decide to what state of life they are called. In a broader sense vocational guidance means help toward choosing, not only a state of life, but also an occupation or profession. Great harm is done when a person decides on a vocation for which he is not meant, especially when he acts under pressure of whatever sort. From God's hand come abundance and variety and uniqueness to each living thing, whether it be the flower of the field or the human person. It is the work of vocational guidance to uncover to the person himself the working of God within him, to make him aware of ultimate values, and to encourage him to use his potentialities to the full.

Young persons are in great need of social guidance. The adult world bequeathed to them is not a Christian society; it is not a unified society. Its confusion of half-truths is reflected in customs and manners. The high-school student is not only gradually entering adult activities and assuming adult responsibilities; he is doing so as a Christian in a non-Christian world, a world still in the throes of breaking from a corrupted Christian tradition and rediscovering Christ. His immediate problems connected with dates, speed-driving, and competitive sports have moral as well as social implications and facets. The same thing is true of his problems when he thinks of how best to attain happiness as a member of society.

The crowning point in all guidance should be moral guidance. As the high-school student comes to decisions about his lifework, his relationships with others, and his ultimate goal, he needs to know what to do and what not to do, and also why or for what reason he does what he does. Immediate questions of conduct that come up may involve several depths of value. Reasons for the same action may differ with different individuals. For example, a group-guidance session may end with general acceptance of the principle that the drinking of alcoholic beverages is not desirable for people of high-school age and that even mature people must use prudence in quenching their thirst. The varsity football player agrees because alcohol will undermine physical fitness. The boy who has seen his father, an alcoholic, struggle in vain against his weakness knows at first hand the lure and strength of such temptation. His sister has understood the effects of the father's drinking on their mother and the family happiness. In agreeing with the group opinion she is refining her social ideals and looking forward to life in her own family. Each person's choice of action flows from his values, his degree of maturity, his experiences, and his response to grace.

Just as a person cannot be dissected and educated part by part, so too he cannot be guided in one area without cognizance of his advance or need in another area. The kinds of guidance overlap and interweave. It is the need of a particular person at a particular time and in a particular situation that determines what guidance is needed and how it should be given. The caution which characterizes the actions of conscientious specialists should stand as a warning to teachers who rashly undertake to guide children in difficult cases. In giving clinical help to a maladjusted child a team composed of psychiatrist, psychologist, and social worker tests and interviews the child, meets his family, studies his school records, and only then in a series of conferences agrees upon a tentative diagnosis and tentative therapeutic program. Children in general are not in need of such specialized services; but to spiritual depth and simplicity a teacher must join a practical knowledge of human development, of the workings of grace, and of the ways of the devil. Above all the teacher must assure the child of sympathy and understanding and inspire his trust. If we do succeed in giving guidance as indicated, there will be happiness for the individual and progress in our social living.

SELECTED REFERENCES

Allers, Rudolf. *Character Education in Adolescence,* Chapter 6, "General and Vocational Guidance." New York: Joseph F. Wagner, 1940.

Arbuckle, Dugald S. *Guidance and Counseling in the Classroom,* Chapter 1, "Guidance in Modern Education"; Chapter 2, "Need for Guidance Services." Boston: Allyn and Bacon, 1957.

Bertrand, Sister M. "Guidance in the Elementary School." *Bulletin National Catholic Educational Association* 51:508-14, August 1954.

Cribben, James J. "A Critique of the Philosophy of Modern Guidance." *Catholic Educational Review* 53:73-91, February 1955.

———— "Guidance: Primary Function of the Catholic School." *Catholic Educational Review* 54:505-15, November 1956.

———— "The Important Guidance Principles." *Catholic Educational Review* 51:520-36, October 1953.

———— "The Modern Function of Guidance—An Ancient Christian Tradition." *Catholic Educational Review* 52:510-22, November 1954.

Crow, Lester D., and Alice Crow. *An Introduction to Guidance; Principles and Practices,* Chapter 1, "The Meaning and Function of Guidance"; Chapter 2, "Development of the Guidance Movement"; Chapter 3, "Problems of Life Adjustment"; Chapter 4, "The Fundamentals of Guidance." New York: American Book Company, 1951.

Cunningham, William F. *The Pivotal Problems of Education,* Part 1, "Ends in Education"; Chapter 6, "The Universal Human Needs." New York: The Macmillan Company, 1940.

French, William Marshall, and others. *Behavioral Goals of General Education in High School,* Part 1, "General Education in High School." New York: Russell Sage Foundation, 1957.

Harcar, George A., and Regis J. Leonard. "Suggested Principles of Guidance for Catholic Secondary Schools." *Catholic Educational Review* 49:260-65, April 1951.

Jones, Arthur J. *Principles of Guidance,* fourth edition, Chapter 1, "Need for Guidance." New York: McGraw-Hill Book Company, 1951.

McCarthy, Raphael C. *Training the Adolescent,* Chapter 19, "The Guidance of Adolescents." Milwaukee: Bruce Publishing Company, 1934.

McDaniel, Henry B. *Guidance in the Modern School,* Chapter 1, "An Overview and an Outlook"; Chapter 2, "Basic Concepts in Guidance"; Chapter 5, "Guidance Needs of Young People." New York: Dryden Press, 1956.

Mathewson, Robert Hendry. *Guidance Policy and Practice,* Part 1, "Fundamental Factors in Guidance Practice." New York: Harper and Brothers, 1949.

Recktenwald, Lester Nicholas. *Guidance and Counseling,* Chapter 1, "The Nature of the Problem"; Chapter 2, "Some Fundamental Concepts in Guidance and Counseling." Washington: The Catholic University of America Press, 1953.

Smith, Glenn E. *Principles and Practices of the Guidance Program,* Chapter 1, "A Point of View"; Chapter 2, "Guidance Services Yesterday and Today." New York: The Macmillan Company, 1951.

Stoops, Emery, and Gunnar L. Wahlquist. *Principles and Practices in Guidance,* Chapter 1, "Guidance: An Indispensable Pupil Service." New York: McGraw-Hill Book Company, 1958.

Willey, Roy DeVerl, and Dean C. Andrew. *Modern Methods and Techniques in Guidance,* Chapter 1, "Guidance as Part of the Educational Program." New York: Harper and Brothers, 1955.

CHAPTER TWO

THE ORGANIZATION

OF GUIDANCE SERVICES

It is difficult to outline a guidance program completely suitable for all schools and applicable under all conditions. Frequently such factors as the organization of the school, the number, training, and traditions of the faculty and other personnel, the grade level of the school, and the community services available to the school will affect the organization of the guidance program. But since every Catholic school has the same general objectives and since every student encounters the same basic problems in achieving Christian maturity, the principles and methods of guidance suggested here can be used, with perhaps some modifications, by all schools. It should be noted that the guidance program deals with matters related to the sanctification and salvation of souls. A thoroughly Catholic character and approach, therefore, must be evident throughout, and the realization of the aims of Catholic education must be deliberately sought in the organization and administration of the program.

INITIATING A GUIDANCE PROGRAM

A guidance program must begin with recognized educational authorities. The person who initiates the program might be the bishop of the diocese, the superintendent of schools appointed by the bishop, an assistant superintendent who has been put in charge of guidance activities, the superior or supervisor of the religious order or congregation that conducts the school, or the principal of the school. In very many cases the program is planned and put into execution by the principal alone, and without his active cooperation a guidance program could scarcely be carried out in any school. In order to simplify our presentation we will speak only of what the principal should do, but without overlooking the fact that the principal may be acting under directives issued by some higher authority. A principal who is carrying out orders received from a superior officer must make his own the ideals of that superior officer if he wishes the program to succeed.

What Is Required of the Principal. The principal who is about to inaugurate a guidance program and who is to be responsible for supervising the program must have certain convictions, must accept certain principles, and must take certain steps. These may be summarized as follows:

1 He must be convinced that there is place for the systematic provision of guidance services in the school and that all the existent informal services will gain strength and effectiveness within an organized program.

2 He takes inventory of the problems and difficulties experienced by students in utilizing their God-given powers, developing their personalities, and solving their social problems, and he is convinced that these needs can be better met through a guidance program than through any other available means.

3 He formulates the general objectives and specific goals he expects an organized program to achieve in terms of the whole school and of the individual student and not merely with reference to problem children.

4 He refuses to limit guidance to any one field or activity, but seeks to have it affect the total school program in curricular, cocurricular, extracurricular, and administrative activities.

5 He plans to secure the cooperation of his faculty by interesting them in the program, and he avoids anything that might interfere with complete faculty acceptance of the program.

6 He must be willing to take the time necessary to organize the program properly, or to make that time available to a staff member, delegating authority to him and giving him continued support and assistance.

7 He needs to appraise the capacity of the school to undertake an organized guidance program, to assess the abilities of school personnel and the availability of outside services, and to provide the funds, time, and facilities necessary for satisfactory results.

8 He looks upon the program as something that must be initiated gradually, he has plans for its maintenance, and he thinks of what its probable growth will be.

Enlisting the Assistance of the Faculty. The principal will not seek to impose on his faculty a guidance program of his own creation, but will call a general faculty meeting to discuss the need for guidance services and the organization of a guidance program. All teachers will have had experiences, within the classroom and without, in which they recognized a student's need for additional social or moral instruction and guidance and felt themselves unable to meet the need adequately for lack of time, of proper facilities and information, or of sufficient training. They will be able to point to specific examples and to enumerate the kinds of need.

The principal then selects a committee to study the needs for guidance services and to make recommendations on all phases of guidance in view of an organized program. The committee should be composed of teachers who have had previous training in guidance and counseling or who are willing to take some in-service training in this field of education, and those who have been constantly sought out by students for advice and informal discussions. The committee will continue in some form, working within the framework of the guidance program; it will meet periodically and should, from time to time, invite other interested personnel to share their problems and suggestions.

After the committee has made its initial report, the principal should appoint a guidance director to coordinate the program. In a school of small enrollment the principal himself may assume this responsibility. In a larger school the guidance director may be assisted by several persons, each responsible for a guidance service: one for group guidance, another for vocational guidance, and so forth. Every teacher, however, should realize the importance of guidance work, should desire to become an active member of the guidance staff, and should wish to share responsibility for the services offered, for homeroom teachers and religion teachers are the key guidance personnel.

The Type of Guidance Program Selected. Every conscientious principal and every devoted teacher has offered guidance services in the ordinary school and classroom activities and outside of school. With the increasing complexity of modern living and the growing school population, however, specialized guidance services have come into being. As guidance services have become more formal and specialized, they have been organized in three types of programs:

1 The specialist type, sometimes called the centralized program, requires the services of experts, particularly of psychologists and highly trained counselors.

2 The classroom type, sometimes referred to as the uncentralized program, depends mainly upon regular teachers under the direction of the principal.

3 The combination type is the adaptation of the advantages of the other two programs to fit the needs and facilities of the individual school.

Catholic schools have ordinarily organized a combination type of guidance program, finding in that type a most satisfactory utilization and integration of their excellent informal guidance services supplemented by expert professional skills. Chart I shows how the combination-type guidance program calls upon the talents and capacities of the entire school personnel and suggests how, with various outside services, such a program may be organized. It is quite evident that few if any schools will employ all the different kinds of persons mentioned in the chart. They are mentioned because any one of them might, for special reasons, be found in a certain school, and also because the services for which they are responsible will usually be integrated into the guidance program. Although all the positions mentioned in the chart are readily understood, a few words

CHART I

Superintendent

Principal

Director of Guidance

Counselors
spiritual
academic
college
occupational
cooperative-education
placement
military

Religion Department
department head
religion teachers
school chaplain
director of religious activities
vocations director

Group Guidance
director
homeroom teachers
classroom teachers
class advisers

Deans
of studies
of discipline
of attendance
of social activities

Health Department
health director
school physician
school nurse
physical-education teachers

Specialists
psychologist
psychiatrist
director of testing services
remedial teachers
social workers
court workers
Catholic Charities staff
other agencies

of explanation for some of them may be helpful as a means of preventing any possible misunderstanding.

By a college counselor is meant one who is specially prepared to guide students in choosing the college that will best meet their needs. By an occupational counselor is meant one who helps students choose a profession or a certain type of work. A placement counselor is interested only in students who do not plan to continue their education beyond high school. He may arrange to have representatives of companies and firms speak to groups of students; he keeps himself informed of openings; he prepares students for interviews and helps them write letters of application. A cooperative-education counselor is needed only when the school has introduced a program of cooperative education, under which students work for alternate weeks or some other period of time in school and in some place of employment. This plan appears to be very rarely found in Catholic high schools, but has been extensively used in a number of smaller communities and in at least one large public-school system.[1] The vocations director is responsible for identifying students who might be fit candidates for the priesthood or the religious life and for giving them the proper encouragement and direction. The military counselor cooperates with Army personnel if the school has a unit of the ROTC. Even in cases in which the school does not have a unit of the ROTC, as will be said in greater detail later, boys today appear to need a very special type of guidance in order to be prepared for the problems that they will meet if they enlist or are drafted to serve for a period of time in the Armed Forces.

Any one of four different situations may be found to exist when there is question of specialists and special teachers. Let us take the child psychologist as an example. A Catholic high school might have a psychologist on its staff, and a very large school or a well-endowed select school might be fortunate enough to have on its staff a teacher who majored in psychology while in training. The second situation occurs in some of our larger cities where there are Catholic clinics or in which the bishop may instruct the Catholic school board to

[1] Delos Walker, "Cooperative Education in the High Schools of New York City 1915-1940." *High Points* 22:8-18, September 1940.

employ a psychologist to serve all the schools. The third situation is found in cities in which Catholic schools can obtain psychological service only from the 'public schools or from other non-Catholic agencies. The fourth situation is found when the school can obtain no service whatsoever in its own area. Many Catholic high schools located in small cities or towns are forced to face the fact that special services of one kind or another are impossible for them to obtain.

Whatever the situation may be, the one who initiates a guidance program needs to know what services will be needed, where and how to obtain them, and how to use them. These questions will be discussed later. The only purpose of Chart I is to give a comprehensive view of the personnel that might be found in a school that is rendering every possible type of guidance. In practice a single person usually assumes responsibility for several of the services assigned in the chart to different individuals. Those initiating the program might decide that certain services are not needed or that their introduction had best be postponed. It is also possible that services not mentioned in the chart are needed in some particular school. In general, the activities mentioned in the chart will be reduced or even increased to meet local requirements.

GUIDANCE PERSONNEL

The size, grade level, and type of the school will determine in a large part the placing of responsibility for the provision of the guidance services. The principal in virtue of his office has authority to organize and conduct the program. In many schools he may be performing a number of the guidance services in the routine course of his work. As a school grows in size, the principal will wisely delegate many of these powers to capable members of the faculty. He may appoint one to handle discipline, another to serve as dean or prefect of studies, another as spiritual director, another as vocational director, and so on. Whatever titles are given, such as dean, director, head counselor, and so forth, the principal ought to assign specific duties and responsibilities to each one. Everyone should know for what he is responsible, where his authority begins, and where his authority ends.

Director of Guidance. For a high school with an enrollment of six hundred or more students, the appointment of a guidance director is a practical necessity. The principal should give the guidance director authority to direct the entire guidance program as it is organized in the school. The director of guidance is the one who is immediately responsible for coordinating and supervising the services which the school guidance program offers. As a rule he will not merely direct the work of others but will himself have certain contacts with students. For example, he may be the one who acts as college adviser, vocations director, and military adviser, while others assist in counseling, placement, or other guidance services. The extent to which the director of guidance is solely responsible for certain areas of the program will depend upon the size of the school, upon local conditions, and sometimes upon directives received from the diocese or the superintendent of schools.

Inasmuch as every teacher is a group-guidance worker and is considered as a possible student counselor, the guidance director should be responsible for guiding the staff members who offer these services. He should assist all members of the staff by providing information, services, and general direction. For new counselors and group-guidance workers especially he should act as a supervisor until they have mastered the best techniques. The office of the director of guidance ought to be a service center for information, supplies, and contact with all the outside agencies whose services may be of benefit to students.

The director of guidance should see that all the work of guidance is carried out by various members of the staff in some part of the total school program. If he decides not to undertake a guidance service, such as remedial teaching, he should have valid reasons for omitting it. He should omit nothing that is essential to a sound program. Where a formal guidance program does not exist, he should survey the work of the school, label those functions that are appropriately guidance, and coordinate them. He should eliminate unnecessary duplications and make needed additions to the program. He should define the limits of responsibility of those cooperating in the program.

Qualities of a Director of Guidance. The principal should select as guidance director one whose classroom teaching career has been characterized by successful guidance and counseling. It is desirable that the person selected should have had formal training in the field or that he be given the opportunity to do advanced work through courses during the school year or in summer sessions.

In addition to the fundamental spiritual qualities to be indicated in the section on personnel training, the director of guidance should excel in judgment and leadership. Interest in his work and a willingness to give an unlimited amount of time in service to others will be needed if this judgment and leadership are to become productive of the best results. Principals ought to be aware of the fact that the most saintly and pious, the most intelligent, or even the best classroom teacher will not necessarily be the best guidance director.

Counselors. Attention to the needs of the individual student will be secured most effectively by the appointment of a personal counselor for each. Members of a school staff should recognize counseling as essential to the Christian development of students. The values to be gained from a guidance program will be dependent upon the work of the counselor in his personal contact with and knowledge of the individual student. Likewise, the direction that guidance is to take and the services that are to be offered will frequently depend upon the extent to which members of the school staff accept counseling as an activity of the greatest possible importance to be undertaken gladly and generously.

Teachers and Advisers. When homeroom and other teachers, particularly in religion and the social studies, are zealous and alert, they carry out many guidance and counseling responsibilities even though they have never been formally appointed counselors. Those who direct the extracurricular activities of an entire class, such as the seniors, are likewise vital members of the guidance personnel. They are often called class advisers.

Other Guidance Workers. Anyone who performs a guidance service belongs to the department personnel. Each person listed in Chart I has some duty connected with the complete program. His functions and responsibilities are treated in succeeding chapters.

The Parish Priest and the Guidance Program. All priests should be interested and active in the Christian development of the young. The vitality of any parish is intimately bound up with the spiritual strength of the young Christian families. The parish priest ought to be aware of the great possibilities that are dependent upon his sharing in the work of the guidance program of the Catholic school. The interest of a parish priest in the work of a high school is naturally greater when the school is a parochial rather than a so-called central high school and is under his own control and direction. The number of high schools owned and operated by parishes is quite small in comparison with the total number of high schools, but it is not at all difficult to convince priests that they should welcome the opportunity of serving in high schools lying outside the limits of their own parishes. A great number of priests in our country are part-time teachers or workers in the high schools of their city. Local circumstances have brought about for these priests a variety of arrangements, such as teaching all the religion classes each day or once a week, rotation plans of teaching religion, classroom visits, the hearing of confessions, the direction of athletic programs, and so forth.

Both priests and the regular teachers of the school may sometimes find these arrangements quite unsatisfactory. Because of the pressure of parish duties a priest may be able to come to the school only infrequently, and there may be irregularity in his attendance. It may be that he does not know how to handle a classroom situation effectively, that students are unable to understand his explanations, and that he is ignorant of the proper methods of giving assignments, correcting papers, and grading. Such limitations interfere with the unity of teaching in a school. These evils do not always exist, are not inevitable, and could usually be eliminated by discussion and cooperation. If a priest, however, does find it difficult to teach successfully, he can with far less difficulty render most valuable service by participating in the guidance program of the school.

Many priests desire a more intimate pastoral relationship to the school. The priest who is able to give only an hour or two a day to the school in his parish or city can render very valuable priestly service to students and still achieve his objectives without the burden of the formal teaching of classes. Instead of accepting a teaching assignment he may arrange to come to the school in the capacity of a counselor to interview students and to provide an opportunity for going to confession. These duties will enable him to give personal spiritual guidance, to promote religious vocations, and to cement a real bond with the parish life of the student. The priest may call for individual students at definite times and be available to students who wish to see him during the time he has so scheduled.

Where the school serves many parishes in an area, regular visits of priests from the parishes for interviews and counseling ought to be encouraged and a master plan ought to be established. In an arrangement providing for this guidance service the priest should leave such areas as academic guidance and testing to members of the regular staff of the school. In any case his part-time work ought to be done professionally as a priest and counselor, and with order and system. He may profitably use many of the forms and procedures outlined in this book. Harmony in the total guidance and counseling program calls for cooperation of the priest with the regular staff of the school and for his attendance at meetings of the guidance personnel.

Sisters Aiding Part Time in the Guidance and Counseling Program. Providing guidance services for all students requires adequate staffing. While it is always more desirable that a guidance worker and counselor be a classroom teacher for much of the school day, some sisters are often available and eager for part-time schoolwork. These may render important services in the guidance department. Often a sister who is unable to teach a full or even a limited class schedule can spend some time each day or week in counseling students. She will then have an interest and continuing devotion to the work of education by providing students with guidance services rendered by an experienced religious. She may undertake the guidance of as many students as she is able to handle and thereby lighten the guidance load of others on the staff. What is said of sisters is equally applicable to priests and brothers, who unfortunately are available in smaller numbers.

There are many wise and prudent members of religious communities whose length of service could be extended by engaging in this work. These religious can lighten the load of others, who then could devote more time to the guidance and counseling of the individuals or groups for whom they are responsible. Years of experience in the classroom and maturity in the spiritual life should have provided these religious with adequate information and knowledge of method. They should nonetheless keep in touch with the minds of youth, with current problems, and with the conditions existing in the world in which the youth live.

The superior of the community or the one assigned to initiate the guidance department ought to take care to unify the work of guidance by these part-time guidance workers and counselors. Care should be taken to select these counselors wisely and to arrange a program that would minimize any disadvantages or foreseeable difficulties resulting from the plans.

THE TRAINING OF GUIDANCE PERSONNEL

In the public-school system of the United States there has been an increasing tendency to place guidance workers and counselors upon a professional level by demanding preservice training. Approximately forty states have established requirements for the certification of guidance workers on various levels.[2] Fifteen to thirty credit hours in such specific areas as principles of guidance, counseling, and occupational information are required for a guidance certificate, in addition to the undergraduate courses in education and psychology. Classroom teaching experience and in-service guidance training are invariably demanded.

The training of a guidance worker and counselor in a Catholic school must be in harmony with the objectives of Catholic education and the concept of a Catholic guidance program. Guidance training, then, must be based on grace and the working of the Holy Spirit. By its very nature the entire training of the priest and the religious

[2] For a listing of state requirements see Royce E. Brewster, *Guidance Workers Certification Requirements,* U. S. Department of Health, Education, and Welfare, Bulletin 1957, No. 22.

to learn and live the spiritual life, "to put on Christ," to develop the Christian personality and character, should be understood as training in Christian guidance practice. Catholic guidance personnel should have a threefold training: teaching experience, educational training, and religious experience.

Teaching Experience. Teaching experience is a real necessity for one assigned to guidance work. One who knows the classroom life, the mind and attitudes of the students, and the problems that are associated with school life can more easily and correctly understand the problems of adjustment in the adolescent. Several years of classroom experience should be sufficient to give a reasonably good concept of the mind of adolescents and some knowledge of how to gain their confidence.

Educational Training. The completion of the required course in education and philosophy fits the Catholic secondary teacher for work in the classroom, but the services which the school is called upon to provide for modern youth and the areas which guidance programs now embrace call for the acquisition of more specific knowledge. The regular courses in Catholic philosophy and theology, educational psychology, sociology, and principles and methods of education will serve well for counseling, group guidance, and religious guidance. Special study in the fields of occupational guidance, remedial methods, testing, and the like, will be necessary if the teacher is to provide trustworthy guidance in the areas in which Catholic guidance programs are often weak and inefficient. Any inclination to depend entirely on outside help should be resisted, for a ready source of referral in these matters is hardly sufficient to fulfill the responsibility of the school. Justice to students requires that those responsible for guidance and counseling should either be trained in such areas through regular courses or make adequate preparation by means of private study.

Contact must be maintained with the current sources of information, such as the state department of vocational education, labor bulletins, professional journals on vocational information, college catalogues, and books and articles on tests and measurements. Knowledge of community and state service agencies and the sources of occupational information is necessary.[3] Membership in state and national groups such as the American Personnel and Guidance Association should be encouraged to keep the staff abreast of current developments. For Catholic teachers there is much to be gained from others and always much to be given.

While courses in guidance, counseling techniques, and related subjects are advisable for those engaged in guidance work, a measure of discretion ought to be employed in enrolling in these college courses. Some true value should be seen as definitely forthcoming. Much time may be wasted if the course is not properly conducted. Confusion or compromise often results from courses in which there is excessive analysis of the very simple relationship of teacher to student and counselor to counselee.

If it is desirable that all those who are to give guidance should have received the training and taken the courses to which we have referred, it is far more important—in fact, it is imperative—that they should have a keen realization of the limitations of the training they have received. Far too many teachers, after a single course in child psychology, in tests and measurements, or in counseling, are inclined to think that they have all the answers at hand and that they can settle any problem with finality. This is particularly apt to occur when courses have been conducted by college instructors who exaggerate the achievements of modern education and the power of tests and scales to measure what a child actually does possess. The principal, the director of guidance, and everyone else who has any authority over staff members should constantly insist upon the necessity of proceeding with caution, of suspending judgment in difficult cases and whenever anything of great value or importance is at stake, and of looking on decisions as subject to possible revision in the light of facts that may be learned later. In other words, a master's degree in education does not render a teacher infallible; it may, as a matter of fact, render him only the more liable to make mistakes, and to make the gravest and most harmful of mistakes, if he has

[3] *The Catholic Counselor* (650 Grand Concourse, New York 51, New York) and both *The Personnel and Guidance Journal* and *The Vocational Guidance Quarterly* (1534 O. Street, N.W., Washington 5, D.C.) are a worthwhile investment.

too much faith in the tests that he uses or if in his conceit he believes that he knows more than he does know.

There are teachers who have done incalculable harm by telling young persons that they would endanger their eternal salvation if they failed to become priests or religious, by creating timidity or encouraging scrupulosity, by solving moral problems on the basis of their own notions and without knowing what is held by approved theologians, and in general by claiming for themselves gifts and rights that even the vicar of Christ neither possesses nor claims. There are other teachers who have made educational decisions concerning students, or led students into making decisions for themselves, which were justified only if the data obtained through tests were altogether true and dependable and if the one who interpreted the data was trained to interpret such data correctly. Students have frequently been put in slow-moving groups when they could have succeeded in fast-moving groups, or have been discouraged from attempting certain subjects or vocations, or have been refused admission to high schools or colleges, all because of test data inaccurate in themselves or inaccurately interpreted.

The entire guidance personnel should be convinced of three things: first, that there is need of true humility and of caution on the part of everyone; second, that there should be retesting, reexamination, and reconsideration whenever a decision affecting something of grave moment is to be made; third, that important decisions should be group decisions rather than individual decisions whenever the obligations of professional secrecy do not render such action improper. If a guidance department is animated by this spirit, it will grow constantly in power to give trustworthy guidance. If it is not animated by this spirit, there is reason for thinking that it might have been better had it never been born.

Religious Experience. The completion of courses in guidance does not necessarily make one a qualified counselor any more than certification as a teacher makes one a truly successful teacher. The basic qualification for a Catholic guidance worker is possession of the *gift of counsel,* which comes from the abiding presence of the Holy Spirit. This point cannot be stressed too much in Catholic guidance. The truth must be emphasized that it is the Holy Spirit who trains souls and that guidance personnel are only the instruments in the hand of God drawing all things to Himself. The guidance worker, then, will be fully qualified only when he himself has been sufficiently formed by the grace of God and when he has habitually activated the virtues, the gifts, and the fruits of the Holy Spirit. The counsel, wisdom, and understanding that are so important in guidance and counseling come only as a result of mature spiritual living.

Some valuable in-service training of Catholic guidance personnel is gained from experience in the life of religion and from the development of one's own spiritual life. Devotion to the Holy Spirit is a necessity for guidance personnel. The seminary or novitiate spiritual program forms only the beginning of preparation for guidance work. Only those who have acquired maturity and experience in the spiritual life and who understand the operation of the Holy Spirit in the lives of men can hope to become intelligent and truly efficient guidance workers.

In assessing the personality qualities needed for capable guidance and counseling, the evaluation of a staff member ought to be made in the light of the cardinal virtues and of the fruits and gifts of the Holy Spirit. Among these prudence and temperance, understanding and counsel, and patience and charity are the foremost.

THE COST OF GUIDANCE SERVICES

As guidance is so closely integrated with the total school program, administrators find it difficult to determine the proportion of cost which should be allocated to it. The guidance personnel also serve as teachers and direct other activities as well. The administrator must therefore determine how much staff-member time is allocated to guidance. If this time has required additional faculty members for the school, the amount of their salary is chargeable as guidance cost. The total guidance time divided into the total school time will give the percentage of personnel time spent on the guidance program. The same percentage of the total amount spent for salaries will give the cost of personnel guidance services.

The principal considerations in determining a guidance budget are the following:

Total time used in school program ....

Total time used in guidance ....

Percentage of time allotted to
    guidance ....

Total cost of salaries ....

Cost of salaries for guidance ....

Maintenance of guidance center and office,
    telephone, records, and so forth ....

Materials, supplies, tests, forms, subscriptions
    to magazines, and so forth ....

Total expenditures of school program ....

Average cost per student ....

Total cost of guidance program ....

Average cost of guidance program per student ....

Percentage of total cost spent on guidance ....

When the average cost per student has been determined, this amount may be appropriately included in the fees to be paid by a student upon entrance to school. This fee may be labeled "Guidance and Tests."

The cost of public-school guidance programs varies greatly with the size of the school, the extent of the program, and the amount of expense borne by other agencies. In 1950 the cost ranged from $6.44 to $12.42 per student. The larger the school, the smaller the per-pupil cost. It has been suggested that adequate guidance services should not exceed $15.00 per pupil and that a satisfactory program may be operated on $10.00 per pupil in the public high schools.

For Catholic schools the cost of guidance services will also vary considerably, but it should be appreciably lower. In most schools $5.00 per pupil would be sufficient to cover the expenses of the program. One third of this amount will cover the cost of personnel salaries; the remainder should be used for the other items, such as tests, occupational information, books, and materials. Considering the value received from the guidance services and the intimate relationship to the school objectives, expenditures for guidance are considerably more justifiable than a similar amount budgeted to fleeting items such as yearbooks, the school paper, admissions to athletic contests, and so forth. If necessary, underwriting the expense of a guidance program can be an excellent project for the PTA, the Mothers Club, the Parents Club, or other school organizations.

SELECTED REFERENCES

Arbuckle, Dugald S. *Guidance and Counseling in the Classroom*, Chapter 9, "Organizing Guidance Services." Boston: Allyn and Bacon, 1957.

Armstrong, John. "The Role of the Teacher in the Guidance Program." *Bulletin National Catholic Educational Association* 54:335-36, August 1957.

Bransby, Brother Elmo. "Developing an Adequate Guidance Program." *Bulletin National Catholic Educational Association* 51:389-402, August 1954.

Crow, Lester D., and Alice Crow. *An Introduction to Guidance; Principles and Practices*, Chapter 5, "Organizing Guidance Services"; Chapter 6, "Implementing the Guidance Program"; Chapter 7, "The Guidance Personnel." New York: American Book Company, 1951.

Deluhery, Joseph C. "Suggestions for a Guidance Program." *Catholic School Journal* 55:115-16, April 1955.

Foster, Charles R. *Guidance for Today's Schools*, Chapter 1, "Who Is Responsible for Guidance." New York: Ginn and Company, 1957.

Gabriel, Brother J. "Guidance in the Catholic High School." *Catholic School Journal* 56:240-41, October 1956.

Hatch, Raymond N., and Buford Stefflre. *Administration of Guidance Services*, Chapter 4, "Organizational Patterns and Personnel"; Chapter 5, "Administrative Problems of the Guidance Services"; Chapter 6, "Budget and Facilities." Englewood Cliffs: Prentice-Hall, 1958.

Jones, Arthur J. *Principles of Guidance*, fourth edition, Chapter 25, "Organization of Guidance and Pupil Personnel Work"; Chapter 26, "Duties, Characteristics, Preparation, and Certification of the School Counselor." New York: McGraw-Hill Book Company, 1951.

Maher, Trafford P. "The Elementary School Guidance Program: Its Personnel and Clientele." *Bulletin National Catholic Educational Association* 53:285-86, August 1956.

Recktenwald, Lester Nicholas. *Guidance and Counseling*, Chapter 11, "Organization." Washington: The Catholic University of America Press, 1953.

Roeber, Edward C.; Glenn E. Smith; and Clifford E. Erickson. *Organization and Administration of Guidance Services*, pp. 26-260. New York: McGraw-Hill Book Company, 1955.

Smith, Glenn E. *Principles and Practices of the Guidance Program,* Chapter 4, "The Guidance Program at Work." New York: The Macmillan Company, 1951.

Stoops, Emery, and Gunnar L. Wahlquist. *Principles and Practices in Guidance,* Chapter 9, "Essentials of a Good Guidance Program"; Chapter 10, "Personnel in the Guidance Program"; Chapter 11, "The Guidance Budget"; Chapter 12, "Public Relations in Guidance." New York: McGraw-Hill Book Company, 1958.

Willey, Roy DeVerl, and Dean C. Andrew. *Modern Methods and Techniques in Guidance,* Chapter 2, "The Personnel of the Guidance Program"; Chapter 3, "The Requirements of an Efficient Guidance Worker"; Chapter 4, "Where, When, and How to Begin." New York: Harper and Brothers, 1955.

CHAPTER THREE

GROUP GUIDANCE

Group guidance is any form of mass instruction and direction the purpose of which is to help the group and the individuals within the group in the making of decisions. It differs from individual guidance, better called counseling, in this, that the work is done with a number of students. It differs from the ordinary classroom instruction in this, that classroom instruction is directed toward the teaching of subjects. Some subjects, such as religion or civics, are not as a rule taught for their content alone and without any reference to problems of personal conduct. It is therefore possible for group guidance to be given by a classroom teacher who is conducting a course in one of the subjects of the curriculum, but in this case the teaching of the subject is the primary objective and guidance is looked upon as a by-product, albeit a very important by-product. The group guidance of which we speak in this chapter is guidance purposefully undertaken for the sake of guidance and not for the sake of teaching a curricular subject.

THE NATURE OF GROUP GUIDANCE

Group guidance ought to result in the making of good and helpful decisions by the students. These decisions penetrate into every phase of life and study, future occupations, family life, political life, and spiritual life. There are decisions that must be made because of needs basic to a period of development, to an occasion that arises, or to a group action in which the student is a participant. For example, introduction into a new and larger social group and the acceptance of new responsibilities and obligations are common to all high-school freshmen. The choice of a lifework and preparation for that work, whether it be by means of further study in college or vocational school or by means of apprenticeship on the job itself, become more pressing as the time for that work draws near. Social relationships create new problems when the opposite sex begins to exercise an attraction unfelt in childhood. The high-school student must face many new problems which, if not solved wisely, can result in failure, frustration, and even lifelong unhappiness.

The Christian guidance of an entire body of students is a great challenge to every Catholic school. Their formation as active Christians devoted to Christ and familiar with the traditions of Catholic culture requires foresight and planning. The guidance director may utilize the school's program, its facilities for cocurricular and extracurricular activities, and various kinds of public programs and services in meeting this challenge effectively.

Group guidance looks to the instruction and formation of students in certain critical areas that are not specifically covered in the curriculum, but which are nonetheless a definite part of their education. At its maximum efficiency this guidance should result in positive development and direction, as well as in the prevention of problems or in the prompt solution of problems that cannot be prevented from arising.

The Objectives of Group Guidance. Group guidance is at once individual and social in nature, directed as it is to the individual within the group. Its objectives are:

1 To set the tone of the day for the entire student body on a truly supernatural level.

2 To keep constantly before students the work of formation of the Christian personality through the steady development of Christian attitudes and ideals.

3 To renew frequently the purpose and theme of the year as set by the principal or by the director of guidance and to employ new means of achieving and evaluating progress toward the goal of the year. Such a theme may be charity, greater sacrifice, more fortitude, the giving of good example, a conscious attempt to exercise influence, and so forth.

4 To establish a goal for each week for which every student in the school is working simultaneously in the true spirit of Catholic action. This guidance involves mass action, group pressure, and united effort stimulated by the individual teacher acting under the guidance director. Thus group participation in a school movement or project takes place.

5 To instill the characteristic Christian spirit of the school by acquainting students with the way in which one lives a spiritual life as opposed to a purely natural life. Teachers should seize the opportunity for emphasizing the specific Christian purpose, ideals, and objectives of the school.

6 To work for the adjustment of the personality of students to life at this school and for a character development making for success in this school. For freshmen this means orientation to a new level of education and to a new school.

7 To provide the opportunity for the influence of the teacher on the student on a nonacademic basis. Here is the time for the teacher to become acquainted with each student as a friend, adviser, and helper with sympathetic understanding and genuine interest. It is the meeting of teacher and students in a smaller group and in a different relationship.

8 To instruct students in the matters which are a definite part of Christian education but do not fall within the scope of the usual class subjects—rules of discipline, manners, study habits, proper motivation, grades, help in the selection of courses for one's vocation in life, and so forth.

The Group-Guidance Period. Group guidance is often satisfactorily carried on during the homeroom period at the beginning of the day when each teacher assumes the role of a group-guidance worker. This period can easily become the core of work done for group guidance, and the proper use of this time can solve problems that otherwise would have to be handled individually.

Although schools may differ in their arrangement of the program of studies, it is essential that the period for group guidance be fixed for each day and that it be maintained. It is desirable, moreover, that the time be set at the very beginning of the school day. A period of ten minutes immediately after the opening roll call, prayer, and other routine activities (for example, the pledge of allegiance) will be adequate. When it is held five days a week, it will be equivalent to one full classroom period. It is also advisable for the regular classroom subjects to begin in the same rooms immediately after the guidance period.

A short period at the beginning of each day is recommended for several reasons. Students are then in the most receptive and cooperative attitude and teachers are close to their daily source of spiritual strength in the Holy Sacrifice and are not yet worn by trials, fatigue, and mounting tensions. The reasons accepted for making a meditation at the beginning of each day serve also as the convincing reasons for utilizing the first minutes of school for group guidance. Furthermore, a program intended to set the tone of the day and foster action on a selected objective cannot realistically be placed at the end of the day.

A ten-minute period allows for the development of a single point and the encouragement of a single, definite action. It limits the material offered by the teacher to the attention span of the adolescent and thwarts the tendency to the lengthy preaching and moralizing which are odious to youth. Periods presenting unified and progressive material on consecutive days offer the advantages to be found in repetition and sustained action without becoming a burden to either student or teacher.

To confine the program to a single full-length period once a week would neither accomplish the objectives of group guidance nor have much effect on students. The work would be doomed to failure if guidance were confined to a single period scheduled for the last day of the week. The inability of the adolescent mind to recall vividly on Monday the importance to his life of principles given on

Friday must be taken into account. To assign students to "take guidance" as a subject or to send them to a room identified with group guidance as such is poor educational psychology. Group guidance should be integrated into the school program at some regular time, and the time for each meeting should be brief.

If on occasion a longer period is necessary, the religion period may be used for the fuller explanation and discussion of moral or spiritual matters and the activity period may be used for matters of social or personal import. If religion follows as the first class of the day, the group guidance will often have been a convenient personalized introduction to the current subject.

Ticket sales, promotions, administrative details, and routine announcements should precede or follow rather than interfere with the objectives of the group-guidance time. Certain drives or "weeks" may be converted into the work of the group-guidance period, as, for example, Brotherhood Week, the Community Chest, and safety campaigns. These offer opportunities for the exercise of Christian virtues and group Catholic action.

A normal class group is a suitable size for group-guidance purposes. Larger groups, such as those in a study hall, do not provide the intimacy, the flexibility, or the freedom for expression that group guidance requires. Guidance groups of more than forty students are too large for the average teacher to handle effectively. Ordinarily the guidance group should be comprised of the same students who are in the first-period classes which immediately follow the guidance period.

METHODS OF GROUP GUIDANCE

Any method that genuinely and truly achieves the objectives of group guidance may be used. One may be more appropriate for a certain subject or in a certain situation than another, but the principal tool in any method is the ever-available grace of God. Emphasis and insistence upon the supernatural aid needed in attaining a supernatural personality should permeate all phases of the guidance program. Catholic schools should make every provision for the operation of the Holy Spirit, the molder of Christian men and women.

The work of grace must first take place in the mind and soul of the teacher. Certainly the example of the teacher's deep and practical spirituality will influence the spirit of the school and of the individual student. The teacher's understanding of the ways of God with men is his best preparation for helping others. His closeness to God is the source of his power to help others.

In the formation of the student the means of training the will to cooperate freely with divine grace must go hand in hand with the best methods of enlightening the intellect.[1] The importance of setting a high tone in the school and of maintaining a fine atmosphere, the value of presenting uniform motives and ideals, and the necessity of setting up goals to be attained and of making attractive the victory that is won by gaining mastery over self are to be emphasized in any method. Guidance materials should always be adapted to the ability of the students and to their experiences, and should be pointed to their immediate needs while providing for future needs.

The Direct Approach. The subject matter of guidance units often requires the direct approach, by which we mean that the teacher states his subject and presents what he has to say without waiting for the students to indicate by questions or in some other manner that they are interested in the subject. Such positive, teacher-centered instruction and direction and teacher leadership of discussion will be similar to the method ordinarily used by Christ in teaching His apostles and disciples, although many of His discourses were provoked by questions asked of Him. An authoritative treatment by the teacher is the most acceptable method in subjects involving moral matters. Students rightly expect clear and authoritative direction from one recognized as a leader and a guide. They come to school expecting to hear, find, and accept the truth in matters pertaining to their Christian formation. Granted that the teacher has the necessary training and experience, direct formation and information in many areas of guidance remain the only correct method.

[1] Johannes Lindworsky, *The Training of the Will,* translated by Arpad Steiner and Edward A. Fitzpatrick (Milwaukee: Bruce Publishing Company, 1929) and Edward Leen, *What Is Education?* (New York: Sheed and Ward, 1944) contain helpful material on will training.

Some educational theorists have maintained that the secondary school ought to encourage students to develop moral codes of their own. The Catholic school can never accept such a principle. Christ gave the world a complete moral code, and conferred upon His Church and upon no one else the power to teach, preserve, and interpret it. No one, for example, is free to decide for himself whether divorce is permissible, since God has told mankind what is to be thought of it. But if discussion of the existence and binding force of God's law is to be discouraged, other kinds of discussion may oftentimes be very desirable. All God's laws fit man's nature as God made that nature and are intended to work for the welfare of mankind and the happiness of the individual. The teacher, firmly convinced himself of the goodness of all God's laws, can encourage students to show how the divine law contributes to the happiness of mankind, even though the individual may sometimes have to suffer for the sake of the common welfare. There can also be fruitful discussions of the ways in which we best keep God's law or of the steps to be taken to avoid infractions of the law. God's law requires that we should love our neighbor, and there can be practical discussions of what this law of love requires of us. We are obliged to avoid giving scandal, and the students can discuss ways and means of giving good example, both to their associates and to the non-Catholic world. In all such discussions students are not developing moral codes for themselves, but are simply studying the beauty of the God-given code and deciding how they can best apply it to their own lives.

It is always to be expected that there should be some students in a school who think that certain of God's commandments are too severe. There will be others who obediently accept the statements of the teacher or of the textbook, but who fail to apply them as they should be applied. On one occasion a teacher discovered, quite by accident, that in a group of unusually innocent and pious freshmen there were many boys and girls who believed in euthanasia. You would kill a dog, they argued, that had a broken leg, so why should you let a person die a painful and lingering death from cancer? The teacher should not allow himself to become upset when he discovers that students have false and objectionable ideas on moral subjects, but should patiently and sympathetically endeavor to clear up the difficulty. A teacher who shows violent displeasure when a radical or unorthodox opinion is expressed forces students to adopt a policy of concealment and hypocrisy. Under such conditions students may give the socially acceptable answer without subscribing to it. Juvenile delinquents have been found to score high on tests of civic attitude. They know what is considered morally right or morally wrong but do not accept society's code. Similar things happen in Catholic high schools. A prudent teacher can, without any lessening of the respect due to God and the Church, make students feel free to speak of their difficulties.

The Indirect Approach. A teacher who is using the indirect approach refrains from selecting a subject on which he wishes to speak. He rather endeavors to set up a situation which will provoke or force students into coming to him for assistance in solving their problems or difficulties. By sleeping during the tempest on the lake Christ led the apostles into acknowledging their terror and begging His help. This may be considered an example of the indirect approach. A teacher should use the indirect approach with caution. He should not permit students to suffer harm because he has waited too long for them to ask for help.

The Student-Centered Approach. The student-centered approach is often confused with the indirect approach. As a matter of fact, the student-centered approach is usually a very direct approach. The teacher deliberately and purposefully organizes the students into a discussion group, appoints committees or provides for their election, suggests topics for discussion, provides materials or references to materials, and in general acts as sponsor and guide. There would appear to be nothing indirect about this approach, for the teacher is using a direct and positive method of getting students to think about and solve their problems.

There are many advantages in the student-centered approach. Aided self-discovery is a fundamental method of learning. Student panels and class discussions can increase interest, lead to independent activity, and cause the student to think and to relate to himself and his life the knowledge he has acquired. Class discussions prepare the student for later work in adult life as a defender of the faith. An ideal which a student has publicly accepted in a class discussion will usually be a more potent force in his life than an ideal with which he is acquainted only because his teacher has insisted that he ought to make it his own. If class discussions are properly conducted, the better students will often do more than the teacher could do to silence and correct students who express narrow, selfish, or rebellious ideas. Finally, class discussions reveal to the teacher points on which students need further information. These are but some of the many advantages of the student-centered approach.

The general purpose of class discussions is to assist in assimilation by helping students see how a fact or truth ought to be applied. If this goal is to be achieved, correct pedagogy requires that the necessary facts and principles be presented *before* the discussion. In matters of faith and morals it is most necessary for students to know that they are not at liberty to entertain or express private opinions or judgments concerning the truth or the reasonableness of the revealed word of God or the teaching of the Church. Their task here is twofold: to endeavor to see more clearly how good and helpful God's truth always is and to think of ways of making that truth function in their own lives. Considerable prudence and care on the part of the teacher are required so that students may arrive at the desired decisions or attitude. As a result of his own self-discovery a student may come to a false conclusion and may determine upon action that is undesirable or even morally wrong, and he may then be most reluctant to conform to objective truth. Opinions at which a student has arrived through a process of reflective thinking are indeed precious things, but not if they run contrary to truth. Group-guidance methods should avoid encouraging the formation of opinions of such a kind. The outcome of all student-centered discussions ought to be the acquiring of Christian knowledge and greater conformity to the Christian attitude.

It is necessary that the teacher should adopt some method for conducting class discussions, but the method may be one that admits of variations from time to time. The debate and the panel discussion are so well known to all that nothing need be said of them. The method of the Sodality of Our Lady calls for dividing the group into committees and subcommittees, each of which is made responsible for some aspect of the work that is to be done.[2] The Phillips 66 method and the kineposium method are methods of breaking down large groups into small groups and of rotating them so that each individual will in the course of time meet with all other members of the entire group.[3] All these methods apply solely or chiefly to the organization of the discussion group. For the fundamental approach to the problem of arriving at truth the teacher could hardly do better than adopt what the Young Christian Workers calls its inquiry technique, which is expressed in the slogan "Observe, Judge, and Act."[4] Constant reference should be made to these three steps. The first step is to observe, by which is meant the gathering of all pertinent facts concerning a problem or situation, and here there is almost no limit to what a teacher might say concerning scholarly methods of gathering, evaluating, and interpreting data. The second step is to judge, or to reach a conclusion, and here the teacher might encourage students to learn to distinguish between conclusions that are certain and conclusions that are only probably true. The final step is to act; that is, to determine to accept some ideal or principle as one's own and to carry it out insofar as conditions permit. Students will also need help in becoming active and useful members of their groups. On this point the teacher will find much excellent material in *My Group and I.*[5] This small manual was written for adult groups organized in associations, but the teacher can easily make a selection of principles suitable for high-school students. It also contains rating scales for evaluating discussions.

Teachers should beware of making the group-guidance sessions into exhortatory "this-must-be-done" or "what-not-to-do" meetings.

---

[2] Daniel A. Lord, *New Sodality Manual.* St. Louis: The Queen's Work, 1945.

[3] *The Summer School of Catholic Action, 1949 Season.* St. Louis: The Queen's Work, 1949.

[4] *This Is the Young Christian Workers,* pp. 37-38. Chicago: Young Christian Workers, n. d.

[5] Gordon L. Lippitt and Warren· H. Schmidt, *My Group and I.* Washington: Educator's Washington Dispatch, 1952.

The student must be able to fit the suggested action into his life and circumstances. He should be stimulated to positive rather than negative action. He must be free to seek depth of principle or the fullness of grace that is offered to him. The unrealistically pious approach or lack of interest and enthusiasm on the part of the teacher hinders the desirable effects of positive leadership and mature development. A sincere desire to understand and a manifest interest in helping the individual will bring favorable results more readily than any studied technique.

A group-guidance leader can also with a bit of ingenuity and disguise convert recognized methods of meditation into group-guidance techniques. The Catholic teacher from his own training should be well versed in the methods of meditation which are easily adaptable to subjects of character guidance. Each period should close with practical and positive applications suggested by the teacher and the students. These applications will be in the form of possible action, new attitudes, and strengthened convictions. The teacher, however, must be sensitive to student reactions in order to make his meditation meaningful to them.

GUIDANCE THROUGH ORGANIZATIONS

The cocurricular and extracurricular program of a school properly organized and carried out provides another group medium for aiding the adjustment and development of students. The club program of a school should be integrated intimately with the over-all work of the school in providing information, expressing individual interests, developing abilities, and encouraging the religious and social virtues. The club program may effectively be related to the subject areas of the academic program of the school. To prevent duplication of activities and to guarantee a well-rounded program, a limit should be placed on the number of clubs or organizations in the school. A sensible plan would provide one club for each of such areas as athletics, science, music, and religion, and one for each of the major interests of students.

The administrator of the school must be able to justify the existence and the activities of any organization by evidence of its contribution to the welfare of the students in particular and of the school in general. The moderator of the individual organization should be made responsible for maintaining a worthwhile objective for the group. Periodic examination of the value of these clubs should be made in order to test their right to continue in operation. Solely recreational or social groups are a luxury for Catholic schools and do not fulfill the prime responsibilities of a school.

In every Catholic school there should be at least one organization devoted principally to the promotion of spiritual values and activities. The name given to this group makes little difference as long as the work is carried out. Whatever technique is used, it should serve the real and long-term needs of the students and the community. A spiritual organization should be looked upon as the most effective group in the school and the one in which membership is most to be sought.

INTERCULTURAL GUIDANCE

Provisions for developing in students an appreciation of the fine arts and for deepening aesthetic and cultural values should be diffused through the entire curriculum of the school. Although an understanding and appreciation of the true, the good, and the beautiful are developed only with time and after considerable education, the guidance department should be watchful for ways by means of which cultural values can be achieved and cultural advances brought about. Special programs, assemblies, inspirational speakers, concerts, and displays can aid in achieving long-range cultural objectives.

True culture implies an absence of provincialism and a knowledge and appreciation of the contributions of other nations. Intercultural education, as the term suggests, is directed toward making one nation more appreciative of the cultures of other nations. Intercultural education is accomplished in part by the exchange of students between nations. The foreign-student program, in addition to being a means of extending culture, provides an opportunity of practicing the corporal work of mercy of harboring the stranger, who because of the ravages of war and because of persecution is often one in great need of help. Since many of the students coming to the

United States are Catholics or from nations whose people are predominantly Catholic, every effort should be made to participate in the exchange-student program.

The National Catholic Welfare Conference occasionally issues appeals for temporary homes for foreign students. Participation with the NCWC involves the raising of money through the school, provision of free tuition and books, and finding a host family to care for a foreign student. The American Field Service Student Exchange Program also offers Catholic schools an opportunity to participate in its program. Information about this program may be secured from the local representative or by writing to the American Field Service Student Exchange Program, 113 East Thirtieth Street, New York City. The major problem of Catholic schools in joining in this program will be the raising of funds to bring the teen-age ambassadors to this country or to send a student abroad. The minimum cost of a foreign student for the school or the sponsoring agency is $650.00. The cost of sending one of our own students abroad for the summer is $525.00. The new school program of AFS now permits young Americans to attend school for five months while living abroad. Oftentimes service clubs and community agencies are willing to underwrite the project and to supply the funds that are necessary for this expression of fraternal charity.

FRESHMAN ORIENTATION

The planning and supervision of the orientation of new students to the particular mode of life at the school is a responsibility of the guidance department. Freshmen especially cannot be presumed to know what to do, where to go, how to study, or how to act in the new educational environment. The first days should be a pleasant experience in which the new student receives aid in making the necessary adjustment and in acquiring healthy attitudes. A carefully devised orientation program should guarantee the adjustment which will prevent problems from arising later.

The objectives of new-student orientation should be:

1 To introduce the new student to the school program, personnel, and plant.

2 To integrate the student into the larger social group.

3 To assist the student to assume responsible school citizenship and self-direction.

4 To form the desirable attitudes and to provide the motivation that are characteristic of the Catholic school in general and of this Catholic school in particular.

5 To establish cooperative home-school relationships.

A program of orientation by which these objectives will be achieved should be drawn up by the guidance personnel. Elements of such a plan would include a classroom unit (offered in the religion, social-studies, English, or physical-education classes), a student handbook, homeroom group instruction, a big-brother-big-sister program, welcome assemblies, group introductions, and so forth. The classroom orientation unit should seek in particular to give the necessary information, to develop needed skills and appreciations, to show the opportunities for personal growth, and to designate clearly the manner in which the student vocation is fulfilled. An opening assembly planned as a welcome to new students can effectively and briefly introduce the new students and accept them into the student community. Study schedules, traditions, manners, and allied topics may be explained in a more individual follow-up in the group-guidance program of the homeroom. The student handbook will be a necessary tool of orientation in a large school. This permanent guide will serve parents as well as students during the school year.[6]

Forms of initiation such as hazing, paddling, and the compulsory wearing of odd types of dress should be prohibited in Catholic schools in favor of more intelligent acceptance of new members into the student community. The orientation services supplied and the welcome tendered by older students ought to be a true expression of the Christian virtues of charity and justice among members of the mystical body. Success in achieving orientation objectives will be evidenced by the love and appreciation which the new student will

---

[6] In addition to parent-teacher conferences a parents' newsletter containing current information on school progress and policies can be an excellent means of promoting cooperative home-school relationships. The letter should be composed by the principal and may be sent regularly with bills for tuition.

have for his school and fellow students. His positive attitudes of cooperation, enthusiasm, and serious work will evidence his adjustment and happiness in the new environment.

The content of the orientation program should be adapted to local school conditions, but will include much of the following:

Objectives and aims of a Catholic high-school education

Curriculum, personnel, and operation of the new school

Healthy attitudes to the new school and its authorities

Rules of attendance and discipline

How to study and do high-school work

Traditions, the religious life of school, Mass and the sacraments

Physical plan of the building, care of property

Names and pictures of school personnel

Names and pictures of student officers

Activities and organizations, curricular and noncurricular

Time schedules

School colors, songs, yells, and so forth

Calendar of special events, sports and social

Special regulations in regard to dress, library, fire and safety regulations, and so forth

Grading system, honors, report cards

Expenses, means of transportation, cafeteria information, and so forth

Guidance and counseling services

HEALTH GUIDANCE

Methods of integration of health services with the guidance program will vary considerably with the size of the school and the available services of trained personnel. Diocesan, state, county, and local requirements for health education also play a part in determining the type of health program. The responsibility for this area of guidance and for giving the required health instruction may be assigned by the guidance director to the physical-education, biology, hygiene, or other related departments.

Counselors should be concerned with the physical and mental health of students whom they interview. In each case the counselor should check as far as possible on the condition of the student's health and on the care that the student is taking of his health, and make the proper referrals in cases of deficiency. Group-guidance teachers will find it appropriate to discuss hygiene and personal appearance during the year. All teachers in general should take note of physical defects or handicaps, sight or hearing difficulties, unhealthy skin conditions, and so forth, and refer the students to the school physician or nurse.

One of the school staff may be selected as health-services coordinator to take care of the supplies and equipment needed for incidental school illness and accidents occurring during the school day. He should administer the details of any health and accident policies in which the school or student body participates, arrange for a school physician, coordinate work with the school nurse, make the arrangements for routine physical examinations, serve as the center for referral of students with handicaps and health problems, and generally supervise health education in the school.

GUIDANCE AND DISCIPLINE

Inasmuch as the management of the discipline of a school is intimately related to responsible guidance, all staff members of a school must share in the maintenance of order and in securing compliance with school regulations by students. Intelligent guidance and counseling supplying effective motivation create a love and desire for good discipline and prevent problems at their outset. Teachers who keep their disciplinary problems to themselves and successfully solve them in a manner that contributes to the welfare of school and students perform an excellent guidance service. The Christian teacher will look upon discipline as instruction in the fourth commandment and as a means of developing the virtues of justice and obedience.

The personnel for the enforcement of discipline in a school ought to be distinct from the personnel in charge of guidance, and the offices used by the two departments ought to be separated. In the minds of the students the work of the deans of discipline should not be closely associated with the work of the counselor. Nonetheless, guidance workers and disciplinarians will have much in common and will strive cooperatively to prevent or solve problems connected with the adjustment of students.

The deans of discipline regularly solve behavior and attendance problems of students themselves. At times, however, they will find it helpful to refer the problem to the guidance personnel or to send the student directly to the counselor. The deans will serve as the liaison officers between the school and student and the home, the courts, and the attendance bureau. In the work of the disciplinarian problems of undesirable student adjustment other than school behavior will frequently come to light and should be referred to the guidance personnel.

Whatever the problem, the objective of both guidance and discipline should be therapeutic even in the punishment of offenders. The deans should be striving for a cooperative and wholesome attitude toward school regulations on the part of students. Students should be made to feel that violations of school discipline are not considered by the dean as a personal offense. The enforcement of discipline and the imposing of punishment should be understood as prompted by respect for authority and the desire to have order maintained for the best welfare of the individual and the group.

Patience, fairness, understanding, judgment, justice, and above all a saving sense of good humor are among the manifold qualities required of the disciplinarian. The ability to command respect and to instill the "fear of the Lord" will facilitate his work of correction. The ability to forget the problems of the day will help the disciplinarian maintain good order in the school without strains that should if possible be avoided.

SELECTED REFERENCES

Allen, Richard D., and Margaret E. Bennett. "Guidance through Group Activities." In *The Thirty-seventh Yearbook of the National Society for the Study of Education,* Part 1, Chapter 5. Chicago: National Society for the Study of Education, 1938.

Allen, Richard D.; Frances J. Stewart; and Lester J. Schloerb. *Common Problems in Group Guidance.* New York: Inor Publishing Company, 1934.

Arbuckle, Dugald S. *Guidance and Counseling in the Classroom,* Chapter 8, "The Student Group." Boston: Allyn and Bacon, 1957.

Bennett, Margaret E. *Guidance in Groups.* New York: McGraw-Hill Book Company, 1955.

Crow, Lester D., and Alice Crow. *An Introduction to Guidance; Principles and Practices,* Chapter 10, "Guidance in Group Situations." New York: American Book Company, 1951.

Foster, Charles R. *Guidance for Today's Schools,* Chapter 6, "Guidance Activities of a School-Wide Nature." New York: Ginn and Company, 1957.

Gordon, Ira J. *The Teacher as a Guidance Worker,* Chapter 7, "The Teacher as a Group Worker." New York: Harper and Brothers, 1956.

Hoppock, Robert. *Group Guidance: Principles, Techniques, and Evaluation.* New York: McGraw-Hill Book Company, 1949.

McDaniel, Henry B. *Guidance in the Modern School,* Chapter 15, "Group Activities in Guidance." New York: Dryden Press, 1956.

Ohlsen, Merle M. *Guidance: An Introduction,* Chapter 4, "Guidance and School Discipline"; Chapter 14, "Counseling Individuals within the Group Setting"; Chapter 15, "Group Activities in the Guidance Program." New York: Harcourt, Brace and Company, 1955.

Ryan, Leo V. "Group Techniques in Vocational Guidance." *Catholic Educational Review* 51:29-42, January 1953.

Willey, Roy DeVerl, and Dean C. Andrew. *Modern Methods and Techniques in Guidance,* Chapter 19, "Group Procedures of the Guidance Program"; Chapter 20, "Group Assistance in Learning to Adjust." New York: Harper and Brothers, 1955.

CHAPTER FOUR

COUNSELING

Counseling is the work of guiding the individual to the most perfect development of his total personality and character by personal attention rather than by group methods. Through conferences with the individual a counselor seeks to use all the means possible to assure the best Christian growth in the spiritual, mental, physical, and vocational areas of the life of the student counselee. The counselor assists the individual soul to choose the ideal goals of life and to make a wise selection of the means by which he will attempt to achieve these goals.

THE NECESSITY OF COUNSELING

A small child depends constantly upon his parents, and especially upon his mother, for help and direction. Even mature men and women often feel the need to ask for advice. Sympathetic counseling is most necessary during the period of adolescence. Adolescence, always a critical period, faces new problems because of the complexity of modern life and the size of the modern school.

The Critical Period of Adolescence. High-school adolescents are at the most critical stage of their development, both naturally and supernaturally. The physical changes that occur at puberty and the resultant interest in sex create serious problems that are completely new and for which adolescents do not always find answers ready at hand. There have been both an increase in their independence of action and a certain relaxation, at least in many cases, of parental control. The groups with which they mingle do not have the innocence and docility of young children and by example or even suggestion may become sources of temptation. The need to decide what they are to do with their lives begins to become imminent and pressing. At this stage of their development adolescents are most sensitive and most responsive to personal direction and assistance. Despite their seeming unwillingness at times to listen or to be assisted, they appreciate the personal interest taken in them. Counselees value the prudent counsel which is necessary if Christian living is to become for them a matter of habit and of intelligent self-direction.

The Complexity of Life. Most of the problems of modern living are far too complex for the adolescent mind to solve. A lack of assistance in these problems, or at least an absence of the opportunity for assistance, leaves the student bewildered. The counselor may not be able to do much about changing or removing the problems; he may succeed only in identifying the problem of the student. On the other hand, the counselor can do very much to enable the student to solve or face his own problems with the security and assurance that comes from counsel. The need of seeking counsel is a priceless lesson for the adolescent to learn. It should be noted that problems are really solved by the student, not by the counselor; it is the student, inquiring and judging and acting, who effects the solution.

The Impersonal Nature of the Large Modern School. The larger the school, the more absolute the necessity of a counseling program. Greater numbers of students increase the possibility that the school may become impersonal, forgetting the individual and thereby forsaking that attention to and concern for the individual soul which are the characteristic mark of Catholic education. In any school in which each teacher does not know all the students, someone must be made responsible for checking on individual student progress and development. Good direction of an effective counseling program should prevent students from getting lost in the crowd.

The Development of Vocations. The Catholic school has the responsibility of preserving and developing vocations to the priesthood and the religious life. A vocation includes a personal call and an individual response, and a student oftentimes needs help in deciding whether he has a call and what his response should be. Personal counseling is therefore necessary if the school is to do that for which it is responsible. At the same time counseling will serve to encourage existent vocations, to uncover the hidden ones, and direct all these vocations to fruition.

The responsibility of building and preserving the tradition of Catholic marriage for the vast majority of students weighs heavily on Catholic secondary schools. To achieve satisfactory results in this area prudent counseling of the individual will be a necessity. These matters cannot be left to chance, nor can they be neglected by assuming that they are cared for at home or in the parish. Personal counseling of every individual in the school on Catholic marriage is a necessity of the first order. The subject is too closely connected with the very core of Catholic education to justify the school in using anything but the surest approach.

COUNSELING IN A CATHOLIC SCHOOL

Those who are responsible for counseling in a Catholic high school should of course be acquainted with the best methods and procedures known to the educational world in general. They should be determined not to permit their zeal and their interest in the young to fall short of the zeal and interest often found in counselors in public schools. But most of all, they should appreciate and make the fullest possible use of those sources of supernatural help that are available to them and that other less privileged counselors do not think of using. They should also be aware at all times of the spiritual objectives that ought to be sought before all other objectives.

The Work of Grace and the Holy Spirit. In a Catholic school the major work of counseling will always be accomplished through the working of the Holy Spirit, sent by Christ to teach us all things. He is the guide and comforter of the individual soul as well as of the Church in general. The operation of the Holy Spirit is even more pronounced in counseling the individual than it is in the guidance of the group. The most effective counseling of a Christian student is brought about through the power of God's grace enlightening the intellect and strengthening the will to achieve the goal of life by making necessary adjustments in one's person and action. Therefore the supernatural basis of counseling is the state of grace, which if absent must be established in the souls of both counselor and counselee. The gift of counsel cannot be fully utilized unless grace is present.

Counsel as a supernatural virtue is operative and effective only with the development of the fundamentals of the spiritual life. The life of grace, the power of the virtues received in baptism, the strength of confirmation, and the gifts and fruits of the Holy Spirit prepare the way for effective counseling. Counseling must rely on these supernatural helps for the realization of the supernatural purpose of living. For the counselor, then, the constant deepening of grace is the first objective. The employment of other techniques and the use of human wisdom and natural prudence may be good in themselves, but they represent a fundamentally imperfect procedure and power. The results of counseling on a natural basis alone will be uncertain, limited, and often faulty in the light of the Christian objectives of a counseling program.

An understanding of supernatural virtues and the gift of counsel are a *sine qua non* of a Catholic counseling program. Guidance workers and counselors must know the working of the Holy Spirit in the souls of individuals in order to see the true meaning of their work and to employ effective methods of counseling. A humble and correct evaluation of counseling achievements must always take into account the role of the Holy Spirit, lest the counselor take undue credit for himself. A counselor should be thoroughly aware that his work is that of facilitating the work of the Holy Spirit, who by the gift of counsel instructs the reason of the counselee in what actions to perform in life.[1]

[1] The chapter on "The Virtue of Counsel and Counseling Skill," in Charles A. Curran, *Counseling in Catholic Life and Education,* pp. 18-39 (New York: The Macmillan Company, 1952), is a valuable chapter for a counselor.

Counseling and the Works of Mercy. Counseling involves the performance of many spiritual works of mercy. It is more than the process of counseling the doubtful; it will also embrace the work of admonishing the sinner, of instructing the ignorant, of comforting the sorrowful, and of teaching others to bear wrongs patiently, to forgive all injuries, and to seek the universal welfare of the living and the dead. The counselee is the doubtful, the ignorant, the inexperienced, the immature student whom the counselor assists through an individual relationship that touches the soul. The removal of sin, ignorance, doubt, and sorrow should be the objective of a counselor.

Phases of counseling which help the student to evaluate himself and his environment, to adjust to present problems, and to be prepared for the changing conditions of the future are correctly interpreted as works of mercy. If the counselor has occasion to add any of the corporal works of mercy, he can practice the highest type of Christian citizenship. Much of what is called training for good citizenship ought to be translated into training for the performance of the works of mercy. True happiness on earth flows from unselfish service for the bodies and souls of others.

The counselor should single out these works as the finest means by which to attain to citizenship in heaven as well as on earth. He should prepare the student for self-direction, self-discipline, and self-activity in the works of mercy. Such counseling, far more than the mere giving of advice, will lead the student to the imitation of the Christian personality and the Christlikeness he sees in the counselor. Good counseling should bring the counselee to wish to serve others through his chosen vocation in life. When the habit of performing the works of mercy out of love of God and neighbor has been established, the true goals of counseling will have been achieved.

OBJECTIVES IN COUNSELING

The principal objectives of the counseling program in a Catholic school are as follows:

1 To carry out the responsibility of the school and the individual staff members for the proper formation of the Christian mind and personality of each student.

2 To help the student know himself and his problems and arrive at a greater degree of assurance and self-direction, so that he may act prudently in the events of his daily life.

3 To direct students in religious matters, aiding them to decide, choose, act, and live in a manner that enables them to perform the work of saving their souls and those of others.

4 To render personal assistance in a manner that will develop the virtues, especially those of responsibility and self-control, in a student who is forming himself socially, morally, and vocationally.

5 To provide guidance in the gradual adjustment of students to new surroundings and to a new period of life with its many accompanying problems.

6 To give the necessary knowledge and to utilize all the means for deciding upon a vocation, applying data and test results in counseling sessions to arrive at the selection of a vocation.

7 To safeguard against the unjust or unwise treatment and dismissal of students.

8 To exercise the virtue of counsel and to provide for imitation a good example of the priestly or the religious life, thereby attracting students to this life.

9 To check on the progress of students in their intellectual life by considering their grades, their choice of subjects, their test scores, their application, and their chosen or probable work after graduation.

10 To investigate and help students to correct any unfavorable condition or to supply needs proper to the student; for example, health, job, companions, morals, home life, influence.

THE DUTIES OF COUNSELORS

In order to carry out the objectives that have been given, the counselor is obliged:

1 To notify his counselees by writing or in person that he is their personal counselor. If counselors are chosen by the students, the best relationship is already established. If counselors are assigned, the counselor must make this initial contact in a friendly and helpful manner.

2 To be available at all reasonable times for consultation. Ordinarily one gives this work a priority over most extracurricular or co-curricular activities.

3 To familiarize himself with the background history of the counselee by reading the cumulative record before counseling.

4 To confer with the counselee once each semester, or oftener as the case demands.

5 To discuss with each counselee the areas given on the counselor guide form.

6 To note carefully the observations of faculty members relative to the counselee's progress and conduct. If advisable, observations ought to be brought to the attention of the counselee so that he can make necessary readjustment or take appropriate action.

7 To protect the interests of the counselee at all times, especially if he is in danger of dismissal. No student should be recommended for dismissal until the counselor has been heard or has been given an opportunity of speaking in support of a counselee.

8 To inquire of each counselee about the possibility of a religious vocation, and generally to assist him in the choice of an occupation or state of life.

9 To inquire of every Catholic about the performance of his religious duties; namely, attendance at Sunday Mass, reception of the sacraments, and daily prayer. Such information normally is a matter of confidence. Similar questions may be put to the non-Catholic student.

10 To complete and file a counselor guide form with the guidance office. (See pages 221-23.)

QUALITIES REQUIRED IN COUNSELORS

To be successful a counselor must possess certain qualities of soul and of mind, of which the former are by far the most important.

Qualities of Soul. To list all the desirable qualities in a counselor in a Catholic school would be to portray the character of Christ.[2]

---

[2] Karl Adam, *The Son of God,* translated by Philip Hereford (New York: Sheed and Ward, 1940), in Chapters 4 and 5 gives a graphic picture of the qualities of the model counselor, Christ.

A truly Christian personality is the finest equipment for counseling work. Such desirable personality characteristics as unselfishness, interest in students, sincerity, patience, enthusiasm, friendliness, tact, cheerfulness, wisdom, justice, kindness, tolerance for the opinions of others, and good humor are in reality only manifestations of the theological and moral virtues and of the fruits and gifts of the Holy Spirit. Together with these qualities of personal holiness the counselor should also possess the ability to radiate in some degree the character of Christ. Good judgment and the ability to act prudently are essential qualities for counseling.

Qualities of Mind. Information on the part of the counselor should precede his work for the formation of the counselee. The counselor ought to have a clear knowledge of the work of counseling, its aims, procedure, methods, and sources of information. Adequate understanding of students with their differences and problems is a necessary prerequisite to the exercise of good judgment in providing for development and in removing conflicts. The teacher who is conscious of the needs of the individual in the classroom will already be performing skillfully the function of the counselor.

By reason of his training a priest or religious should be capable of doing satisfactory counseling. Counselors in Catholic schools, however, will often be inadequately qualified in the area of occupational information. For many years Catholic secondary schools were largely college-preparatory, and the need for occupational guidance was not as obvious as it is today. Private study or college courses in guidance in this area ought to be recommended for staff members who do guidance and counseling work. At least one of the school staff should have made a study of educational and vocational testing programs, so that intelligent direction in these areas may be given to other members of the staff.

THE SELECTION OF COUNSELORS

Questions that occur in connection with the selection of counselors have to do with the use of faculty members, the appointment of a head counselor, the methods of assigning counselees to counselors, and the use of counselors of special kinds.

Faculty Members as Counselors. Every faculty member in a Catholic school is ordinarily considered a counselor sharing the responsibility for the total work of guidance. If a teacher is truly a Catholic at heart, he will want the opportunity to be of service to the minds and souls of students. To mold a character into the character of Christ and to transform a personality into His personality is to do the finest work of education. To do this work directly and individually by counseling is often more effective than teaching a formal subject. Since not all teachers realize this important truth, the desire of a teacher to do counseling should be known before he is assigned to serve in this capacity.

Other factors which might prevent a teacher from undertaking the task of counseling are a heavy teaching schedule, extracurricular duties, personality factors, or the holding in the school of positions not conducive to a good counseling relationship. By reason of the duties of their offices the principal, the deans of discipline, and the superior are not eligible to act as counselors. For them to serve as counselors would restrict their freedom of action in regard to their counselees. Some teachers and staff members will be better suited than others for the work of counselor. The principal should strive to free such individuals from activities or heavy teaching loads in order to enable them to do more of the counseling work.

The Appointment of a Head Counselor. The principal should delegate to one person responsibility for supervising and administering the counseling program. Depending on the size of the school, this person may be the director of guidance or a staff member. The office of the head counselor should serve as a center for counseling activities. His duties are as follows:

1 To provide a source and channel of information regarding counselee problems and direction.

2 To define and make known to the staff the aims and objectives of counseling for any given year.

3 To build, maintain, and check periodically the cumulative file of nonconfidential information on students and to make certain that such information reaches the classroom teacher.

4 To direct the selection of counselors and counselees.

5 To channel information and requests for counseling to the proper counselor.

6 To check on the results of counseling when a referral or request is made.

7 To provide forms, outlines, and questionnaires for more efficient counseling.

8 To keep a current counselor bulletin board or other means of communication with counselors to give them information on the latest developments, especially in the field of college or vocational guidance.

9 To learn which students are maladjusted, specially gifted, or deficient in religious instruction or practice and to assign them to the proper counselor.

10 To serve as a specialist whom others can consult in unusual problems of counseling or to whom cases can be referred.

11 To check on the progress of the counseling program, its quality, and its extent.

The Selection of Counselors by Students. In order to achieve the best results from the relationship of counselor and counselee, students should be permitted to choose their own counselors. This conduces to the acceptance and friendly esteem that are vital to good counseling. A list of eligible counselors from which to choose should be given to students. An exception may be made in the case of freshmen who have not had the opportunity to appraise their teachers or who have not as yet established a friendly relationship with any teachers. After selections have been made by the upper classes, freshmen may be assigned to teachers whose counseling load is light.

When students are permitted to select their counselors, some staff members will be more popular than others. This popularity will last only as long as the staff member is successful in his work. Students will choose the one who actually does the work of counseling, the one who manifests an interest in them, and the one who truly helps them in their growth. To prevent excess counseling loads students should be requested to name an alternate or second choice for counselor. The director of guidance or the principal who assigns and apportions the counseling load should honor the first choices of the upperclassmen. Students in the lower classes should be given their alternate choice only when necessary. The naming of alternates by students makes it possible easily to reassign a counselor in the event of the illness or absence of a counselor or of a breakdown of the desirable counseling relationship.

Teachers who are aware of the importance of counseling and conscious of differences in personality will not look upon this method of selection of counselors as a popularity contest and be offended by students' choices. Staff members should realize that each has his own gift to use in the service of others. Ability in this work is God's gift of counsel implemented by the power of the Holy Spirit, who does not give the same gifts to all (1 Corinthians 12:27-31).

The Selection Form. Students should make out a counselor-selection form in duplicate. One set of these forms (see page 213) remains with the director of guidance and one is given to the respective counselor, that both may have a complete file of names, class schedules, and free periods with which to begin immediately. The form should always ask the student whether he wishes to see his counselor as soon as possible. The answer will tell the counselor which students desire and need immediate attention.

Assigned Counselors. When the local school situation does not make it advisable for students to select counselors, the director of guidance or the principal will make assignments, bearing in mind that any counselor should be acceptable to students and conscientious in fulfilling his duties. Disagreeable or uninterested personnel can do great harm as counselors, for the most important and lasting relationship between student and school is dependent upon that created by the counselor. In a surprising number of instances the strongest impact of Catholic education has been in the relationship between counselor and counselee. To assure the achievement of the aims of Catholic education, assignment of the best-qualified teachers to counseling positions is prudent action on the part of the administration.

Special Counselors. Students who show unusual aptitude or promise should be assigned to experienced counselors or to specialists in programs for gifted children. Similarly, those who give signs of a religious vocation may be directed to a faculty member who is interested and skilled in the development of vocations. Depending on the size of the staff, there may be counselors who are adept at the handling of unusual and difficult cases of various kinds; for example, students suffering from the effects of broken homes or living under impossible home conditions, students with physical handicaps, poor readers, and others who present problems of a special kind. In some instances the director of guidance may prefer to serve these counselees himself and then to make any necessary referrals.

The Number of Counselees. Staff members should realize that every student without exception must have a counselor. Even though the counselor may not be able to interview each student as promptly and thoroughly as he might wish, the counselee should be made aware that he has someone to whom he may go in time of need. The counseling load depends on many factors: the number of available counselors, the extent of the program, the attitude of the personnel to these services, and budget provisions for the work.

The extent of other school duties also helps determine the number of counselees a teacher may be required to serve. The willing and effective counselor may be assigned a greater load than others. For the teacher who has been given one free period per day, the reasonable minimum number is approximately fifty counselees. A much larger number can be handled if the interviews are limited to a brief check on student progress. In any case the important point is that the counselee be interviewed.

The counselor with a true sense of values in the work of education will realize the pre-eminent importance of the counseling function. He will be keenly conscious of the fact that the time utilized in individual contact on matters of personal development and adjustment brings a more permanent good than time spent in routine school and personal affairs, and he will therefore exert every effort to interview each of his counselees in the best manner possible.

THE USE OF COUNSELING TIME

Most frequently the greatest amount of the available time for counseling is spent on those few whose problems are complex, whose home situations are abnormally difficult, or whose healthy development has been prevented by unfortunate circumstances. These cases are vitally interesting to the counselor, but they may also take the time that should be used for an adequate coverage of all counselees. Care should be prudently exercised to prevent the few from utilizing time which should be available for others.

Counseling is not designed to help only the weakest students; it should make the good students better and serve the ablest and strongest as well. A short time spent in counseling normal students will often prevent an undue demand for counseling time at a later stage. Concern should be concentrated upon the counseling of new students who need immediate attention in choosing the right course of action and the right objectives.

There are situations in which some of the time for counseling may be used for social visiting with the counselee. Regularly, however, social "chitchat" is not appropriate to a counseling interview. The counselor has a professional work to do and the counselee has the duty of attending class and of applying himself to study.

A wise counselor should know that some areas and problems often cannot be thoroughly handled at certain times. Accordingly he will indicate to the counselee that he ought to come back later, give the problem some thought, or wait until circumstances have cleared sufficiently to offer a solution. To force a solution, adjustment, or development when all the phases of the problem are not known or present is useless and possibly harmful. Many problems have no immediate solution other than the decision to live patiently with them for a time.

The Length of the Counseling Interview. In the normal or average counseling interview approximately twenty minutes will be sufficient to achieve good results. If counselor and counselee are adequately prepared for the interview, the areas of counseling can be covered rather readily. Some areas may be omitted when both know that all is in order in those areas. A simple remark such as "You seem to be doing very nicely and developing properly in this regard" will provide the student with the necessary bit of incentive and encouragement to continue. He deserves and needs assurance of satisfactory progress more often than he needs correction.

A counselor working efficiently should be capable of conducting three full-scope interviews in the ordinary fifty-minute school period. When the interview does not require full coverage of the areas of counseling, the counselor may contact several more students. The secret of the efficient use of time in counseling is *preparation,* which is aided by regular use of easily accessible cumulative records. When the counselor has records at hand he can immediately familiarize himself with the student, learn what problems have been found to exist, and catch a kaleidoscopic view of student progress. Valuable time will not be consumed in needless questioning when the student realizes that the counselor has a clear profile of his life both at home and in school.

The Times for Counseling. The counselor who is convinced of the importance of his work should be willing to receive the counselee at any reasonable time. In a formal and systematic program the counselor should be permitted to call the counselee from any regular class or activity without objection on the part of teachers. The counseling session itself will frequently achieve more lasting results than the few minutes lost from the classroom. The principal and the guidance committee should establish a policy in this matter, win its approval by teachers, and carefully observe any undesirable results. The counselor record form may serve as a means of ensuring success for the policy.

Whenever a student is called from a class period for counseling, a previous arrangement with the teacher or a courteous note requesting a student interview should be sufficient. Although a special project or an examination scheduled for the entire class may call for rearrangement of the counseling appointment, no teacher should object to the absence of a student if a worthwhile result is achieved. Counselors should first try to interview counselees during free or study time. When this is not possible, the counselor may call the counselee from the religion period, since counseling is intimately related to this area. If a counselee is called from a class, the counselor should strive to make his counseling effective and not a social visit.

Experience shows that students will gladly remain after school hours if they know that counseling is profitable to them. Counselee-initiated calls upon the counselor are naturally more desirable, but the counselee readily learns to expect a call for counseling at regular intervals. If a friendly relationship has been set up, the counselee will be awaiting with eagerness his turn to talk over his problems or to be assured that he is progressing satisfactorily. The counselor will find advantage in posting the times at which he is available and asking his counselees to fill in the time at which they wish to be interviewed. Counselors should not delay in scheduling interviews at the beginning of the year. Examination time and the close of the school year are inconvenient times for counseling.

The Frequency of Counseling. Unless there are circumstances that warrant more frequent attention, two or three counseling sessions for each student per year are adequate and satisfactorily effective. One session early in the year should be devoted to devising a plan for development and for the satisfaction of personal needs. The other sessions should be held just previous to the time of forecasting subjects for the following year. A final summary session with seniors should be had before their graduation. Whenever a need is apparent, counseling should take place without making the student too dependent on the counselor. An excessive number of interviews is not good for counselor or counselee.

PHYSICAL FACILITIES

Ideal physical facilities for the work of guidance and counseling in a Catholic school may not always be possible. Lack of funds, lack of floor space, or the nature of the arrangement of the existing building may prevent the school from providing what should be provided. In such cases it is well to remember that the accomplishment of the work is far more important than the physical surroundings or conveniences that are available. A counselor, for example, may often have to utilize whatever areas are not being used at the moment, such as a vacant classroom, an unoccupied office, the health room, the publications room, the bookstore, or living quarters. For the purpose of counseling even the quiet end of a corridor or the corner of the gymnasium will suffice provided the place permits and encourages a reasonably quiet and confidential conversation. No place in a school should be so sacrosanct that it cannot be used for counseling. The nature of the surroundings will always be secondary to the nature of the relationship between counselor and counselee.

For schools initiating or developing a complete guidance program, and especially for the assistance of those responsible for the building of new school plants, some suggestions may be offered to guarantee an ideal guidance center. The floor plan should take into account the following factors, which have a close connection with the work of guidance and counseling: (1) the location of guidance and counseling rooms adjacent to other school offices; (2) ready access to communication systems and cumulative records; (3) the guarantee of privacy in counseling and the control of student traffic entering the guidance center; (4) efficient storage space and ample area for displays, bulletin boards, and so forth; (5) the possibility of the multiple use of rooms in the guidance area.

Heating and ventilation, lighting and window areas, floor coverings, and other furnishings should of course conform to the acceptable standards in school construction.

An ideal floor plan such as the one suggested on page 68 for the needs of a school in the 1200-enrollment range should allow variations that best meet the needs of an individual school and its existing guidance structure. A smaller school may omit several of the counseling rooms or diminish the size of other rooms, while larger institutions may wish to increase the number and size of guidance-center rooms. Some may desire the addition of special-purpose rooms adjoining the guidance center, and still others may propose to use some of the rooms as convent parlors, parish offices, or meeting rooms in the after-school hours.

Cumulative File and Records Room. The close relationship and the harmony of work that must exist between guidance personnel and the administrative staff make this room the key place of the guidance center and the connecting link with the general offices of the school. Although called a file and records room, it also houses the all-important intercommunication system of the school and the switchboard for Bell telephones. The room should be designed as a part of both the guidance center and the general office, which will be

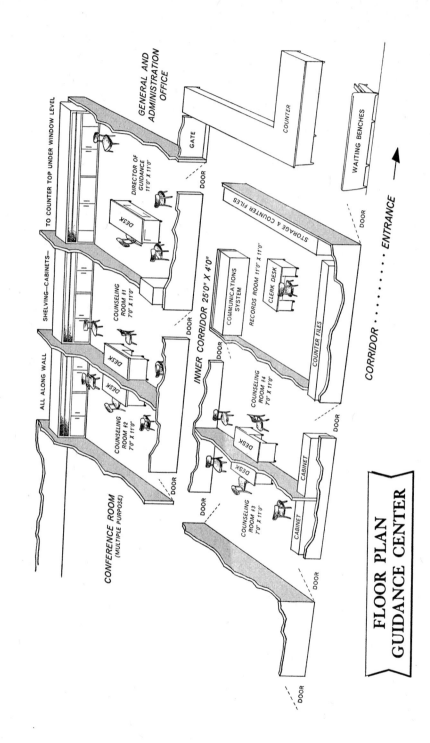

FLOOR PLAN
GUIDANCE CENTER

separated from each other only by a counter. Since the employment of clerical help so often poses a problem for Catholic schools, the plan here suggested for this room helps to eliminate the duplication of office personnel. The person occupying the records room or office will be in a position to carry out any of a number of duties; for example, that of guidance secretary, attendance clerk, monitor of student traffic in the offices, records clerk, receptionist, and when necessary, the work of mimeographing, and so forth.

Under the counters surrounding the two sides of the room cumulative records are kept in two-drawer locked files, each of which will accommodate the records of 150 students. Both counselors and office personnel need take only a few steps to reach the record of a student, and the attendant can easily keep check on the return and refiling of the records. Permanent records and business accounts, along with other valuable documents, should be kept in a vault or other place of safe keeping in another area of the general office.

The communication system located on the inner corridor side of the records room solves the often difficult problem of efficient and quick contact with students and faculty, since through this medium the counselor or attendant may readily deliver a message or request to anyone in any part of the building. While the convenience of an intercommunication system may lead to abuses, the time saved and the efficiency achieved through this equipment justifies its use and location. Administrative officers and counselors in particular must regularly contact many students each day. A polite call for an individual student in a faraway room in the building creates less disturbance of school order than finding a messenger, sending him to the room, knocking on the door, interrupting the teacher and the lesson to ask for the student, delivering the message, waiting for a reply, and finally returning to the office. A brief request on the intercommunication system requires only a word of permission and a nod from the teacher to the student who is wanted. At the office the student can be directed to the person who desires to speak with him, and in this way others will not know whether he is being summoned for counseling, for disciplinary action, or for some other matter that requires immediate attention.

General announcements to the entire school which may be made over this same system can be more readily controlled from the records room. Ordinarily the principal will find it necessary to use the system much less frequently than counselors, and he will not want the system within his office or close at hand when others need it more frequently and he can easily delegate its control to another.

The central telephone may be placed in this records room, from which calls may be directed by the attendant to the proper person by use of the intercommunication system when extension phones are not available. The need and location of extension telephones in the building will be determined by the principal of the school. The guidance center itself should have at least one extension that permits private conversation and referrals to parents or agencies. Where funds are limited, the installation of telephone jacks or extensions shared between counseling offices or the limited use of the central telephone by guidance personnel should be considered.

The main corridor wall of the records room may provide the outside bulletin-board space necessary to the guidance department for the posting of notices, schedules, dates of scholarship examinations, and so forth. Some schools may wish to have a window opening from this room to the main corridor for transactions and inquiries, and in this manner prevent the undue crowding of the inner offices. The records room should be equipped with the necessary filing cabinets, a desk and chair for the attendant, a typewriter, and storage space as needed by the individual school.

The Guidance Director's Office. A separate office for the person responsible for the guidance and counseling program should be provided in a location that lends itself to easy supervision and contact with other personnel. Space may be allocated in this office for the storage, care, and display of guidance materials, tests, and college bulletins on additional shelving and cabinets. The office should be furnished with a desk, several chairs, a telephone, a typewriter, a larger filing cabinet, and several smaller card files.

Counseling Offices. Each office should be so arranged as to be conducive to personal conversation and planning. The position of the desk and chair of the counselor should permit the placing of counselee chairs alongside, and so prevent the undesirable practice of talking across a desk to a counselee. Bulletin-board space, a small cabinet and shelving area, and several small card files for counselee schedules, occupational information references, and placement cards should be found in these offices. A telephone may be added where necessary, and a sliding panel between counseling rooms may also be optional. The counseling offices may be used as confessionals for boys, for waiting rooms, or for parent-teacher conferences when not being used for student counseling. The counseling office adjoining the records room may be converted into a waiting room for the guidance center.

The Inner Corridor. This corridor must be designed to admit light to the other offices through the clear glass above the six-foot level and through the open space above the glass. Below the glass level, bulletin-board space and eight-inch deep shelving may be provided, especially if the floor plan has been expanded to permit a wider corridor. In this case waiting benches may be placed along the walls.

The Conference Room. Directly adjoining the counseling offices 'is an area suitable for other phases of guidance work. The multiple-purpose conference room will provide a place for meetings of small groups of counselees, teachers, and parents, for physical examinations, for a health room, for small-group testing, for student activities, and even for a small classroom. The room ought to be equipped with the necessary tables and chairs, bulletin and blackboard space, outlets, and a sink and running water. Other conference rooms provided in a school floor plan should be located nearby.

The General Offices. These offices, as well as those of the principal and other administrative officers of the school, are indicated in this plan only to show their relative position with reference to the guidance center. The arrangement of this space, so often influenced by individual preference and local conditions, does not lie within the scope of this study.

THE COUNSELING INTERVIEW

The following outline of the principal duties necessary for the successful conduct of an interview should serve as a guide for the counselor in a Catholic secondary school.[3] The practical work connected with the holding of an interview is summarized under the three following phases: the preparation, the interview itself, and the postinterview duties.

I. Preparation:

    A. The counselor should gather information from the following available sources:

        1. The *cumulative record* containing personal history such as date and place of birth, parish, date of baptism, first Communion, and confirmation, schools attended and school from which admitted, parents' occupation, brothers and sisters. Record from the elementary school, current scholastic record in high school, questionnaires administered, record of any correspondence with reference to disciplinary or other matters, record of honors received or demerits acquired, record of previous counseling, and other significant data accumulated by teachers.

        2. The *permanent record* card presenting the over-all picture of current grades, character-personality record, intelligence quotient, results of testing (standardized and vocational), and credit received to date.

        3. The anecdotal reports from parents, teachers, and others who have information pertinent to the student.

    B. The counselor should notify the student that:

        1. He is the counselor assigned or chosen for the year.

        2. He wishes a copy of the class schedule and the free time of the counselee.

        3. There are set times at which the counselor is available.

        4. An interview is desired at a set time. A note delivered to the classroom, a telephone call the evening before, or a message will enable the counselee to be ready for the coming interview. If advisable, the counselor will indicate beforehand the problem or the subject matter of the interview.

---

[3] An extensive analysis of the interview and its technique may be found in the excellent work of Charles A. Curran, *Counseling in Catholic Life and Education* (New York: The Macmillan Company, 1952).

II. The Interview Itself:

A. Sincerity and interest in the student and the matters of discussion are the essential duty of the counselor. Lack of interest is quickly sensed and wholehearted response will be repressed. On the other hand, the counselee will speak readily and frankly to one he knows is concerned and helpful in offering direction as well as correction.

B. The counselor seeks to identify:

1. The present condition and problems of the counselee.
2. The advisable adjustment and the proper action at the present age of the counselee.
3. The nature of the progress made by the counselee.

C. The counselor should judge the areas of discussion most important at this time. To ensure proper coverage he may profitably use the suggested counselor guide form on pages 221-23. He may keep the form in sight as an aid to the orderliness of the interview.

D. The counselor should take sufficient time to achieve the objective in an adequate manner.

E. The closing of the interview should be on a friendly basis with a reminder of the suggested actions or objectives. The conclusion should be such as to serve as a preparation for subsequent counseling.

F. The following precautions should be observed:

1. Do not participate in criticism of teachers or authority. This is neither the function of counseling nor demonstrative of the virtue of counsel. It may be prudent to listen to the complaint and to accept the existence of a conflict of interests; the counselor, however, should encourage the counselee to accept the problem and should offer advice by which the difficulty can be solved or lived with. Counselors should recommend that the student review difficulties with teachers unemotionally and maturely, and accept criticism from those who hold positions of authority.
2. Do not assume the position of admonishing another teacher or staff member for what you might consider unjust treat-

ment of a counselee. Such matters are to be handled by an administrator, the director of guidance, or delegated personnel. It may be proper, however, to discuss the problem with a teacher with a view to discovering a solution or to reaching agreement on the procedure that is for the best interest of the student.

3. Do not personally solve the problem or conflicts of the counselee. The actual solution is the task of the person counseled. The counselor seeks only to help devise the solution and adjustment. A counseling interview will aid in the development of maturity when the student thereby grows in ability to face the changing circumstances of his present and future life and to solve the problems they present.

4. Do not inform a counselee of his recorded IQ when evaluating his scholastic ability. Intelligence-quotient figures are inexact and because of the influence of many factors the true intelligence quotient often varies greatly from the intelligence quotient derived from a test. Students and parents as well rarely understand correctly the meaning of an IQ. For sufficient reasons they may be told that the counselee is above or below average in intelligence.

5. Do not allow an interview to be generally negative criticism of the counselee except in extreme cases. A bit of deserved praise and encouragement will bring better results and stimulate further mature development.

6. Do not fill out a counselor record form or write a report in the presence of students. Such a practice prevents them from talking freely and honestly. In any case a better evaluation can be made upon a completed interview when all parts of the picture have been put together. If notes are taken, a counselee ought to be able to see or read them.

7. Do not record or place confidential information in the cumulative file. This file is for the use of all the school staff. If there is significant confidential information that affects the education of a student, a simple notation, "refer to _____," will serve to ensure correct treatment. The

rule to avoid recording moral or spiritual failures or lack of proper spiritual condition in a student should be absolute. To note on a counselor record form that a student is living an exceptionally good spiritual life may be helpful.

III. **Postinterview Duties:**

A. The counselor should make notes on the interview and fill out an interview record while the information and judgments are still vivid in his mind.

B. He should make the necessary referrals if there are any.

C. He should send the interview record to the guidance or counseling director, who places it in the cumulative file.

D. He should carry out promptly any services promised to the counselee and be alert to aid him when possible.

E. He should return any other records to their proper place immediately.

F. He should respect the professional confidence of the interview to the extent necessary. The counselee should realize that the information he gives may be used as a means of assisting him in his development. If complete secrecy is advisable, both counselor and counselee should understand the nature of such confidence.

THE TECHNIQUES OF COUNSELING

Counseling. Very much has already been said about the techniques of counseling in the section on the counseling interview (see pages 71 ff.). It may be helpful to speak briefly of informal as opposed to formal counseling and of directive as opposed to nondirective methods.

Informal Counseling. Informal counseling occurs in a casual and incidental meeting with a student during which there is discussion of his problems and progress. There will be general inquiry about his life as a student, specific questions about a difficulty, and some words of direction and encouragement. This meeting may take place after a class period, during lunch hour, in the corridor, at school activities, and at other times outside of school hours. Interest thus manifested in the routine matters of the school life of the student is helpful to the entire counseling process. The informality of the interview promotes an effective relationship of considerable benefit to the student. This type of counseling has been one of the great characteristics of Catholic schools.

Formal Counseling. Formal counseling is the planned meeting and discussion with the counselee. The counselee has come of his own accord with an objective in mind, or he has been called by the counselor for a discussion of general or specific points. Notice of the coming interview should stimulate both parties to prepare themselves for the formal counseling session. Both counselor and counselee, particularly the counselor, will give previous thought to areas in which counseling should take place. All the phases of development should be discussed at some time in formal counseling.

Directive and Nondirective Counseling. Much discussion and debate have occurred in recent years over the relative merits of directive and nondirective techniques. The counselor in a Catholic secondary school will not be unduly concerned with this debate if he remembers that counseling is largely the work of the Holy Spirit. He will choose accordingly the method or technique that prudence and the other gifts of the Holy Spirit suggest. The power of the grace of God and the sincere interest of the counselor will constitute the best elements of any counseling technique. When the subject matter or area of an interview calls for greater participation and initiative on the part of the student, the method should naturally be more nondirective on the part of the counselor. When the knowledge and experience of the counselor are essential to the welfare of the student, the counselor will assume a more directive role.

The choice of technique will therefore be determined by the objective sought in the interview. The objective may be to inform, to explore, to diagnose, to solve, to form, to adjust, to incite positive action or choice, to defer action, to negate a course of action, to persuade, to advise, to direct clearly, or not to direct. It may be the place of the counselor at times to listen rather than to talk, but in most instances it should be a combination of both. There are times when counselees should be permitted to express themselves quite freely. To permit one "to get something off his mind" may be therapeutic as long as it is done without sin and within the limits of reasonableness.

The routine interview with a Catholic adolescent will very frequently be directive on the part of the counselor. In areas of the moral and spiritual, whenever there is question of submission to authority or of the acceptance of an absolute truth, the counselor should be directive. In nearly all the areas of counseling an adolescent, the mature, trained, and reliable counselor regularly is expected to give positive aid, encouragement, and correction by directive counseling. If it cannot be safely presumed that the counselor is more informed and reliable than the counselee, the former should not act as a counselor; a referral should be humbly made to some competent source. If the counselee is not moved by ordinary methods to self-direction and action, circumstances may dictate that he be compelled to act as directed by the counselor.

The counselor should adapt his approach to the needs of the counselee and to the nature of the problem. Where there is a good relationship between the two, the interview will be a mutual work of securing the objectives of the counseling process. Some of the best counseling takes place in the small school where the teacher knows every student well and has an active interest in his welfare. The natural relationship of friend to friend will determine the technique most suitable and effective for the individuals concerned. With sufficient knowledge on the part of the counselor and with the state of sanctifying grace in the souls of counselor and counselee, the interview will be properly carried out, regardless of so-called scientific techniques. Counseling is meant to be a normal human relationship unrestricted and unharmed by excessive analysis.

THE AREAS OF COUNSELING

Since Catholic schools profess to educate students for full Christian living, counseling must cover all the aspects of an individual's manifold activity: the physical, the social, the religious, the moral, the mental, and the vocational. Three areas are most important: the mental, since the purpose of the school is the development of the intellectual virtues; and the religious and the moral, since a Catholic counseling program is concerned principally with the growth of souls. From the viewpoint of the place or purpose of an individual's activities counseling must embrace the total experience of life: home, church, school, leisure, and social, vocational, and occupational life. The suggestions on the following pages cover counseling in the areas of the physical, the social, the religious, the moral, the mental, and the vocational.

The Physical. Sufficient inquiry should be made concerning the physical health of each student. The health-record card in the personal file of the student should show whether more care is needed for the body as the vehicle of the soul. When necessary, the counselor should help the student to arrive at better personal living habits and hygiene. The counselor should observe the general appearance and the dress of the counselee. He may appropriately add a remark about care of the body as care of the temple of the Holy Spirit, a suggestion about physical strength as a gift, a reminder that attractiveness and beauty are desirable first in the soul, or a reference to the eyes as the windows of the soul. When special problems of health or physical handicaps are noted the counselor ought to make the necessary referral to the school nurse or to the local public health agency. Rehabilitation centers in every large city make aid available to adolescents with handicap problems. The counseling director, if he has the real welfare of the handicapped counselees at heart, will keep himself informed about all possibilities of aid in his community. A telephone call to the proper agency will provide preliminary contact and information.

The Social. The counselor will seek to determine whether the student is socially adjusted, merely accepted, maladjusted, or not accepted by fellow students. If it seems that a student is not making the proper adjustment or is not truly appraising his adjustment, the counselor should give some practical direction. He should suggest and seek means by which the student can reach greater social competence. A counselor should discuss the home situation and experience in such questions as: "How well do you get along with your parents, brothers, and sisters?" or "What are your points of disagreement?" or "What is the amount of guidance or supervision at home?" or "What do you feel is your predominant problem?" or "Is there anything that specially bothers you in this regard?"

In discussing the work experience of the counselee a counselor should indicate that ability to hold a job, to do it well, and to make a favorable impression on an employer is most valuable and indicative of success in the future. Work experiences ought to be related to the future and to the problems of selecting a vocation. A counselor should determine whether the hours spent in work interfere with progress in school.

In the area of leisure-time activity the counselor may open up a discussion of the ways in which a counselee spends his leisure time. The fact that hobbies and interests tell much about character and personality and that they may affect vocational and occupational choices may be conveyed to the student. The use that a student makes of his time is another important item of inquiry. Acceptance of the principle that the habit of using time well is a priceless quality is most important for the young.

A counselor will be concerned with the companions and associates of the counselee. A frank discussion of the desirability of companions of certain types may bring good results at a later time. A word of warning or a word of encouragement may be needed. Criticism should refer to types, not to individuals.

The boy-girl relationship should be a definite area of discussion. Normal development should include some reasonable interest in the opposite sex. A counselor should aid his counselee to picture the ultimate purpose of this relationship either as one of the means for the reliable selection of a spouse for marriage or simply as a practical necessity in learning to understand and get along with members of the opposite sex.

This discussion can naturally lead to other related areas, such as the problem of "going steady." Once the counselor learns what the individual means by "going steady," he can point out the dangers involved, analyze the problems already experienced, and point out the necessity of breaking up the steady dating arrangement. It should be accepted as a principle that "going steady" in the case of high-school students is to be discouraged in almost every instance.

Here a counselor should take the opportunity to uncover incorrect, puritanical, and impure attitudes to sex. Regular sex instruction is the responsibility of the parent and should be given by a counselor only when delegated by the parent or when the parent will certainly not provide that instruction. The development of a healthy, controlled, common-sense attitude on the subject of sex is an objective of counseling in the social area. The interview dealing with the social area is highly important in Catholic high schools of both coeducational and separate types. This phase of counseling should give encouragement to better Christian social development and to whatever contributes to protection against moral hazards.

The Religious. The priest or religious who is counseling an adolescent will be intensely concerned with the religious development of the counselee. A counseling session should never be completed without some discussion of spiritual affairs, or some encouragement to a finer religious life, or some indication about the pre-eminent importance of this phase of student growth. The first points of information to be sought from the cumulative record should be the fundamental facts of baptism and confirmation and the extent of religious instruction already received. As a result of discussion and by arrangement with the counselee provision should be made to supply any lack in the fundamental or spiritual development. This work should take priority over all the other work.

Prudent inquiry should be made into the general spiritual condition and spiritual attitude of the student and his regular reception of the sacraments, particularly if the counselor is a priest. These things, however, are quite correctly a matter of concern for any Catholic counselor, and students ought to learn to expect inquiry and discussion on fundamental essentials of Catholic education. Questions such as "How often do you go to Mass (during the week)?" or "How often do you go to Communion and/or confession?" are legitimate questions and necessary topics of discussion. Catholic teachers and counselors must create right attitudes and urge good habits in these matters. If no interest and concern are shown, counselors fail in connection with the primary objectives of the Catholic school that are the very cause of its existence.

When counseling directly facilitates the work of the Holy Spirit in student life by encouraging the use of the means of grace, the greatest amount of good is accomplished. Herein Catholic guidance has the most powerful of all the counseling aids. The use of the sacraments and of prayer, attendance at Mass, and prayer for light and strength to solve problems are basic helps not to be minimized in any way. On these matters the counselor can and must be most forthright; he should speak with authority and conviction; he must show forth the ideal, encourage the student, and even seriously warn a careless counselee.

The counselor can exercise a tremendous personal influence when he indicates specific ways and means of spiritual living or singles out areas of spiritual experiences, deeper spiritual life, and aids to progress. Personal spiritual direction is often all too rare in Catholic schools. A counselor should recall that he really is serving as a spiritual director and that in so doing he renders the greatest eternal service to the soul. His own spirit of prayer will assure the intervention of divine aid.

With the welfare of the Church and the subsequent care of souls in mind, the counselor ought to be interested in the parish loyalty and interest shown by a counselee. He should keep a broad view of the work of the Church and not participate in unfavorable comparisons or criticisms of dioceses, parishes, religious communities, priests, brothers, and nuns. Catholic high schools are not meant to be seminaries or novitiates, but they must be concerned with developing a vital and informed Catholic laity. The school must seize every opportunity to make students parish-minded and to encourage them to develop loyalties and to build a bond with the parish for post-school life.

In Catholic schools there are undoubtedly a significant number of students who are prepared for some deeper spirituality by a regular program. Many will welcome the opportunity and will come seeking such a program. The counselor will be of untold help to the spiritual happiness and progress of a student if he personally gives the student a simple basic program of religious practices. In a few brief minutes a counselor can outline some basic elements of a personal rule and practice. The counselor should then indicate that this is but a beginning with such a remark as, "We'll see how you do with this and then give you the next steps after you have worked on this for a while. Come back and tell me how you got along."

The suggestions given to the student obviously must be simple. Every priest, religious, and mature Catholic teacher knows the basic means of grace and the fundamentals of spiritual living, which he learned either at home, in the novitiate or seminary, or in the experience of life. A simple program of spirituality should avoid sweet piety and unusual devotions and should concentrate on fundamentals. The devout and more frequent participation in the sacrifice of the Mass, the more thoughtful reception of the sacraments, the addition of prayers or intentions to morning and evening prayers, concentration on the development of a virtue, the practice of the presence of God, the examination of conscience to overcome one's predominant fault, and some work of penance and reparation are the elements of a program to be given to selected counselees.

The Moral. Moral development here refers specifically to growth in Christian virtue, to personality traits and attitudes. Moral counseling should make clear the fact that "This is the time at which you are forming permanent habits. This is the period in your life when it is easiest for you to change. You want to develop the most desirable qualities of character. It will not be long before it will be difficult to change your ways. Perhaps you already find it difficult to change and grow."

Counselees may be asked which points of character and personality in their acquaintances they most admire and which they most dislike. The counselor should then urge a deliberate pursuit of the good and avoidance of the evil. He should present a model by indicating the manner in which Christ showed desirable qualities. A counselee should see how grace strengthens virtue and overcomes vice. A thorough self-examination to determine what must be developed or remedied within a specified period of time may be recommended. When a counselor points out what he and other teachers have observed as to the qualities lacking in the counselee, he should indicate how these are best supplied. Since many traits and moral virtues of the counselee will be as yet undeveloped supernaturally, a good counselor will show the student how a virtue, a habit, or a character trait is built. He should describe the specific practices by means of which a particular characteristic can be developed. Examples can be drawn from the life of Christ, His Mother, and the saints. The imitation of parents and of religious and lay people known to a student can also be effective.

Emotional control presents a great difficulty to the adolescent and very often marks the difference between the mature and the immature. Every adolescent wants to be grown up. He should see that mastery of the emotional is an indispensable factor in acquiring maturity. Stimulation to this ideal may come from such questions as: "How much can you take? Can you be fairly sure of how you will react in certain situations, or don't you know what you will do? How do you control your temper, your tears, your enthusiasm?" A counselor can effectively single out for comment the tremendous control of Christ during His Passion. The restraint and control of some person known to the student may be an effective incentive. Influencing the counselee to see that emotional control is both a challenge and a desirable objective may mark the step that puts within grasp the noble traits of personality and character. Such traits can be made to become more and more prevalent if students, having been convinced of their desirability, are encouraged by being shown the effect of grace in strengthening the will to win mastery over the emotions.

The counselor will investigate the attitudes of the counselee which inevitably condition the formation of favorable character and betray the presence of the undesirable. A word of praise will encourage the continuance of the wholesome traits and will assure the counselee that he has at least done well in this respect. When there are poor attitudes such as quarrelsomeness, jealousy, suspicion of others, or a critical approach to school or home life, a student may often not be aware of the extent of the harm done. The counselor should suggest these questions: "Do you know that this is the impression you are creating?" or "What seems to be the trouble?" After singling out specific instances in which the undesirable attitude was betrayed, the counselor ought to show how the attitude can be changed by deliberate work on the development of the opposite virtue.

When a poor attitude or trait has been studiously acquired, or when the student seeks to defend it, the skill and wisdom of the counselor will be tested. Quite often the attitude stems from a problem or situation that the student has not faced and solved, or from inculpable deficiency or failure. Some discussion of the strength needed to face problems cheerfully, of the necessity of starting anew after failure, of the value of being able to be patient and tolerant of others and their weaknesses, and of the merits of sacrifice and the willingness to change attitudes is often needed to bring about improvement.

The counselor may need prudently to point out to the student that he is much too young to have adopted permanent attitudes. The student must understand that he should be ready and able to adjust himself when later experiences prove an attitude to be wrong. When all else seems to fail, the counselor will prudently give stern advice or a command, telling the student: "Such an attitude is only going to bring you heartache and unhappiness. The sooner you change it and learn how to live with others and your own problems, the better it will be for you." Or further, "How do you think your future husband (or wife) is going to be able to tolerate this attitude?"

Emphasis on the positive sides of habits and attitudes is in general the best counseling procedure. The desire to excel and to be flawless is present in all normal individuals, especially at this age. Encouragement to be perfect, to love and be loved by others, to be respected for character and person, to be admired for virtues, will stimulate counselees to better performance and to greater imitation of the Divine Model. The counselor of boys should point out these traits as definitely manly, requiring courage and strength; for girls these characteristics should be shown as truly womanly qualities, looked upon as desirable in them by others and bringing respect for their person.

Encouragement ought to be given to participation in activities of the school program which develop the moral virtues. Drama, debates, athletics, intramurals, journalism, and social affairs afford opportunities for practicing fortitude, temperance, prudence, and justice. Counseling should suggest a purposeful effort to develop the virtues through these activities.

The Mental. Attention to mental development and progress will mean that a counseling interview will not be satisfactory without examination of the past and current record of the student. A study of grades and of facts concerning the student's application, of test results, of placement in class sections in relationship to the intelligence quotient, and of known abilities or interests should provide the counselor with the information needed for profitable discussion. The counselor ought to determine whether or not the subjects the student is taking are suited to the interests and abilities manifested. A check should be made to see if the program of studies adequately meets his occupational needs, prepares him for a chosen vocation, or satisfies the requirements for college. A student must realize the need for good performance in his subjects as the preparation for his future work and for success in life.

Educational counseling involves development in a student of two fundamental intellectual virtues: an understanding of what should be done and wisdom in choosing the means of doing it. A counselor must check on how well the student is improving in knowledge of what to do and how to think. Because God's gift of intelligence to the individual is not the same for all, there will be differences in ability. If a student is perfectly fulfilling his vocation, he will be working efficiently to the limit of his ability. Grades will be supernaturally meaningful only if they represent best performance in the state of grace. Supernatural merit, moreover, will often be in proportion to the extent to which one works to capacity.

It is always a challenge to a student to be asked if he knows just how much he is capable of knowing and doing. One may stimulate action by asking: "Have you ever found out just how much you can do, how much you can learn, how good a grade you really can earn? Have you really ever explored your own abilities and talents? Is there a whole area of learning that you are missing? Are there areas that you could master?" A counselor will try to create in students a curiosity about undeveloped personal abilities, unused talents, and undiscovered strength.

Finally, a counselor will remind the student that God asks only that the individual do the best he can with the talents and equipment given to him. The virtue of humility requires the student to recognize limitations as well as abilities. Low-ability students have opportunity for praiseworthy development of the virtue of humility. Counselors should be urged to teach this virtue to the superior students, who moreover need awareness of the necessity of gratitude for the gifts God has given them. Superiority and inferiority complexes may be righted by the humility and justice taught by the counselor.

Counselors should discuss homework and assist teachers in demonstrating its relationship to satisfactory learning. In discussing progress in knowledge the counselor should check on the relationship of counselees to teachers. Clashes of personality and misunderstandings sometimes prevent the development of the intellectual virtues. Students at times will not accept a teacher as qualified or as really seeking to help them. Counselors as a rule should not involve themselves in differences between teachers and students. Students should handle their own problems with the teachers by going like grown men and women to discuss the difficulty calmly and to arrive at a reasonable solution. Finally, the counselee should be directed to accept the authority of the teacher and act accordingly.

His future education ought to be planned with the student. Ignorance and misinformation as to colleges, scholarships, and the kind of a college program required to accomplish a chosen occupational objective must be replaced by up-to-date information and sound advice. A well-staffed guidance department should have a specialist in the preparation of students for college. The counselor can be invaluable in directing students to Catholic colleges, and he should point out the necessity and the advantage of such a selection.

The counselor must also be familiar with the meaning and import of the testing program. He should apply to the individual student the results of all the tests taken and should draw for him practical conclusions. Often the counselor may be the only one to construct a complete composite with which to orient the student to his present intellectual condition and to plan for the satisfaction of his future needs. To direct counselees intelligently in the choice of courses the counselor must likewise be sufficiently familiar with the academic program. He should know the needs and ability of the student, and with them in mind he should outline the educational pattern the student must follow. Further explanation of educational guidance will be found in Chapter Seven.

The Vocational. In guidance and counseling increasing attention is now being directed to the vocational future of students. Catholic schools by reason of their philosophy and aims have always devoted much effort to help students choose that vocational life which will best assure their eternal life. Because of the emphasis given to the priesthood and the religious life, students may often think that these are looked upon as the only truly worthy vocations. Considerably less attention is too often given to the great majority of students who are called to the professions or to mechanical or manual work in the world.

The counselor should look for indications of vocational future in the scholastic and activity record of the student. A counselee may often reveal in an interview his ambitions, goals, and dreams about the future. A counselor should learn the results of any vocational testing that has been done, or he should recommend such testing as an aid to the development of a vocational plan. Some routine questions such as "Have you figured out what you want to do when you graduate or leave school? How do you intend to make a living? What do you like to do?" will often lead to further discussion and thought on the subject.

A simple set of questions such as the following may initiate occupational direction:

1 Do you like to work with your head or your hands?
2 Do you like to work indoors or outdoors?
3 Do you like to work alone or with others?

Answers will throw the future into broad categories of occupations of which investigation should be made by the student. The questions should direct the younger students to awareness of need for organized thought concerning the future. A prudent counselor will not immediately dismiss as unsuitable the answers to these preliminary questions. Young people often have unrealistic pictures of their abilities and their future, but an indication of possible success in a related field may be present.

Once the student has conceived an idea of a desirable and possible occupation, the counselor should discuss three further questions:

1 What capabilities do you have to do this work?
2 What opportunities exist to make this practically possible?
3 Will this work bring satisfaction and happiness?

1. *What capabilities do you have?* The counselor should learn from the school and home life of the student if capabilities exist in a degree sufficient to enable him to earn a living. The physical, mental, and moral requirements for any given occupation need not be possessed in an unusual or outstanding degree. For those interested in medicine, for example, there are many occupations in the field that are just as important and satisfying as being a full-fledged doctor and that do not require the same kind or amount of ability. Charts of occupations given by the *Kuder Preference Record* help to visualize for the counselee the many variations of occupations. Younger students particularly ought to limit occupational choices to a broad category of work for which they are capable instead of choosing and preparing for some limited field.

As an aid in finding capabilities, occupational inventories and aptitude tests give results which are significant in counseling. The help of the state employment services, departments of vocational and occupational education, city and county vocational-guidance centers, and private employment agencies may often be obtained. A counselee should be urged to test his capabilities by seeking work in his favorite field during vacations. Consultation with the parents can frequently lead to valuable information concerning the capabilities and aptitudes of students.

2. *What opportunities exist in this field?* The counselor should know the answer or have a ready source of information on this question. Current knowledge of local labor and professional conditions will prevent leading students into blind alleys of employment. Counselors will make use of communications from federal, state, and

local labor agencies, vocational-guidance manuals and periodicals, business reports, bulletins of professional societies, and contact with the personnel of state and private colleges. Sources for the student are described in the chapter on vocational and occupational guidance, pages 96-120.

Contacts that can result in placement in an occupation should be encouraged. Relatives working in the field can give first-hand information and oftentimes can make known special opportunities. Occupation in which Christian influence can be exercised constantly and on a greater number of individuals ought obviously to be favored and encouraged by the counselor.

3. *Will this work bring satisfaction and happiness?* A safe guide for the selection of occupational future will be the student's expression of attraction to a certain occupation. Inquiries such as "What kind of work gives you the most satisfaction? In what vocation do you think you would be the most happy? In which kind of life do you think you could do the most good for others?" often bring to light the proper occupational choice. Counselors should be wary of directing a student into work in which he is going to be discontented. Wages and pay scales, advancements and responsibilities, in themselves will be insufficient to offset unhappiness resulting from the type of work. A lesser position in work which gives satisfaction can be approved by a counselor in view of the fact that God certainly intended individuals to be happy in the work to which He has called them. On the other hand, the attraction and satisfaction of doing a work which first of all renders service and brings happiness to others should be brought to the attention of the counselee. Although selecting an occupation is a personal choice, it should not be the result of completely selfish considerations, especially if the satisfaction that is sought is material in nature.

Since training is necessary for any occupational future, the student should be advised to choose his occupation on the assumption that he will receive the proper preparation. A counselor may ask, "Would you like to do this kind of work if you were trained for it?" Before making a decision a student must know what training is required and ought to consider realistically the possibility of securing it. The counselor should assist him by discussing the required courses of study, the available training programs, and the places and people to contact. Consultation with persons actively engaged in the work and the reading of pertinent literature in the occupational library should be encouraged. The course in cooperative or distributive education offered in some schools as "on-the-job training" for students may be a further help to a sound occupational choice.

Counseling Religious Vocations. Vocational counseling in a Catholic school must always include inquiry about the possibility of a vocation to the priesthood or religious life. This legitimate opportunity should be omitted only when it is obvious and certain that this student can never qualify for such a vocation. The counselor should ask: "Have you ever considered the priesthood or religious life? Have you prayed for a vocation? Have you satisfied yourself and your conscience that you do or do not have this vocation?" The counseling interview may be the only occasion in which a staff member of a Catholic school has personally asked many students to consider the possibility. It is not unusual for a few students to be besieged with suggestions from teachers who have conceived a special admiration for them, while the great majority of the students receive no suggestions.

The counselor should insist that the question of a religious vocation be answered before other choices can be considered. He should explain that the answer must have a more mature basis than previous decisions which may have been made in grade school. When a counselee feels some attraction to this vocation but is nevertheless in doubt, he should be urged to begin a program of inquiry, prayer, and sacrifice to learn the answer. The priceless gift of a vocation comes only after prayer and sacrifice and requires serious thought without hurry and impulsiveness. If the student cannot make a decision after a program of prayer, he should be told that more reflection is evidently needed, that inability to decide is not proof that a vocation does not exist, and that the possibility of responding at a later date may still remain.

When the answer is negative the counselor should remind the counselee that other vocations must also bring about sanctity and lead to salvation. If the student responds favorably to a religious vocation, the counselor must give the needed direction and advice for safeguarding the vocation.[4]

Further discussion of religious vocations will be found on pages 101-04. Counseling for students who plan careers requiring higher education will be discussed in the chapter on guidance for college entrance, pages 121-37.

Special Problems. When all of the foregoing areas have been covered the counselor should ask if there are special problems or questions in connection with which he may be of service. This procedure may bring to light any omissions and may uncover adjustment difficulties that are not readily identifiable with any single area. The counselee should sense that he has been counseled rather completely in all the phases of his development.

THE COUNSELOR RECORD OF INTERVIEWS

Written records of counseling interviews are indispensable to effective guidance and counseling services. The counselor of a large number of students needs these tools for efficient work. Despite the additional burden and some disagreement concerning the advantages of keeping counseling records, the greatest possible benefits result from this summary of every interview. These records will serve:

1. *As an aid to the counselor by:*
    a. Assisting him in recalling the areas to be covered in a counseling session. Refer to the form on pages 221-23.
    b. Serving as a check list for inquiry and a list of essential questions to be asked.
    c. Presenting an orderly method of approach to the areas of counseling.
    d. Providing a rating and evaluation sheet for checking students as excellent, good, or poor.
    e. Serving as a source of reference to progress or failure in given areas.

[4] The methods of counseling and directing vocations are well treated in such works as Godfrey R. Poage, *Recruiting for Christ* and *For More Vocations* (Milwaukee: Bruce Publishing Company, 1950, 1955).

f. Recalling the content of previous interviews by another staff member, especially in the case of a counselor change.

g. Giving evidence that the student has been counseled in the event he says he has not been contacted previously.

h. Providing valuable help in the vocational direction given to older students.

2. *As an aid of the counselee:*

a. To ensure better counseling and coverage of areas of development and formation.

b. To eliminate the necessity of referring to many staff members when information about a student is needed immediately.

c. To provide a readily available cumulative record giving a fairly accurate understanding of students and their problems.

d. To enable a vocation director to pick out likely candidates for the priesthood or the religious life.

e. To give an over-all picture of the state of student life and of progress in the whole school program, its spirituality and major problems.

f. To guarantee correct attention to the needs of the individual student, his proper placement, his selection of courses, and related matters.

SPECIALIST COUNSELING AND REFERRALS

Problem children will often require the services of a specialist. Counselors should never hesitate to seek advice from other members of the school staff or to refer the problem to someone outside the school who is qualified to render adequate service to the problem student. Problems in reading, placement, or discipline, or problems encountered when dealing with handicapped or gifted students, may often be solved more readily if the counselor refers to an agency or a member of a department of the school prepared to handle such problems. A referral to the head counselor or to an agency should be followed up by a check on the results. A note regarding the referral should be placed in the counseling record and cumulative file. A referral should not mean a surrender of responsibility for the welfare of the counselee.

The guidance director or head counselor ought to survey the services available to Catholic students in the community. Both counselors and students should be aware of the many agencies, public and private, which aid individuals faced with specific problems or living in difficult situations. Where friendly cooperation and good public relations have been established, satisfactory arrangements can be made to refer students to public agencies and school systems for remedial-reading classes, classes for the hard of hearing, special training programs for the physically handicapped, classes for those with speech defects, appointments for special occupational testing. Arrangements may be made with the local Catholic college or university, and at times with other universities, for the clinical testing and treatment of unusual cases in their psychological-services department. An advanced college-work program for the gifted child may be cooperatively planned with the college or university.

A close and harmonious relationship should exist between the juvenile-court authorities, professional social workers, homeroom teachers, and the local school-attendance or truancy officer. An invaluable service is frequently offered to Catholic students by the local health department and regular visits of the public health nurse may be provided. Reports of the nurse on visits to the home of the student will frequently add significant information for counseling.

SELECTED REFERENCES

Arbuckle, Dugald S. *Guidance and Counseling in the Classroom,* Chapter 4, "The Counseling Process"; Chapter 5, "Teacher-Counselors in Action"; Chapter 7, "A Case Study in Counseling." Boston: Allyn and Bacon, 1957.

Arnold, Magda B., and John A. Gasson. *The Human Person,* Chapter 15, "Counseling as Therapy and Self-Integration." New York: Ronald Press Company, 1954.

Barry, Gerald M. "Impact of Personality Theory on Counselor's Approach." *Catholic Educational Review* 53:611-20, December 1955.

Beatrice, Sister M. "Every Teacher a Counselor." *Catholic Educator* 28:134-36, October 1957.

Biestek, Felix P. *The Casework Relationship.* Chicago: Loyola University Press, 1957.

Brayfield, Arthur H. *Readings in Modern Methods of Counseling.* New York: Appleton-Century-Crofts, 1950.

94

Curran, Charles A. *Counseling in Catholic Life and Education.* New York: The Macmillan Company, 1952.

Drasgow, James. "Intake Interviewing in Counseling." *Personnel and Guidance Journal* 35:100-02, October 1956.

Foster, Charles R. *Guidance for Today's Schools,* Chapter 4, "Teamwork and Counseling in the Guidance Program." New York: Ginn and Company, 1957.

French, William Marshall, and others. *Behavioral Goals of General Education in High School,* Part 2, "Capitalizing the Results of This Study"; Part 3, "Organization of Proposed Behavioral Outcomes." New York: Russell Sage Foundation, 1957.

Gordon, Ira J. *The Teacher as a Guidance Worker,* Chapter 8, "The Teacher as a Counselor." New York: Harper and Brothers, 1956.

Hahn, Milton Edwin, and Malcolm Shaw MacLean. *General Clinical Counseling in Educational Institutions.* New York: McGraw-Hill Book Company, 1950.

Harvey, John F. "Counseling Is a Complex Art." *Catholic Educator* 27:513-17, April 1957.

Knapp, Robert H. *Practical Guidance Methods,* pp. 55-71. New York: McGraw-Hill Book Company, 1953.

Leonard, Edith M.; Dorothy D. Vandeman; and Lillian E. Miles. *Counseling with Parents in Early Childhood Education.* New York: The Macmillan Company, 1954.

McDaniel, Henry B. *Guidance in the Modern School,* Chapter 6, "Principles of Counseling"; Chapter 7, "Progressive Steps in School Counseling"; Chapter 12, "Vocational Counseling." New York: Dryden Press, 1956.

McIntyre, John P. "Counselor-Centered Acceptance." *Catholic Educational Review* 56:299-305, May 1958.

Maryolf, Stanley S. *Psychological Diagnosis and Counseling in the Schools.* New York: Henry Holt and Company, 1956.

Ohlsen, Merle M. *Guidance: An Introduction,* Chapter 12, "The Counseling Relationship." New York: Harcourt, Brace and Company, 1955.

Poage, Godfrey R. *For More Vocations.* Milwaukee: Bruce Publishing Company, 1955.

――― *Recruiting for Christ.* Milwaukee: Bruce Publishing Company, 1950.

Recktenwald, Lester Nicholas. *Guidance and Counseling,* Part 4, "Counseling Principles and Practices." Washington: The Catholic University of America Press, 1953.

Sanderson, Herbert. *Basic Concepts in Vocational Guidance,* Part 4, "Counseling with Adolescents." New York: McGraw-Hill Book Company, 1954.

Smith, Glenn E. *Counseling in the Secondary School.* New York: The Macmillan Company, 1955.

Smith, Glenn E. *Principles and Practices of the Guidance Program,* Chapter 8, "The Counseling Service." New York: The Macmillan Company, 1951.

Stoops, Emery, and Gunnar L. Wahlquist. *Principles and Practices in Guidance,* Chapter 6, "Counseling." New York: McGraw-Hill Book Company, 1958.

Strang, Ruth. *Counseling Technics in College and Secondary School.* New York: Harper and Brothers, 1937.

Tooker, Ellis D. "Counselor Role: Counselor Training." *Personnel and Guidance Journal* 36:263-67, December 1957.

Truax, William E., Jr. "Critical Requirements of Small School Counselors." *Personnel and Guidance Journal* 35:103-06, October 1956.

Warters, Jane. *Techniques of Counseling.* New York: McGraw-Hill Book Company, 1954.

Weity, Henry. "Counseling as a Function of the Counselors' Personality." *Personnel and Guidance Journal* 35:276-80, January 1957.

Willey, Roy DeVerl, and Dean C. Andrew. *Modern Methods and Techniques in Guidance,* Part 3, "Techniques for Using Information about the Student." New York: Harper and Brothers, 1955.

Williamson, E. G., and M. E. Hahn. *Introduction to High School Counseling.* New York: McGraw-Hill Book Company, 1940.

Wrenn, C. Gilbert. "Counseling with Students." In *The Thirty-seventh Yearbook of the National Society for the Study of Education,* Part 1, Chapter 4. Chicago: National Society for the Study of Education, 1938.

———— "Status and Role of the School Counselor." *Personnel and Guidance Journal* 36:175-83, November 1957.

Zerfoss, Karl, editor. *Readings in Counseling.* New York: Association Press, 1952.

CHAPTER FIVE

VOCATIONAL

AND OCCUPATIONAL GUIDANCE

Pius XI, in his encyclical on the Christian education of youth, defined education as the preparation of what one must do and be here below in order to attain the sublime end for which he was created. "What one must do" cannot be interpreted as referring only to moral behavior. It refers also to the lifework that one chooses as his own, and it therefore implies a call to Christian schools to carry out an effective program of vocational and occupational guidance.

The Christian concept underlying the program of vocational and occupational guidance is this, that each person is called by God to work out his salvation in some definite way of life. The meaning is not that God wishes Alice, for example, to become a teacher and Helen to become an interior decorator, but rather that He wishes all individuals to choose intelligently something that is suitable and good for them. The choice should not be based on natural and selfish motives but on supernatural motives, and these motives ought to be higher and more perfect in proportion to the graces and opportunities granted by God. The work should be morally unobjectionable and socially useful. It should be possible of accomplishment in view of the health, intelligence, and talents of the individual. It should enable the individual to provide for his dependents. It should be work in which the individual can be happy and contented. This is the general description of the work to which God calls all men; but since health, intelligence, talents, and interests vary, the nature of the work will not be the same for all, and its choice is a very personal matter. After an individual has chosen wisely, he may look upon God as wishing him to apply himself to his work and to persevere in it, since both sloth and inconstancy are displeasing to God.

Cardinal Newman once said: "God has created me to do Him some definite service; He has committed some work to me which He has not committed to another. I have my mission. . . . I may never know it in this life, but I shall be told it in the next." This statement can only too easily be misinterpreted. Cardinal Newman was emphasizing in this place the greatness and the all-embracing extent of the providence of God. Since God wishes men to cooperate with Him in raising up saints, He undoubtedly wishes some men to be an encouragement, an assistance, and an example to others. If they are faithful to the law of God, they may accomplish this mission even though they are unaware of it. When told in the next world what their mission was, they will understand why God in His providence permitted certain hardships or required certain sacrifices. Cardinal Newman suffered because of his faith, and that suffering even today is an inspiration to other men. Such "missions" may indeed remain unknown to the individual; but God cannot impose upon a man the obligation of being a surgeon rather than an architect and then make the discovery of that fact impossible. There is no eleventh commandment against which we can sin despite the fact that we know nothing of it. Counselors and students should have clear ideas of what is meant when we speak of the obligation or of the possibility of "learning the will of God."

SOME GENERAL CONSIDERATIONS

Before discussing in detail vocational guidance and occupational guidance, we may speak briefly of certain facts or principles that are applicable to both.

The Goal in Choosing One's Lifework. It is not unusual for a false emphasis to creep into guidance work. Students are sometimes encouraged to make their choices on the basis of what can be expected to lead to personal contentment or on the basis of what is most lucrative. It is true that God wishes men to be happy and to be able to support themselves and their families, but neither of these goals is the ultimate goal of man's activity. The ultimate goal is to serve and glorify God and thus to save one's own immortal soul. Moreover, Christ Himself has told His followers that they cannot achieve this ultimate goal unless they freely render service to humanity. He made the performing of the works of mercy a condition of salvation, and He represented refusal to perform the works of mercy as a sufficient reason for reprobation.

When Christ at the end of the world sits in judgment upon all mankind, He will tell the elect to enter into the joy of heaven because "I was hungry and you gave me to eat; I was thirsty and you gave me to drink; I was a stranger and you took me in; naked and you covered me; sick and you visited me; I was in prison and you came to me" (Matthew 25:35-36). And when the elect ask when they did these things for Christ, His answer will be: "As long as you did it for one of these, the least of my brethren, you did it for me" (Matthew 25:40). Thus social service has been made an essential condition of salvation.

Whatever one's vocation or occupation in life may be, it should be related to the performance of the works of mercy. It should be chosen, among other reasons, because it facilitates the performance of these works of mercy and it should not be chosen if it renders their performance impossible or extremely difficult. Newman has expressed the further thought that "I am a link in a chain, a bond of connection between persons. He has not created me for naught. I shall do good. I shall do His work."

Just as members of the guidance personnel constantly tell students that the works of mercy are necessary, so they can tell themselves that the giving of guidance is also a work of mercy. It is ordinarily what is called a spiritual work of mercy rather than a corporal work of mercy, but it is a work of mercy nevertheless.

Two Decisions: One's Vocation and One's Occupation. By rather common consent vocation is understood to refer to the state of life in which one lives, without reference to the kind of work that he does. There are, broadly speaking, only three possible states of life: the priesthood or the religious life, married life, or single life in the world. For the sake of orderliness in guidance work, counselors should remember that the first decision of a student is vocational. Youth must choose one of three types of future: the married life, single life in the world, and the priesthood or the religious life. The vast majority of young people are called to the vocation of marriage; relatively few are invited by a special call of God to embrace one of the other vocations. Because of the special character of the vocation, every Christian student must satisfy first the obligation of considering whether or not God has called him to the priesthood or the religious life. Marriage or the single state cannot be accepted as one's vocation until this question has been considered.

The second great decision to be made is occupational. This decision must be made even by one who has decided to be a priest or a religious, for there are great variations in the kinds of work that priests and religious do. The occupational decision calls for prayerful investigation, occupation analysis and survey, humble study of one's own abilities to learn in what work or in what manner one should live this vocation of the married, the single, or the religious life. Neither decision can be made quickly: both demand prayer and the grace of God to enlighten the intellect; they require time, patience, and checking and rechecking on the part of both counselor and counselee. Assisting the student to arrive at a decision which is comfortable to the will of God and wise in the view of the student's life in the world is one of the more difficult tasks of the guidance program.

The Obligation of Providing Vocational and Occupational Guidance. The serious responsibility of the Catholic school to offer balanced and sufficient vocational and occupational guidance is one easily overlooked. Too often there is much concentration on religious vocations and too little attention devoted to marriage and the accompanying occupations that are God's will for so many. The first step of the school administration in satisfying its responsibility will be that of motivating the staff to carry on deliberate guidance with respect to all vocations and occupations. The school personnel should be urged to infuse practical guidance into all the phases of the work of education. Teachers should be challenged by being shown the need for relating subject matter realistically to the future life of the student by showing how what is being learned has an application to lifework and by picturing virtuous action as a basic and essential preparation for any vocation.

The second step in discharging the obligation to youth will be that of offering ample means and materials to assist students to know their vocation and select their occupation. While ordinary classroom instruction is clearly insufficient to provide adequate guidance in today's world, the extent to which the school must go to supply the means for making decisions and for preparing for the work that has been chosen will vary according to the nature of the school and the social and economic needs of the community. For these same reasons a fixed pattern of vocational guidance is difficult to establish. To know what are the effective means and how best to employ the materials for aiding youth to discover the work which God has intended for them and to learn how to render service for others is the special problem of the vocational counselor or guidance worker.

Because a vocation or occupation is tailored to fit the individual, fulfilling these guidance responsibilities is singularly difficult for school personnel. The responsibility is not solely theirs, for in making a decision of prime importance the adolescent should always prudently consult with parents, who hold the first responsibility for his welfare. At the same time he alone must make this decision calling for mature thinking; parents and counselors cannot make it for him. Moreover, the adolescent, who ten years from now will not be what he is today, must arrive at a decision that concerns his needs in an unknown future as an adult. Because of such factors counselors will ordinarily prefer to keep advice and direction general in nature. Assistance in making a choice in general fields of vocations and occupations is better for students than counseling which leads to very specific choices, since it makes it possible for students to adapt themselves later to changing circumstances.

GUIDANCE IN THE VOCATIONS

The preparation of young people for the careful selection and successful living of the priesthood, the married life, or the single state is correctly identified as *vocational* guidance. It is the heart of a Catholic guidance program. Increases in religious vocations and the stability of Catholic marriages will be evidence of the effectiveness of guidance work within the Church and its schools. At the present time, when so much analysis and emphasis is directed to various forms of school guidance, confusion as to its proper content and objectives is often prevalent. The Catholic school personnel should be alert to keep the true concept in mind and to continue the concentration on leading youth to the right *vocation*.

The Priesthood and the Religious Life. Fostering religious vocations has always been an overwhelming concern for Catholic teachers. The same diligent care and interest given to religious vocations, however, should also be directed to the preparation for marriage, careers, college, and employment. Undue emphasis by priests and religious upon their own state may result in neglect or discouragement of the other vocations and occupations. Christian guidance should not permit incorrect concepts that the married and single states are unworthy vocations. The priesthood and the religious life are indeed nobler vocations, but they are intended for comparatively few. For God to call all men and women to them would be opposed to His own purpose of having the human race "increase and multiply." The vocation in which God wishes the majority of mankind to live cannot be ignoble or unworthy.

The guidance of youth to the priesthood and the religious life may form the model for other phases of the guidance program. Our aim in encouraging young men and women to become priests or religious is to form other Christs and to recruit volunteers for the work of social service. We have the same purpose in every kind of guidance, for Christ called upon all men, not only upon priests and religious, to become branches belonging to the same vine, to imitate

His virtues, and to save their souls by serving mankind. The desire to aid growth and to help toward adjustment to a vocation is present in all kinds of guidance. When there is question of the priesthood or a religious vocation we obey the mandate of the Church by insisting upon complete freedom of choice and action on the part of the one who is called, but the principle that decisions must be made and action taken *by the student* with the help of the counsel of parents and teachers is accepted in all guidance. The effectiveness with which vocations are fostered will indicate to a degree the effectiveness of the total guidance program if the same attention is given to the other phases. There is no need, then, to propose a program for developing religious vocations that is independent of the general guidance program, and our aim here is to outline the duties and activities of the personnel responsible for this work of guidance toward religious vocations.

The Director of Religious Vocations. The administrator or guidance director of a school should designate the best-qualified person of the staff to head and coordinate the work of others in finding and guiding vocations. The vocation director should possess the essential qualities of influence over the students, prudence unlimited, personality and acceptability, sociability, and Christlikeness. He must work closely with the diocesan and community vocation director to realize a twofold objective: information and formation.

The director of religious vocations will gather the methods and means of fostering vocations from the excellent works on the subject,[1] from his own experience and that of others, from vocation workshops, from conferences, and from prayer and meditation. His enthusiasm and the example of his devotion to this work will strongly influence, not only the faculty, but the students as well. The more the vocation director consults with counselors and staff concerning problems and possible candidates, the more "vocation conscious" others will become.

Duties of the Director of Religious Vocations. In addition to the general duties of informing and forming students by the means de-

[1] Godfrey R. Poage, *Recruiting for Christ* and *For More Vocations*. Milwaukee: Bruce Publishing Company, 1950, 1955.

vised for the individual school, the vocation director should perform the following specific duties:

1 Acting as a central source of information on all actual and prospective vocations. The director should be acquainted with all the likely candidates, while a staff member may be aware of only a few.

2 Urging the counselors to ask each boy or girl this question: "Have you given serious consideration to the priesthood or religious life?" No child should pass through a Catholic school without some sort of check on the possibility of his having a vocation. A Catholic school in our time cannot afford to neglect the opportunity offered by counseling contact or to overlook the possibility of God's call in the case of a single individual. God gives the call to those whom He, and not the school, chooses.

3 Searching elementary-school records, registration blanks, and questionnaires to find indications of vocations in the student body. Conversation with the grade-school teacher may be a great help. When students who may have vocations have been found, the vocation director will guide them himself or assign another faculty member to the care of the prospective vocation.

4 Acting as an adviser to counselors and others on the best means of developing latent vocations. He should check upon the proper direction of individual vocations by staff members and should emphasize the necessity of the candidate's undertaking a program of prayer, sacrifice, and faithfulness to the sacraments.

5 Investigating and advising on impediments to acceptance as a candidate for the priesthood or the religious life; observing prudently to prevent undue influence and unhealthy relationships in vocational direction, since undue influence is forbidden and since excessive attachment to some teacher may lead to an unwise decision.

6 Enlisting the interest of parents and others in the fostering of vocations among students. This work is not merely the private concern of the religious teacher. In all cases parents ought to be consulted before, rather than after, a vocational decision. The local Serra Club or auxiliary or other Catholic organizations may

provide help through speakers, funds, and the supplying of transportation for visits to seminaries and novitiates.

7 Conferring and cooperating with the pastor of the prospective candidate. This is wisely and prudently done before a decision is made, and certainly must be done after a declaration of intention to become a priest or religious, since the recommendation of the pastor is usually required.

8 Keeping records of those who enter seminaries and novitiates, of those who complete their preparation by ordination or profession, and of those who discontinue the pursuit of this vocation.

9 Attending when possible the investiture, profession, and ordination ceremonies of students who had attended the school.

Marriage. The great majority of students of Catholic secondary schools are called by God to the married state. In every aspect of school life there should be a form of guidance which prepares young people to establish holy and successful Catholic marriages, and this guidance should have a twofold objective: (1) to enlighten the intellect by providing the necessary knowledge of the state and (2) to strengthen the will by the means of grace, by the encouragement of self-sacrifice, and by the building of a strong conviction.

Teachers of religion and of the social studies will bear the responsibility for the major part of the guidance directed toward preparing students for happy marriage. Other teachers should share in this responsibility and seek in their own classes or guidance work to help equip the student for this vocation. The curriculum and the courses of a school should be evaluated with respect to the extent to which they make adequate provision for preparation for marriage.

A survey of former students may be conducted to learn the following facts: the students who have married, how soon after high school they married, how many married Catholics, how many married outside the Church, how many marriages have failed, and how this picture compares with what is found in other Catholic high schools. One teacher should maintain a visible interest in the courtship and marriages of recent graduates of the school. He might also keep a current record of marriages of all former students by enlisting the help of an alumni or alumnae association. Conclusions drawn from facts thus collected can suggest improvements in the work of preparing present students for the married state.

Single Life in the World. The guidance to this vocation should ordinarily be carried out in individual counseling and in religion classes. The nature of the vocation demands careful thinking and a clear understanding of what is involved. Girls, particularly, may plan to become "career women" when they should be preparing themselves for motherhood and family life. All too frequently students are permitted to entertain the impression that the single life is a state for the "leftovers" which is forced upon those who have neither been called to the religious life nor sought in marriage. Still others may conclude that the single life means independence of responsibilities to others and the freedom to pursue selfish objectives. They should realize that this vocation is justified only as the unselfish following of God's will.

The true picture of the lay single life should be clearly portrayed, and students should be made to understand that there must be a good reason for choosing this life in preference to both the religious life and marriage. The call of God to the single life in the world implies a divine command to a life of virginity. One who lives a lay single life may observe virginity in the usual manner without a vow, but with the advice of a confessor may be permitted to take a vow of chastity. Such a person in the world may be engaged in a secular work satisfying the needs of others. In a more unusual manner, however, the lay single person may be a true apostle and make a total consecration of self to the work of religion.[2] A totally consecrated single person lives a deep spiritual life in the world, places himself or herself under the direction of the Church, pledges full obedience, and performs whatever work for souls God proposes to him through the command of the bishop.

Selection of the single lay state often requires more prayer, more counsel, and more impartial advice from others than the choice of

[2] Explanation of the work of secular institutes and other such forms of the lay apostolate will depend on accurate knowledge. In the absence of an available printed work on such institutes, the best source of information will be a well-informed priest.

another state in life. Preparation and counseling for the life of the consecrated lay apostolate may need to be more serious and intense because of the difficulties and challenges that are ordinarily encountered by one who chooses this state of life.

OCCUPATIONAL GUIDANCE

Occupational guidance may be divided into three principal services: (1) providing students with adequate information, (2) gathering information from and about the student, and (3) relating the information to the student.

Providing Adequate Information. Supplying a wealth of information to the student is a characteristic of a good occupational-guidance service. Considerable thought and ingenuity will be required to render all the sources and tools of information readily accessible and to cause them to be utilized by students. Teachers can often give valuable guidance by correlating occupational information with classroom subject matter. Classroom work and assignments may generate a better understanding of the nature of many occupations when discussion, research, or reports in English, social studies, and other classes are built around topics dealing with occupations. For this purpose there are at least 35,000 occupations from which one may choose.[3]

Units devoted to occupations in the social studies should result in an abundance of knowledge that will be of assistance to students. A survey unit can be provided for freshmen and sophomores; more thorough units, appropriately integrated with such courses as sociology and economics, should be taught to juniors and seniors. The minimum provision in the curriculum for occupational information and study should call for one complete unit at some time in the four years, while the maximum would offer one unit during each of the four years in addition to an elective semester course in occupations.[4] Another course in cooperative or distributive education

---

[3] *Dictionary of Occupational Titles,* obtainable from the Government Printing Office, Washington, is the best reference for lists of occupations.

[4] E. A. Leonard, *Vocational Citizenship* (New York: P. J. Kenedy and Sons, 1947) is a very satisfactory text for Catholic schools.

arranged with local employers as an on-the-job training program may be considered. The difficulty of securing a sufficient number of employers and qualified teachers for this type of service in Catholic schools, however, may sometimes make the adoption of this plan inadvisable or even impossible.

In an occupational-guidance unit teachers might assign to each student a project or a research study related to the several occupations in which the student is interested. An outline is given on page 110. The work should lead students to learn how an occupation may fulfill God's will, how it may be of service to others, and how it may provide a living. If this work is not done as a class assignment, the counselor might suggest it to the student as a practical means of determining his occupational future. In any occupational guidance, school personnel should not fail to infuse the idea of service, not only to the souls and bodies of all who belong to the mystical body of Christ, but to those of others as well, since the command to love our neighbor as ourselves obliges us to love all members of the human race.

Library of Occupational Materials. The creation and maintenance of an occupational library is relatively simple and inexpensive for any secondary school. The guidance director and the school librarian should be responsible for the library and should cooperatively work out a plan for its contents and operation. They should evaluate the materials already on hand, examine the bibliography of the class unit in occupational guidance, and add the basic tools that may be absent from the collection. The *Dictionary of Occupational Titles* and Leonard's *Vocational Citizenship* provide an essential foundation. The bibliography and list of sources of information about occupations contained in the latter will serve as a guide to the titles and sources of the most practical materials to be included in the library. Supplemental references for teachers and audio-visual aids are also given. The *Occupational Briefs,* which are part of the SRA Guidance Service and which are issued by Science Research Associates,[5] may be secured as the means of keeping the library content

---

[5] 57 West Grand Avenue, Chicago 10, Illinois.

up to date.[6] The daily mail delivers a quantity of assorted occupational material which may be added to the library collection after evaluation by a guidance worker. Unbound materials acquired for an occupational library soon become worthless without an efficient filing system. The following filing systems are recommended:

1 The Chronicle File (coded according to the *Dictionary of Occupational Titles*) published by the Chronicle Guidance Press, Moravia, New York.

2 The Guidance Index (offered with Science Research Associates Guidance Service).

3 The Bennett Occupational Filing Plan (arranged alphabetically) published by Sterling Powers Publishing Company, 1512 Lincoln Way, La Porte, Indiana.

The library of occupational materials should be given a prominent place in a location that attracts use by students. A section of the main library may be reserved for all such materials used in the guidance program, or the guidance center itself may provide space for maintenance of the occupational library. Whatever location is selected, the attention of students should be drawn to it by the librarian, teachers, and guidance workers.

A mobile file of occupational and vocational materials may be used as the practical solution of the problem of facilitating access to the materials and of encouraging their use. Constructed by students in manual-training classes or at home, this combination bookshelf, filing cabinet, and display cart can travel to the classroom at any time of need. The middle part of the mobile library contains a filing and storage cabinet and the card index. The bottom (or one side) is built for adjustable bookshelves, while the top (or sides) is constructed as a tilted display space which opens out to provide further storage. Obviously, the mobile file should not be built wider than the narrowest classroom door.

A great deal of care must be exercised in the selection and use of occupational filmstrips on guidance. The guidance director should consult the catalog for visual aids available through the

---

[6] Occupational monographs in quantity lots are available from the National Association of Manufacturers, 2 East 48th Street, New York 17, New York.

public or state library. Industry and professional societies frequently provide a source of supply for these visual aids. Merely viewing a film may be a help to the student, but the follow-up analysis and discussion render the greatest service.

Speakers and Interviews. Visits to the school by men and women actively engaged in an occupation furnish a valuable source of first-hand information. A survey of parental occupations drawn from registration data will reveal available speakers in a variety of occupations. The creation of a parental-occupation file will serve as a great help to administrators in other ways. Although thought must be given to ability to speak well and to convey information, the mere opportunity of contact with someone in a given occupation is a service to students. Invitations to parents to speak on their occupations, moreover, arouse the interest of the students and result in active participation of parents in the work of the school in the education of their children.

A schedule of occupational talks may be arranged with local labor councils, the apprenticeship program, professional societies, and the department heads of colleges. Parents and other competent speakers who are invited should be provided with an outline or suggested guide in order to ensure the orderly and worthwhile instruction of students. A suggested speaker's guide is presented on page 110. Provision should always be made for a question-and-answer period following the talk, and when possible, time should be allowed for personal interviews with the speaker.

Visits of capable speakers are usually more effective when made on the classroom level. The smaller group allows more intimate contact and enables the teacher to correlate the talk and discussion with classroom work. Nonetheless, the appearance of speakers before large groups or assemblies during such times as Occupation Week is of appreciable worth.

Career Conferences. A survey should be made among students to determine which occupations are favored. An organized schedule of talks to all students can be arranged with a minimum of effort on the part of the guidance director. The career conferences may be integrated with the activity program of the school. Speakers could

SUGGESTED GUIDE FOR SPEAKER OR OCCUPATION STUDY OUTLINE

I. *Description of the Field*
  A. Nature of the work—hours, working conditions
  B. Attractive features—associations, social status, pensions
  C. Undesirable features—hazards, strains
  D. Present outlook—demand and supply

II. *Requirement of the Occupation*
  A. Education and Training—amount, nature, time, expense
     1. School subjects most essential
        Ability to use good English
        Ability to write well and legibly
        Mechanical skill
     2. Recommendations as to where to obtain training, credentials, licenses, and so forth
  B. Personal Qualifications
        Mental ability, personality types, special interests appearance, age, ability to get along with people, ability to follow directions, ability to lead other people, common sense or good judgment, orderliness, system and neatness, initiative, resourcefulness, punctuality, perseverance, industry, thoroughness.
  C. Physical Qualifications
        Special demands on health, nerves, lungs, feet, endurance, vision, and so forth

III. *Rewards of the Occupation*
  A. Financial—pay scale or reasonable income
     1. How paid—salary, commission, wage, bonus
  B. Security—pensions, retirement allowances, tenure
  C. Possibility of transfer to related occupations
  D. Opportunity for advancement—promotions
  E. Personal—service to others, associations, prestige, self-expression, benefit to community and Church
  F. Spiritual—fulfillment of God's will, care of family, opportunity for grace, and so forth

IV. *How To Get Started*
  A. Where to apply
  B. Placement agencies, unions, associations of workers
  C. Sources of future information

be invited to come at the time of the regular activity period designed for club meetings and small-group activities.[7] Under this plan fifteen to twenty-five occupations presented each year will give an excellent view of all major fields of occupations. A well-planned half-hour period is adequate for an overview, but a full-length period permits better treatment and goes farther toward attaining the objective of the career talks.

Career nights attended by parents as well as students have become a familiar event in many American communities. This occupational-information program consists of talks by men and women in various fields who describe their respective work in three periods of approximately forty-five minutes each. Those attending are asked to select the occupation in which they are interested and the speaker they wish to hear and to go to the room assigned to the speaker. The outline guide ought to be given to the speakers and evaluation sheets to the audience. Arrangements can be made to permit Catholic school students to attend career conferences at the neighboring public high school if such a program cannot be presented at the Catholic school. The career night has the disadvantage that one can hear a maximum of only three speakers and so be informed about only a relatively small number of occupations.

Field Trips. Providing an opportunity for students to view workers on the job is perhaps the most effective means supplying occupational information. Because of the schooltime that must be sacrificed it is difficult to arrange an adequate program of field trips. An equally satisfactory means of securing the value of field trips, however, is an arrangement for interested individuals and small groups to make such trips after school or on some holiday. Trips may be assigned as a project in the classroom and a written report may be required of the students.

On-the-Job Information. Students should be advised to secure a part-time or summer-employment position in the field in which they are interested. Work experience in an occupation is the certain and reliable method of deciding upon one's work for the future. Students

[7] Group meetings and assemblies designed to entertain may more suitably be scheduled for after-school hours rather than conflict with occupational conferences.

should be reminded to appraise this experience in terms of happiness for themselves and of service to others instead of in terms of the resultant amount of money or security. While it is obvious that high-school students are in very many cases incapable of doing the work required in an occupation, they can learn much by serving as office boys, messengers, receptionists, or helpers, by observing what is being done, and by asking questions of those with whom they are thrown in contact.

Apprenticeships. Guidance personnel should be acquainted with state apprenticeship laws and practice and should establish contact with the local apprenticeship committee. The objectives of this relationship are the obtaining by students of adequate information on the apprenticeship program, the encouragement of apprenticeship training, and the careful selection of an apprenticeable occupation. A school counselor should provide an assembly or a career conference on apprenticeships during the course of the school year to inform students on the occupations which are apprenticeable, the number of persons regularly permitted to secure the training, the rate of pay, the length of training required, and the trades which can be entered without previous apprenticeship training.

Since regulations governing apprenticeships vary from state to state, the vocational-guidance personnel and the local apprenticeship council must cooperate in giving such information to students. The instruction of apprentices is frequently organized by the school district in cooperation with the state department of vocational education.

Vocational Schools. Knowledge of the opportunities afforded by technical and vocational schools of the area, trade schools, beauty colleges, technical institutes, and so forth, is of further assistance to students. Bulletins from these organizations should be evaluated and posted. A working arrangement of cooperative instruction in high school can often be devised to reduce the length of time spent in apprenticeship or trade school. A Catholic school ought to recognize its own limitations in the field of actual vocational or occupational instruction, should such exist, and explore the possibilities of cooperative instruction.

Vocational Rehabilitation and Programs for the Handicapped. Many states now offer an excellent service of testing, training, and placement for individuals who suffer from some disability. The occupational-guidance personnel should be aware of the great extent and value of rehabilitation services. Parents of students who may qualify for aid from agencies should be properly informed of these possibilities. Early in the year the head of the occupational-guidance services of the school should make a survey of all students who have health and disability handicaps and problems. With such a list he may systematically confer with and direct these students to sources of adjustment or rehabilitation. Emotional and other problems resulting from handicaps may call for patient counseling and assistance to "one of my least brethren."

Occupational Bulletin Board. The bulletin board for display of informational materials is a simple means of arousing interest in occupations. An adequate amount of material should be posted in a prominent place in traffic centers of the school. A counselor should be given responsibility for the care, posting, and regular variation of materials that will stimulate the interest of students. Little time, effort, or expense are required to provide this substantial help.

Gathering Information from Students. To assist in the choice of occupation and to give a counselor facts for occupational guidance, a four-year plan of gathering information and testing should be devised and carried out through social-studies classes. All the data assembled should be placed in the cumulative record. This program should aim at determining specifically the occupational interest and preference of a student at the time of testing. Interest and the desire to perform a certain service to mankind are normally the best guideposts in the selection of a vocation or occupation. A post-high-school plan may be built upon information secured in the following manner:

In the freshman year a questionnaire should be administered in which the student is asked directly what he would like to be and do. This may be a part of an inquiry made in the process of registration or orientation of new students. The reliability of answers to this initial questionnaire will not be great because of the immature mind of the freshman student. The answers do become significant, however, in evaluation by the counselor after more information has been gathered in later years. The questionnaires should be filed in the cumulative record of the student for use by the counselor.

A simple tool for use with freshmen is the *Vocational Interest Inventory.*[8] This inventory gives a general picture of significant interests of the student based upon likes and dislikes in nine areas: commercial, mechanical, aesthetic, manual, agricultural, academic or professional, scientific (professional), general service, and domestic. The inventory is simple to administer, inexpensive, and may be reproduced without permission.

In the sophomore year the occupational-guidance plan calls for another statement of what students would like to be and do. This may be furnished through the following means: an autobiography or essay entitled "My Future" assigned in an English composition class; a vocational-interest test for sophomores given in the registration room; an occupational study completed in an English class; the Lee-Thorpe *Occupational Interest Inventory;*[9] a second administration of the Germane and Germane *Vocational Interest Inventory;* and a first administration of the *Kuder Preference Record.*[10] In addition, students should be asked what their vocational-occupational choice would be if it had to be made at the time of the inquiry.

For juniors a study of interests and abilities related to their occupational future may be recommended. Personality and temperament analysis tests and measurements may be employed to gain further information on the adolescent development at this point. A study of several fields of occupation may again be suggested and the form filed in the cumulative record.

In the senior year of high school (or in spring of junior year) the *Kuder Preference Record* should be used as a reliable form of interest analysis. Administered within a unit on vocational guidance in the social-studies classes, the profile sheets and manual should be studied carefully by the counselor and student. The study should be

[8] Charles E. Germane and Edith C. Germane, *Personnel Work in High School* (New York: Silver Burdett Company, 1941) contains this inventory. The time required for its administration is about forty-five minutes.

[9] California Test Bureau, 5916 Hollywood Boulevard, Los Angeles 28, California.

[10] Science Research Associates, 57 West Grand Avenue, Chicago 10, Illinois.

correlated with other materials in the cumulative record. The *Kuder Preference Record* is designed to measure ten areas of interest: outdoor, mechanical, computational, scientific, persuasive, artistic, literary, musical, social service, and clerical. For economy, sufficient booklets may be purchased for one class only; answer pads and profile sheets, however, should be secured for each student taking the test. The time needed to administer the test is forty minutes.

Another means of gathering information for the occupational guidance of a student are the records of the scholastic achievement and scores in standardized achievement tests. The existence in a student of scientific ability and interest, for example, can be discovered by noting high grades in science subjects. An intelligence test covering language and nonlanguage factors will be a further tool for occupational guidance. The more extensive tests designate the more specific types of intelligence which will indicate aptitudes classifiable as abstract, mechanical, clerical, artistic, practical, and social. Data from permanent record cards will be of significance to a counselor in the guidance of a student to a proper occupational choice.

For seniors who do not plan to go to college, and for those who drop out of school after the age of sixteen, a general-aptitude test battery is advisable. This state employment service is often free of charge to high-school students. Recognized private agencies and college psychological testing services require a fee.

Relating the Information to the Student. All the information for occupational choice and adjustment will be of little worth unless the counselor applies it to the individual student. As the file of information grows, the counselor and student together should make evaluations of the interests and abilities which point to a general field and at times to a specific occupation. The more data there are in the cumulative record file, the better will the counselor be able adequately to guide the student.

As an example of how this work might be done, a counselor might suggest an occupational future to a student in the following manner: "This was your choice in freshman year; the vocational-interest inventory gave a good indication; grades and tests in related subjects were satisfactory; you made a study of the work in sophomore year; your self-study indicates your suitability for this type of work; the *Kuder Preference Record* confirms it." At this point the counselor might advance the idea of the good that can be done for others by speaking of the Christopher movement, the lay apostolate, work in labor unions, social work, and so forth.

For a satisfactory program of occupational counseling the file of information should be examined with the counselee, at least at the time of choosing subjects to be taken during the year to follow, and again early in the senior year. In the spring of the senior year a vocational plan or questionnaire can be made out with students in the social-studies class and filed in the cumulative record for future reference. The completeness and good sense of these plans will give a broad picture of the effectiveness of the vocational-guidance program through the years.

Job Placement and Employment Services. Related closely to the occupational-guidance program of the school is the maintenance of a job-placement bureau. A file listing students with special aptitudes may be compiled from test scores, the results of counseling, and other data. Another file should contain the list of available jobs. All students should be asked to fill out an employment card to be placed in a third file. This system will enable the placement service quickly and properly to place a student when requests for workers are made through the school. Bulletin-board notices of jobs available should be posted regularly.

Although the proper placement of students and good occupational guidance are the first objective of the program, a small fee may be asked for registering or for placement in an occupation as a means of helping to meet the expense of the operation of the placement service.

At some place in the school program, to be determined by the guidance director or the guidance committee, students should be shown how to write a correct letter of application, how to secure references or recommendations, and the manner of conducting themselves when asking for employment and when being interviewed.

The data to have ready for a prospective employer include the social-security number; three references with names, addresses, and telephone numbers (permission should be received previously from references); a record of any past employer and his telephone number and address, the date of employment, type of work, rate of pay, and name of supervisor; and a record of yearly averages in school and the major courses taken. Students need to be reminded not to withhold information pertinent to employment. An excellent course or unit of instruction on income-tax matters may be secured free of charge from the local Internal Revenue Office.

Follow-Up Study. At periodic intervals a follow-up study of the occupations and vocations of graduates and of "dropouts" or "school leavers" can provide guidance personnel with valuable information. These studies may be made by the staff or by a college graduate student. If there are active alumni, this work may be given to them as a project. The group will have to devise a satisfactory means of contacting all the former students of the school before the study is valid. Revaluation and change of educational services may result from conclusions reached in regard to the school curriculum, teaching methods, and the guidance program.

MILITARY-TRAINING GUIDANCE

The advent of universal military training has made the guidance of high-school boys considerably more difficult. Changing regulations and varying ages for draft calls make it necessary for someone among the guidance personnel to become fully informed on the military obligation. Appointment as a selective-service adviser may be secured from the local selective-service headquarters. In schools where most of the boys will be entering military service soon after graduation, some form of group preinduction orientation ought to be offered.[11]

Providing information about the various ways of satisfying military obligations may be accomplished by means of printed materials and bulletin-board displays and by scheduling speakers from the military services. Each branch of the service will be eager to send

[11] The National Catholic Welfare Conference has issued a *Teacher's Handbook for Pre-Induction Training.* The National Catholic Community Service offers a popular booklet, *Greetings,* by Reverend Thomas J. O'Donnell, C.S.C.

representatives to the school. A panel of all the services is easily arranged and offers the most balanced presentation to students approaching military age. The visits of military personnel for conferences and panels may be properly restricted to after-school hours. An evening session allowing the participation of parents is worthy of consideration because of their vital concern in the future of their children.

The school administration and guidance personnel will be cautious in seeing that pressure and undue influence are not exerted upon students. The school should not be used as a recruiting center, either by representatives of the service or by students participating in reserve and other military programs. Counselors themselves should be wary of advising a certain branch of the service unless there has been previous consultation with the parents. The guidance department should frequently remind boys of the obligation, manner, and place of registering for selective service on their eighteenth birthday.

Counselors will find that the necessity of military service often hinders a satisfactory vocational or occupational choice. Students will be inclined to delay their choice until military-service obligation is completed. They should be advised to make their vocational decision first and then to use the time of military service as much as possible for training and preparation in their chosen occupation. Among the multiple guidance problems that military service involves, the counselor should remember that the decision belongs to the student.

Guidance personnel should instill the correct mental attitude toward the fulfillment of the military obligation. A Christian student should look upon the acceptance of this obligation as compliance with the fourth commandment, as an opportunity to develop the virtue of loyalty, and as an opportunity for service to country. In addition, he may gain maturity in vocational training and competency in social living. Military service should not be considered by the student a source of unhappiness, an unwarranted intrusion, or an unjust infringement of his rights.

Students should be motivated to use the period of military service for demonstrating their Christian morality and life and for drawing definite conclusions on their vocational destiny. The possibilities of bringing souls closer to Christ, of winning converts, of giving good example, and of exercising influence should not be overlooked. Young Christian men in the military have a vast field in which to work for the glory of God and the welfare of society.

In this chapter we have limited a vocation to a call by God to one of the three great states of life and have defined an occupation as a profession, a position, a job, or in general as the kind of work that one chooses as his own. Strictly speaking, vocational guidance is concerned with helping students decide upon a state of life, while occupational guidance is concerned with helping them choose the kind of work that they will do in the world. We do not consider it either necessary or practical to insist upon this distinction at every point in the remaining chapters of this book. Educators in general and the authors of innumerable books and magazine articles use the term "vocational guidance" to indicate both kinds of guidance, but more particularly guidance toward an occupation. Vocational schools, vocational curricula, and vocational courses prepare high-school students for jobs, not for states of life. We will therefore feel free to speak of vocational guidance even when the problem under discussion is occupational.

SELECTED REFERENCES

Allers, Rudolf. *Character Education in Adolescence,* Chapter 6, "General and Vocational Guidance." New York: Joseph F. Wagner, 1940.

Baer, Max F., and Edward C. Roeber. *Occupational Information: Its Nature and Use.* Chicago: Science Research Associates, 1951.

Crow, Lester D., and Alice Crow. *An Introduction to Guidance; Principles and Practices,* Chapter 19, "Guidance Toward Occupational Adjustment." New York: American Book Company, 1951.

Dictionary of Occupational Titles. Washington: Government Printing Office.

Forrester, Gertrude. *Methods of Vocational Guidance.* Boston: D. C. Heath and Company, 1944.

——— *Occupational Pamphlets; An Annotated Bibliography.* New York: H. W. Wilson Company, 1948.

Foster, Charles R. *Guidance for Today's Schools,* Chapter 10, "Guidance in Exploring the World of Work"; Chapter 11, "Guidance and Self-Analysis for Occupational Goals"; Chapter 12, "Classroom and School Projects in

Vocational Guidance"; Appendix A, "A Specimen Career-Day Program." New York: Ginn and Company, 1957.

Frederick, Brother. "Promoting Vocations in the High School." *Bulletin National Catholic Educational Association* 49:245-53, August 1952.

Hussey, Philip J. "Fostering Vocations in Non-Catholic Schools." *Bulletin National Catholic Educational Association* 52:100-02, August 1955.

Isabel, Sister Mary. "A Plan for Fostering Vocations in the Elementary School." *Bulletin National Catholic Educational Association* 49:254-61, August 1952.

Jarlath, Sister Mary. "The Teacher's Relationship with Parents in Fostering Vocations." *Bulletin National Catholic Educational Association* 53:340-41, August 1956.

Joan, Sister. "Fostering Vocations in Colleges." *Bulletin National Catholic Educational Association* 52:110-13, August 1955.

Jones, Arthur J. *Principles of Guidance,* fourth edition, Chapter 14, "Methods for the Investigation of Occupations"; Chapters 19 and 20, "Methods of Vocational Guidance in Secondary Schools." New York: McGraw-Hill Book Company, 1951.

Josephs, Devereux C. *Guide to Career Information: A Bibliography of Recent Occupational Literature by Career Information Service.* New York: Harper and Brothers, 1957.

Knapp, Robert H. *Practical Guidance Methods,* Chapter 3, "Helping Youth through Vocational Guidance." New York: McGraw-Hill Book Company, 1953.

Leonard, E. A. *Vocational Citizenship.* New York: P. J. Kenedy and Sons, 1947.

McDaniel, Henry B. *Guidance in the Modern School,* Chapter 11, "Occupational Information"; Chapter 12, "Vocational Counseling." New York: Dryden Press, 1956.

O'Connor, Paul L. "A Syllabus for Pre-Induction Religious Training." *Bulletin National Catholic Educational Association* 49:325-33, August 1952. (Contains a very good bibliography for military guidance.)

Ohlsen, Merle M. *Guidance: An Introduction,* Chapter 16, "Vocational and Educational Planning." New York: Harcourt, Brace and Company, 1955.

Philip, Brother Arthur. "Vocational Guidance by the Classroom Teacher." *Bulletin National Catholic Educational Association* 52:376-82, August 1955.

Stephanie, Sister Mary. "Fostering Vocations on the Secondary Level." *Bulletin National Catholic Educational Association* 52:107-09, August 1955.

Stephenson, Richard M. "Realism of Vocational Choice: A Critique and an Example." *Personnel and Guidance Journal* 35:482-88, April 1957.

Stoops, Emery, and Gunnar L. Wahlquist. *Principles and Practices in Guidance,* Chapter 5, "Information about Opportunities: Vocational." New York: McGraw-Hill Book Company, 1958.

CHAPTER SIX

GUIDANCE

FOR COLLEGE ENTRANCE

Students who find that the vocation or occupation of their choice requires more than a high-school education and those who have not come to a final decision about their lifework but who possess the ability and the desire for higher education have need of guidance in preparing for college. The number of high-school graduates going on to college has increased 200 per cent in the last generation. This increase has been due to a number of causes, among them the need of industry for college-trained technicians, the establishment of new colleges and technical schools and the expansion undertaken by institutions already existing, the greater variety of courses offered, various plans for helping deserving students through scholarships and in other ways, and the growing number of students being graduated from high school and eligible for college entrance. Causes such as these have all conspired to increase the number of high-school students who are planning to attend college.

Parents are not usually well informed about the requirements of various colleges and about the cost of attending them. They rely largely upon the judgment of high-school counselors in the matter of helping their children decide upon which college to attend and how to meet its admission requirements, but they are vitally interested in their choice if only for the reason that they will be called upon to finance or help finance the venture. The responsibility for adequate academic preparation also weighs more heavily on high schools as colleges become more selective in their admission requirements, for as more and more students apply for entrance, colleges of necessity become more demanding.

The guidance program must, therefore, offer the following services to students who are of college caliber:

1 It must provide encouragement to attend college for those students who possess the qualifications that are necessary for success in higher study.

2 It must provide such guidance that those who apply for admission to colleges will be found to meet at least the minimum educational requirements.

3 It must make available to students all the necessary information concerning colleges of various types, their curricular offerings, their requirements, and their fees.

4 It must assist students in applying for admission to the college of their choice and in obtaining admission.

5 It must make some provision for gifted students in accelerated classes or in an enriched program. Such a program will be discussed in detail in the chapter on educational guidance.

REASONS FOR ATTENDING COLLEGE

When the director of guidance and his staff urge high-school students to plan to enter college, they are of course thinking of the welfare of the individual student, but they also have in mind the needs of the Church as a whole. It is imperative that Catholics should exercise leadership in the intellectual and scientific world and that respect for moral and spiritual values should be maintained in higher education and in the general life of society. The secondary-school guidance personnel must prepare prospective college students to meet the challenge of modern society, which urgently needs to be influenced by Christian principles and ideals if it is not to become materialistic and pagan. Students should be motivated to develop their intellectual capacities for the glory of God and the service of mankind, and must be encouraged to seek that education which will give them the greatest possible Christian influence.

The increasing percentage of high-school students who desire a higher education is due largely to the nature and demands of modern society. A college education has become the key that unlocks doors to many opportunities. The secondary-school staff as a group, however, should not emphasize worldly success as the reason for attending college, but should encourage students to entertain higher motives. Counselors in particular should awaken in students a desire for further truth and knowledge, an ambition for the intensive development of intellectual powers, and a craving to know about God and the wonderful works of His creation. A greater appreciation of the varying circumstances of life, a deeper understanding of people, and an enriched social and spiritual living are other values to be emphasized. Students furthermore should be impressed with the fact that education brings with it the consequent privilege and duty of rendering greater service to God and mankind.

Since high-school students often have faulty impressions of college life, they may desire a college education for reasons that are not thoroughly Christian. Some will want to attend college only as the necessary means to a larger income and to a higher material standard of living. Others may have in mind some specific profession but may exert themselves to do no more than fulfill its minimum requirements, without thought of the opportunities for greater service that they are thus losing. Such goals as having a good time, leading a glamorous social life, taking part in nationwide athletic competition, making social or business contacts, of the mere filling in of time until marriage or military service becomes possible are objectives to be discouraged as a waste of precious opportunity. The outcome of guidance should be the growth in students of a desire to develop fully their God-given abilities, to explore wider areas of truth, and to render conspicuous service. The ideal cannot be presented successfully if it remains a mere theory or abstraction. Counselors must be ready with facts concerning national needs and the service rendered by men and women living today. They should also be prepared, on the basis of what they know about their counselees, to suggest to individuals interesting kinds of work in which it would be possible for them to be successful.

Just as students may have undesirable motives for wishing to attend college at all, so they may have poor reasons for choosing a non-Catholic college in preference to a Catholic college. When a counselor is satisfied that a student has sufficient reason for wishing to attend a non-Catholic college, he should in accordance with the laws of the Church instruct the student to obtain the necessary permission from the bishop or his pastor. The fact that students are known to have enrolled in non-Catholic colleges without permission does not of itself prove that the bishop has reasons for not wishing to insist on the strict observance of the law; in case of doubt the counselor may inquire of the chancery. Careful preparation is highly important in the case of those students who actually will enroll in non-Catholic and secular institutions after graduation from high school. All possible steps should be taken to prevent these students from adding to the alarming percentage of Catholic high-school graduates who lose their faith on secular campuses. Students should go to these campuses determined to wage a zealous apostolate for the dissemination of truth and for conversions to the Catholic faith. In addition to negative cautions positive means should be suggested for meeting religious difficulties and intellectual error, for answering the objections and criticisms so frequently heard in secular classrooms or for turning to the right place to obtain an answer, and for remaining immune to the infection of religious indifferentism that is almost certain to be encountered.

Films, posters, and other visual aids should supplement personal encouragement to seek a higher education and to seek it with good motives. Visits to the high school by college representatives, college alumni, and college students can also serve to stimulate the desire to obtain a college education.

IDENTIFYING STUDENTS OF COLLEGE CALIBER

Surveys and questionnaires administered during the years of high school will bring to notice the students who are definitely college material. Questions and discussions at the time of planning a student's program of studies with him will give the counselor further information about his desires and abilities. In the last year of high school every student should answer a specific questionnaire on college education which asks: "Why do you intend to go to college? To which college do you plan to go? How do you plan to finance the cost? What curriculum or major do you intend to follow? Do you know how to apply for scholarships and admission?"[1]

The substantial number of students who do not know clearly whether they wish to pursue a higher education but who possess the necessary qualifications should as a general rule be encouraged to attend college. The counselor should assist such individuals by advancing the reasons for further educational preparation. When it is possible and seems advisable, these students may be urged to try at least a year or two of college and then decide on the necessity of additional college work for their chosen vocation or occupation. Personal factors, such as family conditions of various kinds, the availability of the necessary funds, and the possibility that the student may have a religious vocation, must be considered in all cases of college counseling.

Intellectual Qualifications. Some high-school graduates who are willing to try further study may not be intellectually capable of it. Under normal circumstances the upper two thirds of a senior class are considered capable of beginning and profiting from courses at college. The satisfactory completion of college work usually requires average mental ability, that is, an intelligence quotient of 95-105. A survey of high-school academic record, class rank, and testing data will reveal the students who are intellectually qualified. Data on the scholastic ranking of students should be available as early as the end of the second year of high school to facilitate counseling for capable students who are not working as they should and who as a result may fail to qualify at the end of high school. This type of student should be detected as early as possible and the reason for his poor achievement should be ascertained. He should be warned of the possible consequences of his deficiency in achievement, prevented

[1] See pages 226 and 228 for sample questionnaires.

from scheduling easy courses, and stimulated to more effective application and study. Counselors may advise refresher courses and additional private instruction or study as a remedy for lack of adequate preparation in these students.

Depending upon the standards set by the individual college, students possessing less than average mental ability may be able to profit from some college training for a period of time. Many of these individuals, however, should be counseled to pursue other opportunities instead of going on to a college or university. A grade average recommended for college entrance which has been determined on the basis of the average high-school grade known to be necessary should be printed on reports to parents and transcripts to colleges. This minimum standard will help to guide teachers as well as students in deciding whether success in advanced education is possible. Very high averages and very low averages can be accepted as they stand; but borderline cases should be studied with care, since a student's work in high school can be affected by causes not associated with mental ability.

Educational Requirements. As a general policy students who possess average and superior mental ability should be placed in courses largely college preparatory in content. At the time of forecasting student programs counselors should be careful to see that college-destined students receive this broad background of English and the language arts, mathematics, science, and social studies. The traditional curriculum of Catholic secondary schools continues to lay the best foundation for college study. Most schools of higher learning desire such preparation even for those students who contemplate a limited and technical program.

The subjects required for beginning college work in certain fields should be demanded of qualified students in the high school. The specific subject and grade requirements for college entrance given in the catalog should be explained thoroughly, and as soon as the student has been able to make an occupational choice in his program should be checked against the requirements found in the catalog. For example, beginners in engineering must have taken high-school courses in advanced mathematics (advanced algebra and trigonometry), and science, nursing, and premedical students must have taken the "solid" or difficult high-school science courses. If a capable student has definitely chosen these or similar professions, the guidance personnel must not fail to give correct information about the credits he needs for college entrance.

PROVIDING INFORMATION ABOUT COLLEGES

In the entire work of guiding adolescents safely to their vocation or occupation in life, sufficient information is essential to intelligent choice and adequate preparation. The wise choice of an occupation may depend in part on the kind and length of necessary preparation. The special work of providing information concerning further education may be made the special responsibility of a guidance staff member. Since this area is so intimately related to vocational and occupational guidance, the principles, methods, and suggestions given in Chapter Five should be kept in mind.

A student needs information to answer three preliminary questions: (1) Shall I go to college? (2) What course should I take? (3) Which college should I attend? Informational material, an orientation program, and contacts with college representatives will help provide answers to these questions.

Informational Materials. College counselors should motivate students to explore the following sources of information and should make them easily available:

1 Materials in the vocational and occupational library.
2 Bibliography and materials of the social-studies unit on educational sociology.
3 Articles, periodicals, and books concerning occupations that require college training.
4 Publications of corporations, industries, and professional societies.
5 Career manuals, brochures, and pamphlets from technical schools, state departments, and other organizations, such as Science Research Associates.
6 Publicity materials, newspaper articles, and other publications from colleges and universities.
7 College guides and catalogs.

College catalogs may be secured by a routine request to the registrar, and constitute the most important source of information. The college counselor or the librarian should be certain that the collection of current catalogs is reasonably complete and that duplicate sets are maintained in the library and the counseling offices.

Practical college guides are especially directed to the student who desires a summary of all the necessary information and advice. The *Catholic College Guide,* issued annually by the Catholic University of America, lists major and minor courses, expenses, and other pertinent facts for all the Catholic schools of higher education in the nation.[2] This work should be on the list of required materials in every Catholic secondary school. *The College Handbook* is another valuable source giving similar information on many other colleges and universities.[3] *Mapping Your Education, A Guide to Planned Education* is a cooperative project of the Interstate Council on High School-College Relations in the Pacific Northwest.[4] This unique offering, which may serve as a model for assisting students in other areas of the country, devotes chapters to planning a career, planning education after high school, and choosing a college. The book offers an excellent orientation in all the phases of college that need to be understood and considered by high-school students.

With his extensive knowledge and experience, the college counselor should be a reliable source of prudent advice on the standards of instruction and the rating of the departments of many colleges. Occasional trips to the campuses and meetings with admissions officers will be profitable for him as well as for the students he counsels. Interviews with graduates now attending college will also offer additional information for guidance purposes.

An Orientation Program. An assembly program or a social-studies unit devoted to college orientation each year will present

[2] Published by The Catholic News, 251 Fourth Avenue, New York 10, New York. The *Annual Directory of Catholic Colleges and Universities* is a well-edited booklet listing programs of study and essential information of schools belonging to the Catholic College Bureau, 109 North Dearborn Street, Chicago 2, Illinois.

[3] Published by the College Entrance Board, 425 West 117th Street, New York, New York.

[4] Published by Abbott, Kerns, and Bell Company, 338 N.W. Ninth Avenue, Portland, Oregon.

detailed information and direct the preparation for college. A counselor placed in charge of this program should explain the fundamental facts of the nature and purpose of a college education, the types of colleges, and the way in which they operate. He might consider the following questions often asked by students: (1) Who can go to college? (2) Who should go to college? (3) Why go to college? (4) What should I take? (5) What is meant by majors, credits, grade points, transcripts, and so forth? (6) Where do I find the information? (7) How much will a college education cost? (8) What scholarships or other aids are there? (9) Where should I go? (10) Why should I prefer a Catholic college? (11) What requirements must I fulfill? (12) What steps do I take to enroll?

Contact with College Representatives. The experience of a personal visit to a college campus can be of the greatest value to a student who wishes to prepare himself for higher education. A purposeful visit should provide a view of the essential educational character of the college rather than the distracting impressions of the social and extracurricular activities of campus life. The visits of college representatives to the high schools should be of similar value. Admissions officers and public-relations departments are eager to work with high-school personnel in introducing students to college life.

If a college does not schedule a visit to the high school, a letter of invitation or a request should be sent. The Catholic high school should not neglect its responsibility to encourage attendance at Catholic colleges and should readily cooperate with Catholic colleges in arranging for representatives to confer with or call upon prospective students. High-school-college conferences should be scheduled between January and March because it is during this period that seniors usually make decisions about college. An earlier date will be needed for colleges which admit a limited number and require an earlier application or entrance examination.

Inasmuch as parents ultimately bear the responsibility and the expense of the college education, information ought to be supplied to them as well as to the students. Conferences scheduled for the evening hours enable both parents and students to meet representatives personally and to confer on special problems, thereby making better-informed and more satisfying choices. At high schools where such conferences have been held, the evening program has met with enthusiastic approval.

To arrange a conference the counselor in the first month of school should set the date and send invitations to participate to the regional colleges. He may wish to arrange a joint meeting to which he invites Catholic and public schools, or he may decide to limit the program to the Catholic colleges of the area. He must prepare publicity on the coming conference to ensure parent and student interest and attendance.

Before the meeting both the guidance director and the students should fill out the data sheets to be presented to the college representative. Each student should make out a student-data form for each college in which he is interested. The guidance director will supply from the school records other information desired by the representatives of the colleges. The data sheets for each college should be gathered into a folder and given to the representative, together with directions for his part in the program.

The following program is suggested for an evening conference:

7:30 p.m.	Welcome, introductions, and explanation of the purpose of the program
7:45 p.m.	First session
8:30 p.m.	Second session
9:00 p.m.	Third session
9:30 p.m.	Fourth session
10:00 p.m.	Evaluation

The first session should be of greater length because it will always represent the first choice of students and will result in more questions to be answered by the speaker. Representatives of the participating colleges are assigned to individual rooms, at the doors of which the names of the colleges are posted, and here parents and students can call upon the representatives of the colleges in which they are interested. The representatives remain in the same room for the entire evening except for the session at which they address all the parents and students. A responsible underclass student may be assigned to act as host and to assist the representative in every way possible. At the close of the fourth session a coffee hour will afford a pleasant atmosphere in which an evaluation of the program can be made. As an aid to future planning the high-school counselor may ask the college representatives to fill in the evaluation form.

This program will enable parents and students to listen to or confer with representatives of four colleges, and weigh their comparative merits. Preliminary arrangements for entrance to college are possible at this meeting when college counselors or admissions officers come supplied with materials and application blanks. These representatives might arrange to be available on the following day for individual appointments.

A similar college conference program may be presented during a class day. In the morning students could be given the opportunity of visiting at least three of the representatives. Appointments for individual conferences might be scheduled for the afternoon hours. Representatives may find it possible to consult teachers about prospective college students or to speak about the progress of graduates who are now in college.

The student data sheet to which reference has been made will be found on page 227. A "Student Study of Individual College," to be filled out by the student by consulting the college catalog, by taking notes during the public session, and by asking further questions during a conference with the representative, will be found on page 228. A "College-Conference Evaluation Sheet" is reproduced on page 231.

Appointments to Service Academies and Special Schools. Students who are interested in the Army, Navy, Air Force, and Coast Guard academies need to know that application for appointment must be made by personal letter to one of the congressmen of the state in which they live. The congressman will notify the student of the conditions, the qualifications, the time and place of examination, and any other preparation necessary in order to be considered for appointment. The letter to the congressman should be written not later than the spring preceding the senior year of high school. Appointments may also be won through other avenues, for example, in reserve programs. Information about such appointments should be available from the source of the appointment.

APPLICATIONS AND TRANSCRIPTS

After a student has definitely decided to attend a certain college, there will be at least one printed form that he must fill out. The guidance department, which has assisted him in the making of his decision, should now assist him in taking the final steps.

Applications for Admission and Other Forms. The guidance director or college counselor should keep an adequate supply of the necessary application forms. Folders containing forms to be used in applying for admission, scholarships, and aid or employment and forms used for recommendations and transcripts of grades should be maintained for each school at which students regularly enter. Upon request for an application form the college counselor should instruct the student on the proper method of making out the form, check the choice of college against occupational intention, make certain that the student can afford the expense involved, and request the required recommendation from his counselor or other qualified person.

This conference affords an opportunity for the counselor to discover any deficiencies, to verify the character and personality recommendations, to review the grade record, and to encourage an application for a scholarship if it is indicated. After the student has completed his part of the form, it should be returned to the counselor or guidance director to check and to complete with school records and recommendations. These documents should always be sent by the school directly to the college.

Transcripts. To prevent unnecessary duplication and waste of time by the clerical staff, requests for transcripts should be directed through the guidance office. The issuance of transcripts to a college before the completion of seven semesters is ordinarily of little value. A notation of the date and the school to which the transcript is sent should be made on the permanent record card. In larger schools equipment for photostating transcripts represents a wise investment.

Three incomplete (seven semesters) transcripts and one complete transcript are usually issued without fee. Students should be notified that additional transcripts will be sent for the usual fee of one dollar each. Transcripts are sent directly to the college, and under no circumstances are they given to the student to deliver.

The guidance office will be able to determine the percentage of students entering college by keeping separate lists of transcripts sent to the colleges. Since not all colleges send either enrollment lists or progress and grade-point reports to the high schools from which the students came, and since not all students requesting transcripts actually enroll, the list of transcripts sent to a college may be forwarded with the request that it be checked against actual enrollment lists. The percentage of students entering college over a period of several years may have a significant bearing on the evaluation of the high-school curriculum. A follow-up study of the progress of graduates in colleges will also be useful for any such evaluation. Statistics on the number of students who have enrolled at Catholic colleges and universities are worthy of careful analysis on the part of the guidance personnel and of the administration. This work may be done in connection with a study of transfers and dropouts. A post-high-school occupational or educational plan questionnaire given to students can serve as source material for a follow-up study of graduates.[5] Filing these plans in a cumulative record folder will facilitate any future reference to the student or his work.

SCHOLARSHIPS

An unprecedented rise in the number and value of scholarship opportunities in recent years should stimulate students of Catholic schools to compete and apply for the various types of financial aid. Colleges have shown an increasing interest in superior students and have been enabled by grants from industry and various foundations to offer more scholarships to them. Assistance given by high-school guidance personnel to promising students may save them a substantial amount of money.

[5] A sample questionnaire will be found on page 226.

Information about Aid. Guidance personnel will recognize awards as desirable for the individual student and as a recognition of the quality of instruction found in the school, and so will render a valuable service to both school and students by publicizing scholarship opportunities. A listing of the many forms of aid may be secured from the United States Bureau of Documents, the guidance departments of public schools, and the innumerable notices coming to the school. Many of the posters sent by colleges, private industry, and other organizations contain data regarding qualifications and the method of application. Information about opportunities for scholarships should be made known visually by bulletin-board displays and personally by counseling superior students to apply for several scholarships.

As scholastic average and rank are frequently the criteria for awards, encouragement to seek scholastic recognition and financial assistance ought to begin in the lower grades of high school. A summary of all the opportunities presented to all students early in the year will be an impetus for the younger students to earn higher grade averages before reaching the senior year. Guidance personnel may consider a program of pretesting to establish a scholarship group to whom a special course of study and advanced work may be offered.

The routine work of filing applications will require some assistance from a staff member to guarantee that all the necessary documents and recommendations have been properly cared for and that deadlines are met. He should request the office staff to send the official transcript and he should see that all the requirements for the scholarship have been met.

Policies and Goals. The guidance committee should adopt a clear policy governing the promotion of scholarship. Whatever else it may decide to do, it should accept the principle that a scholarship program (1) serves as motivation of students to greater excellence in the use of God-given abilities, (2) rewards the praiseworthy fulfillment of the student vocation, (3) promotes deeper interest in and stimulates attendance at Catholic colleges by cooperative planning of scholarships, (4) recognizes the financial need of students as a factor with a Christian implication, (5) acknowledges that the conditions and stipends attached to scholarship are legitimately determined by the granting college, (6) appreciates in true humility the prestige and honor resulting from scholarship awards, and (7) conforms to local standards and seeks the best welfare of the student in aids given on the basis of athletic ability.

The staff of a guidance department should set up goals to be achieved annually in the program. Some goals worthy of achievement are the gaining of one scholarship to each Catholic college in the region, recognition of some kind in at least one national competition, and some award for excellence in each major area of the high-school curriculum (for example, religion, English, science, mathematics, music, the drama). In addition to these goals the guidance personnel may encourage the underwriting of scholarships by local civic bodies, business groups, industry, or private foundations. Staff members may concentrate on the preparation of students for competitive examinations by pretesting, special study, and training in the mechanics of tests. If the Catholic high school is achieving the standards of its educational program, a substantial number of grants-in-aid should be forthcoming.

The National Merit Scholarship Program. This recently developed scholarship program has provided a great stimulus to private agencies and corporations to provide aid for top students on the high-school level. The program gives promise of consolidating and simplifying the many different forms of application and the qualifications for scholarships now offered. Participation in this nationwide examination results in an impartial national ranking of students and the possibility of substantial aid from sources with which the school and its students would have no previous contact.

The College Entrance Examination Board. In preparation for college admission and in competition for scholarships the College Entrance Examination Board tests have been increasingly important.[6] The guidance officers and counselors of a high school should explain

---

[6] Detailed information on College Entrance Examination Board tests can be secured from College Scholarship Service, P. O. Box 592, Princeton, New Jersey or P. O. Box 27896, Los Angeles 27, California.

the nature of the College Entrance Examination Board and urge the abler students to take the tests at the designated times. A supply of application blanks should be kept on hand and prospective candidates should be instructed on their proper filing before the deadlines. Counselors should note that the morning scholastic-aptitude tests are required for admission to many colleges, and special attention should be paid to the afternoon program of achievement tests in specific subjects. Individual colleges frequently require the test results before acting on applications for admission.

Junior-year students of exceptional promise should be encouraged to take the Board tests in the spring as a preparation for testing in the following year. The experience will also prepare them for similar examinations in the Merit Scholarship Program or in other competitive scholarship tests. Scores of juniors in the afternoon achievement tests may be used later to satisfy requirements for college admission. College counselors might give consideration to a requirement that all senior students contemplating attendance at college take the scholastic-aptitude test. Preparation for the examinations will be aided by reviews, refresher courses, and special outline studies of specific subjects.

Interpretation of scores on the CEEB tests is highly important in an evaluation of a high-school educational program. A study should be made of these scores and the evaluations given by teachers. The interpretation of scores as a guidance measure for juniors was always permitted. Beginning with the tests of December 1958 it became permissible to make scores known to seniors as a means of apprising them of their aptitudes or achievement.

The Scholarship Service Program. Since accurate determination of financial need is a serious problem for counselors, they should be aware of the additional services rendered to students by the Scholarship Service Program of the College Entrance Examination Board. This service is designed to provide an impartial estimate of the financial need of students when scholarships are awarded on that basis. Application forms will be provided upon request.[7]

---

[7] College Scholarship Service, P. O. Box 176, Princeton, New Jersey or P. O. Box 27896, Los Angeles 27, California.

For the benefit of gifted students the college counselor should familiarize himself with the Advanced Placement Test program of the CEEB. Advanced placement in college on the basis of high ability and of achievement shown in these tests may be gained at certain colleges.

The Expenses of Attending College. "Can you afford it?" ought to be one of the initial questions in college counseling. Experience shows that students often plan attendance at colleges where expenses are prohibitive and completely beyond their financial means. As a class project a chart showing the costs of a college education can be constructed and posted on a bulletin-board section reserved for college information. Students should consider the possibility of paying their way through college by work. Colleges have employment and placement offices to which the student should be directed, and the catalogs will indicate the available student-loan funds for those in need of long-term aid. The limitations of working while carrying a full college program should be pointed out to students and advice given on their ability to do so.

SELECTED REFERENCES

Amadeus, Sister M. "High School Pupils and Their Parents on the Value of Going to College." *Catholic Educational Review* 54:252-55, April 1956.

Foster, Charles R. *Guidance for Today's Schools.* New York: Ginn and Company, 1957.

"Go to a Catholic College." *Catholic Educator* 27:307-24, January 1957. (A complete listing of all Catholic colleges and universities in the United States.)

Ohlsen, Merle M. *Guidance: An Introduction.* New York: Harcourt, Brace and Company, 1955.

O'Neill, J. H. "Guiding Youth toward Catholic Colleges and Universities." *Catholic School Journal* 52:195-98, June 1952.

Traxler, Arthur E., and Agatha Townsend, editors. *Improving Transition from School to College.* New York: Harper and Brothers, 1953.

CHAPTER SEVEN

EDUCATIONAL GUIDANCE

Guidance personnel are concerned with basic educational matters, such as the nature of the curriculum and the courses of study, methods of grouping students and of evaluating their progress, and so forth. Although such topics are related to the direction of students and the satisfaction of individual needs, an extensive treatment of them is not intended here. Discussion of the philosophy of education, which sets forth objectives, and of the curriculum and courses of study, which aim at achieving objectives, is left to authorities in these and related fields.[1]

In educational matters the guidance department starts with the following premises: that the philosophy of Catholic education sets forth the true purposes of education and the basic needs of students; that the curriculum of the high school is designed to fulfill these objectives and satisfy these needs; that the student must be placed in the course of study appropriate to his specific needs and abilities; and that his progress should be evaluated correctly in the light of his achieving his greatest excellence as a human being.

[1] John D. Reden and Francis A. Ryan, *A Catholic Philosophy of Education* (Milwaukee: Bruce Publishing Company, 1956); William F. Cunningham, *The Pivotal Problems of Education* (New York: The Macmillan Company, 1940).

The distinctive approach of guidance personnel to this phase of guidance work should be a determination to guarantee the characteristic Catholic education of individuals by building the intellectual virtues in the fundamental and essential areas of learning. Despite all the current discussion of "the enriched curriculum" and the many confused variations of a "democratic-experience" concept, students will continue coming to Catholic schools in search of basic truths and in definite need of efficient instruction in the fundamental subject areas first of all. Assistance in maintaining this core curriculum while attending also to the various other needs of students should be the role of the guidance department, which may, on the basis of data on student progress, recommend modifications of the curriculum.

Accordingly the purpose of this chapter is to consider the following duties of the guidance staff in regard to educational guidance: (1) to provide data for the proper placement of the student, (2) to suggest methods for evaluation of student progress, (3) to recommend a minimum testing program for Catholic high schools, (4) to furnish a plan for follow-up studies, and (5) to offer the data necessary for an evaluation of the curriculum.

PLACEMENT OF STUDENTS

The director of guidance will determine methods of placing the individual student in an educational program that best fits his needs, objectives, and ability. His appraisal of the freshman or the transfer student will be based largely on records forwarded to the school, but these should be substantiated or corrected by tests and achievement records within the school program.

Data for Placement. Immediately upon the enrollment of a new student the guidance personnel should request personal information from the school last attended. This information should include mental-test results (test, date, score); reading-test scores (test, date, grade or age equivalent); arithmetic-test scores; attendance and health record; and memoranda on behavior, personality or disability problems, and special abilities.[2] An official transcript of scholastic

---

[2] Sample request forms are given on pages 199-202.

record and credits should also be requested. This will supply a basis for placement of the student and will guarantee the continuity of the cumulative record. The school should send similar information when a student transfers to another school.

A program of counseling and testing should supplement past records with firsthand data for the proper placement, grouping, or scheduling of students. For new students a combination of the results of intelligence testing (language and nonlanguage factors), elementary-school achievement tests (secured from the school attended or from testing upon entrance), and the recommendations of previous teachers or of the counselor after an interview upon entrance will serve as the best basis for placement.

Forecasting. For students registered in the school the forecasting of subjects to be taken the following year will be the method to use for obtaining proper placement. This forecasting should be done in the spring term as a cooperative work of teachers and students. Data on ability-test and achievement-test results, vocational and occupational interests, college choices, and teacher recommendations will be required for intelligent forecasting. Parents may be asked to participate by approving or suggesting changes in the forecast.

The forecast should be a continuation of a tentative *educational and vocational plan* created jointly by the counselor and the student in the freshman year.[3] The plan should stimulate the student to select his vocational or occupational goal and to know the means necessary for accomplishing his plan. Although the goal and means may be changed as the student grows and becomes able to evaluate his desires and abilities more accurately, the plan or forecast should be filed for use in succeeding years.

Ability Grouping. Since guidance personnel, especially in large schools, will be interested in placing a student in a program that will best meet his needs and guarantee his greatest development, they will consider the merits of homogeneous grouping. Grouping students according to ability should not only offer a challenge for the fullest development of God-given capacities, but should also provide

[3] An example of a student forecast or educational plan is given on page 218.

a built-in system of satisfying the different needs of the gifted, the average, and the low-ability students without provoking boredom or frustration. Both ability and achievement must be taken into account in this grouping. The periodic evaluation of individual performance may call for changes in grouping, and these should be effected as soon as teachers and guidance personnel deem them advisable.

Providing for the Gifted Child. The individual creation of the human soul with its powers of intellect and will and the varying influences of heredity and environment are manifest in the individual differences and varying abilities of students. More provision has been made recently for retarded and handicapped children, but the exceptionally bright student also has claims on the services of the guidance program. The urgency of providing for the fullest development of the capacities of the gifted is keynoted by the call of church and state for leadership in the complex crises of modern society. The parable of the Talents (Matthew 25:14-30) and the obligation of making good use of greater abilities purposely given by God should motivate the guidance of the gifted.

The Catholic school should manifest a predominant interest in those gifted spiritually, since they should be the powerful forces in a Christian society.[4] The physically gifted ordinarily have sufficient avenues of development in school athletic and physical-education programs and in the larger world of sports. The socially gifted receive normal attention in the cocurricular activities of school and community. The responsibility for the guidance of those with exceptional mental endowment may be met by a careful selection and grouping of students and by an enriched program of study which may entail modifications of the curriculum and of methods of evaluating progress. It is discussed on pages 154-56.

EVALUATION OF PROGRESS

The first objective of educational guidance is to place the student in a course of study that will best prepare him for his life goal to the extent or at the rate that his abilities will allow. The task is not

[4] See pages 80-82 on counseling in the spiritual area.

over once the freshman has started his program of studies. There must be schoolwide methods of measuring progress that will give the students and their parents an accurate account of achievement and that will stimulate greater effort and prevent failures. Beyond this, the guidance staff may judge more detailed information necessary in understanding and guiding the student. Whatever provides deeper knowledge of the person, his attitudes, and his aspirations will result in more effective educational guidance.

Written Reports of Progress. Regardless of what methods of grading are used in the school, the results should be utilized as regular tools of guidance. Students, parents, and teachers should analyze reports to note progress and to determine what further effort is required for satisfactory completion of classwork. Progress reports, "pink and blue" slips, and similar reports, issued in the middle of grading periods, are valued guidance devices. These additions to the regular card should indicate reasons for satisfactory or unsatisfactory progress and should prepare the way for conferences between parents, students, counselors, and teachers when necessary.[5]

The principal should designate someone on the staff, preferably the counselor, to check educational progress at definite intervals. Since praise is often the key to more intense effort on the part of students, reference must be made to praiseworthy development and achievement as well as to deficient work. Where unsatisfactory progress or failures are found, teachers and counselors should endeavor to discover the cause as well as the remedy and discuss both in individual interviews or, if a whole group is affected, in group-guidance periods. How to study, note-taking, retention, how to prepare for examinations, the meaning of grades, the causes of failure, various reactions to failures in life, and other such topics provide worthwhile subject matter for these groups.

Conferences with teachers and parents should be encouraged as a regular part of educational guidance. If a student is in danger of not graduating, a letter of warning should be sent to the parents several months before graduation. Advance notice will protect school

[5] A report on reasons for failure is given on page 219.

personnel from unpleasant situations and will serve as an impetus to satisfactory and passing work. The practice of awarding a certificate instead of a diploma should be explained to parents and students. Unlike the diploma, the certificate does not recommend a student for college entrance. Students who are to receive certificates should also be notified as early as possible.

Honors. Recognition of commendable work through honor programs and award systems will also encourage effort throughout the school. Frequent variations of the form of honors assemblies is advisable to prevent them from becoming routine and meaningless functions. Affiliation with the National Honor Society establishes a noteworthy honor program. The awarding of honors may take place before or after the sacrifice of the Mass in an appropriate ceremony to encourage thanksgiving for the honor and to refer it to the glory of God. Distinctive awards presented at graduation for proficiency in each of the subject areas and in cocurricular activities and the granting of scholarships have an excellent effect on students.

TESTING IN THE GUIDANCE PROGRAM

Few areas of guidance are more confusing, controversial, and varied than the area of testing. Administrators, guidance workers, and teachers agree on the need for an efficient and simple testing program, but a definite identification of tests for a workable program is not always possible. Extensive studies of evaluation tools may still leave considerable doubt as to the most valid tests. Quantitative measurement of essentially mental values and traits is always to be approached with caution. Furthermore, the results of measurements call for expert interpretation and careful use, since these results are conditioned by a variety of factors.

A diocesan or community specialist in testing can recommend a broad program to suit the desired purposes and to coordinate the work of Catholic schools. When available, diocesan and Catholic college guidance and psychological centers offer invaluable services, particularly in the area of aptitude and personality testing.

The Purposes of Tests. Tests may be used for a number of purposes. They are of help in classifying students, in understanding pupil needs, in discovering specific guidance and counseling needs, and in measuring achievement. There are five general classifications of available tests related to guidance needs: scholastic aptitude, achievement, specific aptitudes, interest, and personality. Some provision should be made for testing in each of these classifications. The type of testing program must always be determined by the needs of the school population and the objectives that the school wishes to accomplish by tests. Since happy and successful work by every student under classroom teachers is an objective of supreme importance, provision should always be made for conveying knowledge of test results to teachers and even for checking up on the extent to which teachers draw sound conclusions from test data.

The administrator and the guidance staff should know exactly *why and what* they wish to test. In any school the general purpose should be to gain an objective measurement of scholastic ability and achievement in subject areas and information about the special aptitudes and interests of students. Relatively inexpensive tests are available to satisfy these purposes.

Sources of Information about Tests. In order to find appropriate and reliable tests *The Fourth Mental Measurements Yearbook*[6] may be consulted. This source gives a fairly complete listing of tests with an evaluation of each one. Publisher's catalogs will furnish additional information. Guidance personnel should also make an effort to learn what tests are generally used by other schools for similar purposes.[7] Frequency of use, however, does not mean that the test is suitable to the individual needs of a given school.

As the next step specimen sets of selected tests should be secured from the publisher or from the area university or school of education. A study of the specimen sets should then be made to determine their purposes, reliability, validity, norms, objectivity, ease of administration, and cost. An achievement test should be examined for comparison of its content and objectives with the course-offered con-

[6] Oscar Krisen Buros, editor, *The Fourth Mental Measurements Yearbook*. Highland Park: Gryphon Press, 1953.

[7] Lester Nicholas Recktenwald, *Guidance and Counseling,* pp. 32-34 (Washington: The Catholic University of America Press, 1953), contains tables of tests.

tent and the teaching objectives of the Catholic school. This analysis is highly important in a subject such as social studies where the scope, sequence, and objectives of the course will reflect a definite Catholic approach. Other factors to be considered before the final selection of tests are time limits, scoring, the possibility of reuse for other groups, the approximate date on which tests will be administered, and the inclusion of aids to score analysis. Cooperation with diocesan and community systems in the selection of tests will ensure economy.

Educational Testing Service,[8] Science Research Associates,[9] and the California Test Bureau[10] provide the most complete test programs. ETS and SRA will assist in formulating a program. ETS offers an evaluation and advisory service that furnishes excellent professional assistance on testing problems. Scholastic Testing Service, organized in 1951 to provide a Catholic-school testing program, presently has an elementary-school battery, a high-school placement test with well-established national norms, and achievement tests for freshmen. In addition diocesan testing programs are offered.[11]

Recommendations for a Minimum Program. Few tests will fit every school situation throughout the country equally well. Nevertheless, the following tests recommended for a minimum program may be used in most schools.

Scholastic Aptitude Tests. The measurement tools offered by Educational Testing Service can satisfy a variety of needs for any school. The new form of intelligence testing, *School and College Ability Tests* (SCAT), is an improvement over the already excellent form, *American Council on Education Psychological Examination for High School Students* (ACE). The latter will be discontinued by ETS in favor of SCAT in 1959.

A simple and easy-to-administer form of intelligence test is the *Henmon-Nelson Test of Mental Ability*. The *Otis Test of Mental Ability* is in common use in many school systems. The *Ohio State*

---

[8] 20 Nassau Street, Princeton, New Jersey and 4640 Hollywood Boulevard, Los Angeles 27, California.
[9] 57 West Grand Avenue, Chicago 10, Illinois.
[10] 5916 Hollywood Boulevard, Los Angeles 28, California.
[11] 3774 West Devon Avenue, Chicago 45, Illinois.

University Psychological Test seems to be more valuable for higher-ability students. The *California Test of Mental Maturity* gives a very reliable measurement of both language and nonlanguage factors and is therefore helpful in testing the poor reader. For individual testing the *Stanford Revision of the Binet Intelligence Test* is worthwhile. The *Wechsler-Bellevue Intelligence Scale* will serve especially well as an individual test for students with unusual backgrounds. Trained examiners for both the Stanford-Binet and the Wechsler-Bellevue tests will be found to be necessary.

Achievement Tests. The Cooperative Test Division of Educational Testing Service provides survey tests of general proficiency in social studies, natural sciences, and mathematics. These *Cooperative Achievement Tests* (American Council on Education) are available in all individual subject areas. Timed for forty minutes, they form a very satisfactory program of achievement testing and offer a reliable basis for comparison with other schools.

The *Iowa Tests of Educational Development,* published by Science Research Associates (SRA), provide a comprehensive profile of a student in social-studies background, natural-science background, correctness of writing, quantitative thinking, interpretation of reading materials in social studies, interpretation of reading materials in natural sciences, interpretation of literary materials, general vocabulary, and use of sources of information. These lengthy tests, which require 480 minutes for their administration, show both the potential high achievers and those students in need of remedial work, especially in reading.

The *SRA Achievement Series,* Grades 6-9 (360 minutes) and the *Iowa Every Pupil Tests of Basic Skills* for the second semester of Grades 5-9 (420 minutes) supply a good measurement of basic skills and ability to use what has been learned.

In testing religion content the standardized tests published by Loyola University Press (forms A-D) are the most satisfactory.[12] These tests ought to be used at the beginning of freshman year and at the end of each year's work.

---

[12] 3441 North Ashland Avenue, Chicago 13, Illinois.

For a diagnostic reading test to be given to all incoming students the *Iowa Silent Reading Test, Advanced Form BM for High Schools and Colleges*[13] is recommended. The diagnostic reading test issued by Science Research Associates and the reading test of the California Achievement series are both satisfactory.

In mathematics the *Lankton First Year Algebra Test* (Form BM),[13] the *Columbia Research Bureau Algebra Test*, and the *Cooperative ACE Algebra Test* are effective tools of evaluation. The *Blyth Second Year Algebra Test* (Form BM) and *U.S. Armed Forces Institute Second Year Algebra Test* (High School Level, Form B)[14] are very good end-of-the-year tests.

In physical education standardized tests arranged by state departments of education should be used.

Interest Tests. Interest tests are of considerable value in vocational guidance and counseling. The Germane and Germane *Vocational Interest Inventory* is a simple and inexpensive means of stimulating the vocational thinking of younger students.[15] Followed by a brief unit in vocational guidance, this inventory may be the basic tool in a simplified program. It is often available from state departments of vocational education.

The most widely used interest inventory is the *Kuder Preference Record*, available from Science Research Associates. The *Kuder Vocational Form C* shows the relation of interests to classes of occupations or to specific jobs. It may be used several times as a check on changes in vocational interests. There is an advantage in using the Kuder while a social-studies unit is being taught. When followed by classroom discussion and individual counseling this instrument is well worth the cost. The *Vocational Interest Blank* by Edward K. Strong has forms for both men and women and compares student interest with that of successful persons in given occupations.[16]

---

[13] World Book Company, 2126 Prairie Avenue, Chicago 16, Illinois.

[14] Veterans Testing Service of the American Council on Education, 5741 Drexel Avenue, Chicago 37, Illinois.

[15] This test may be reproduced with permission from Silver Burdett Company, 45 East Seventeenth Street, New York 3, New York.

[16] Stanford University Press, Stanford, California.

Aptitude or Special-Ability Tests. A variety of aptitude tests is available from test distributors. Unless there is a diocesan or community guidance and testing center or a person specially trained in testing, and unless the test can be followed by capable counseling interviews, the administration of these tests is not advisable, except perhaps in individual instances. Ordinarily these tests or their equivalent may be taken at the local or state employment office, a local college or university, a psychological service center, or one of the growing number of psychological and aptitude testing agencies. SRA has a number of aptitude tests and the battery of *Flanagan Aptitude Classification Tests* (FACT).[17]

Personality Tests. Personality inventories should be used with much care. The judgments of teachers seem to be more reliable than existent tests, at least in identifying personality characteristics. In a Catholic school personality and character are gauged in accordance with the philosophy and purpose of Christian education and the notion that natural interests should be developed into Christian supernatural virtues. The *California Test of Personality* will help to identify causes and patterns of reaction in personality, and when administered carefully in a social-studies unit may provide valid information for follow-up counseling. Serious cases of personality maladjustment and character defect should be referred to a competent priest as well as to a reliable psychologist or psychiatrist.

College Entrance Examination Board Tests. Unusually good students in the junior year should be strongly advised to take the May examinations of the CEEB. Seniors seeking scholarships and asking admission to colleges requiring specific examinations must take the CEEB tests at the time indicated by the college. Guidance personnel should seriously consider a policy requiring the morning examination (scholastic aptitude) of all seniors planning to enter college. The acceptance of students for admission will be facilitated, especially in the case of students who have received lower grades as a result of taking the more difficult courses in high school.

[17] Lester Nicholas Recktenwald, *Guidance and Counseling,* pp. 39 ff. (Washington: The Catholic University of America Press, 1953) contains an evaluation of many of the aptitude tests and gives the sources from which they may be secured.

At the present time, when institutions of higher learning are becoming more selective in admissions, the CEEB results offer the best criteria for impartial judgment of scholastic ability and achievement. Application blanks for these tests should be kept on hand in the guidance office as a service to students.[18]

A SUGGESTED MINIMUM TESTING PROGRAM
FOR CATHOLIC SECONDARY SCHOOLS

Test	*When To Be Given*
1. Henmon-Nelson or Otis test of mental ability or *California Test of Mental Maturity, Iowa Silent Reading Test,* or *School and College Ability Tests* (SCAT)	At entrance and placement
2. *Vocational Interest Inventory* (Germane and Germane) or *Kuder Preference Record*	Grade 9, January
3. *Cooperative Achievement Tests* (ACE) in desired subject areas	At end of each year
Loyola University Press *Religion Test for High Schools*	At end of each year
4. *Iowa Tests of Educational Development*	Grade 10, October
5. *Kuder Preference Record*	Grade 11, Spring or Grade 12, Fall
6. *Iowa Tests of Educational Development*	Grade 12, Fall
7. College Entrance Examination Board tests, depending on college and scholarship requirements	Grade 12
8. CEEB scholastic aptitude or National Merit scholarship tests for juniors, especially those of high ability and those who desire it	Grade 11, Spring

CHARACTER AND PERSONALITY RECORDS

Guidance personnel should strive for the encouragement of desirable traits in a student, for correction of undesirable traits, and for

---

[18] Applications may be secured from College Entrance Examination Board, P. O. Box 592, Princeton, New Jersey or P. O. Box 27896, Los Angeles 27, California.

the balance of all those qualities that make up the ideal Christian person. Before adjustment and development can go forward on a sound foundation, however, teachers and students must have true concepts of a mature character and a Christian personality.

A reliable method for making a character and personality analysis is needed as a guidance and counseling tool. This analysis will serve, not only for purposes of evaluation, but also as a teaching and counseling device for the achievement of Christian social living and the fuller development of personal capacities. A record of this evaluation may also be used to satisfy the increasing demand of colleges, military agencies, and employers for an expression of opinion concerning the character and personality of a student whose application is being considered. The guidance department is obliged to supply a just and accurate means of evaluation. Although personality tests and rating scales furnish some help, especially in analyzing factors in personality traits, measuring devices which omit spiritual values are not reliable and adequate.

Composite Subjective Evaluation. The subjective evaluation of character and personality presents a danger in that an individual teacher may not possess sufficient information about any one student to make a judgment of such a serious nature. The teacher's evaluation may also reflect his biases or prejudices in spite of his efforts at objectivity. Since many factors may render difficult a fair evaluation by an individual teacher, the composite judgments of staff members should be sought. As a further aid to evaluation teachers may ask students to rate themselves on their own qualities of character and personality. The student rating may serve as a guide for teacher judgment and as an instrument for guidance and counseling.

The guidance department of a Catholic school may wish to devise a rating chart based upon the virtues, gifts, and fruits of the Holy Spirit. This form of analysis of the Christian personality and character might present an excellent picture for the use of school personnel, but it would sometimes be difficult for those outside the school to interpret.

A Character and Personality Record. The rating and analysis shown on page 215 is suggested as a dependable means of creating a composite record of the usual character items: scholastic ability, industry, influence, concern for others, responsibility, integrity, manners, appearance, and emotional stability. The items of such a standard form will show the profile desired by colleges and employers. Upon request for a recommendation the guidance department may duplicate the record or may use it as the basis for completing the specific form requested.

A composite record is built in the following manner. In the spring of each year three teachers (for example, teachers of English, religion, and social studies) are asked to make a rating of the character and personality traits of students in their classes. The dean of discipline and the counselor rate students with whom they are familiar. Each rater is required to check items on a three-point to six-point scale, depending upon the trait. Raters are instructed to refrain from checking an area in which they lack information sufficient to justify an expression of opinion.

A chart or record for each of the students is placed in a binder, arranged alphabetically and according to the scholastic year. These binders are kept with the guidance folders and permanent records in the school office. At the termination of the enrollment of the student the record should be placed in the guidance folder.

FOLLOW-UP STUDY

The guidance department may be made responsible for gathering significant information about graduates and students who leave school before graduation. The objectives of such a study should be (1) curriculum research and revision to meet the changing needs of students and community, (2) the evaluation and improvement of guidance work, (3) the gathering of vocational information to aid in counseling, (4) modifications in the preparation of students as a means of coping with problems of occupational or college adjustment, and (5) the prevention of failures and dropouts or additional assistance for those who leave school before graduation. The Catholic school will always be interested in learning as far as possible of the faithfulness of former students to the Church and the problems encountered in their adult Christian living.

To conduct the follow-up study the guidance personnel will (1) prepare the list of names and addresses of persons to whom a questionnaire will be sent, (2) construct a record card, (3) prepare the questions to be asked, (4) arrange the questions in the best order possible, and (5) tabulate and evaluate the replies.

The plan developed for conducting a periodic study will depend upon local school conditions and the help available to the personnel assigned for the work. Use may be made of questionnaires, interviews, class meetings and alumni reunions, the telephone, and other contacts that may be made, not only with the former students but also with parishes and individuals with whom a former student is now associated. The objective of any questionnaire should be to discover the present vocational status of graduates and the services preparing students for the needs of postschool life which the school gave or failed to give.[19]

When a student intends to drop out of school a counseling interview should seek to establish the reason for leaving and to provide the student with a plan for meeting his future needs. The student should be required to complete with the assistance of the counselor a form which will supply this information. Guidance workers should be alert to the possible causes for students' leaving school and should attempt to help them solve the problems which are forcing them to discontinue their education.

The keeping of records of the activities and experiences of high-school graduates requires considerable time and expense which can be justified only by the value of the information received and its use in reappraising curriculum content and classroom teaching. The large Catholic high school will not be able to afford the expenditure unless a special study must be made. The smaller school ordinarily will have sufficient information on its graduates through the usual channels of community and parish life. A simplified form of follow-up may be efficiently achieved by asking the senior class to provide the information about the previous graduating class. The alumni

[19] The *National Association of Secondary School Principals Bulletin* for March 1953 and February 1954 contain sample forms of follow-up and dropout studies. We give a questionnaire for school-leavers on page 229.

organization director may prepare a form[20] and submit it to the seniors, who may then pool their information to provide a very satisfactory record.

CURRICULUM EVALUATION

A careful evaluation of changing community and student needs and of the educational preparation necessary for meeting these needs will help determine curricular offerings. With the aid of surveys, questionnaires, and consultation with parents, staff members, and students, guidance personnel will discover what these needs are. A goal of the department will be to analyze all the data and to suggest necessary curricular modifications.

Tools for Evaluating the Curriculum. Examples of the type of data essential to the evaluation and reconstruction of a curriculum are the numbers of students going to college, to military service, to seminaries and novitiates, or soon after graduation into marriage; the number immediately starting employment; the kinds of work and professions selected; the nature of the training required for these vocations and occupations; accurate information on current trends of employment; and so forth. The information obtained by a guidance department through periodic studies of graduates and those leaving school prematurely will be highly desirable for curriculum revision.

Forecasting, although its primary purpose is to help the student choose from the existing curriculum the course of study that best meets his needs, also serves as a stimulus to serious vocational planning on the part of the student, and the administration may therefore discover in it implications of desirable curricular changes and developments. Ability grouping and the examination of teaching methods for the different ability levels lead to more detailed curricular planning. The results of the minimum testing program of the guidance department also have bearing on curriculum revision. Whatever plan is adopted by the individual school for assessing itself, the guidance personnel will be concerned about the extent to

[20] See page 231.

which the curriculum, its objectives, and the methods of teaching are geared to meet the true educational needs of the students.

The Enriched Program. Schools seldom find difficulty in adapting the course of study for students of lesser ability. The difficulty lies rather in developing a program for the gifted student. Enrichment should go beyond offering college courses for high-school students. Any curriculum revision for the gifted student should challenge him to use to the full his greater ability, should be geared to a high level of comprehension, should assure the development of the basic skills of reading, writing, and arithmetic, and should develop the student's qualities as a Christian leader.

Teaching methods in the enriched program should have definite characteristics. For example, the teacher vocabulary in presentation of new material should fit the level of the student, there should be analysis and synthesis with emphasis on logical reasoning, and the lecture method should be used more extensively. The seminar should encourage student participation in the teaching progress and should avoid discussions which may just waste time. The activities of the gifted group should be creative rather than repetitive. Stress should be laid on the obligation of using talents for the honor of God, of alleviating the burdens of those less gifted, of removing ignorance, and of performing the other spiritual and corporal works of mercy. Any effective method will stimulate critical thinking, wider reading, and positive action in all fields of human experience.

An enrichment program itself should be designed to fit the ability and assets of the individual school. The principal should name a committee to study the guidance of the gifted as well as to provide for low-ability students in the school. The recommendations of one such committee at Central Catholic High School, Portland, Oregon, will suggest the ways in which the challenge of educating the gifted student may be met.

ENRICHMENT AND THE GIFTED STUDENT

We recommend that the following be considered in forming any future plan for curriculum enrichment or any future plan to care for our gifted students:

1. That we adopt a *unified policy* with the emphasis on enrichment rather than on acceleration of subject matter, and that this be a thoroughly planned program that will carry through the four years in each department.

2. That we consider the experience and plans of the Portland Public Schools and consider the possibilities of a similar plan; that is, a plan to provide our top students with work in *small, seminar-type groups* in the subjects in which they excel. The possibility should be investigated of enlisting the aid of the local Catholic colleges in this effort.

(a) That scholastic tools, in other words, should be the point of our emphasis. Portland schools participating in the Ford Foundation Plan place the emphasis on research methods, study methods, improvement of reading, and so forth.

(b) That no gifted student in such a plan may be given a grade less than 85 per cent, or whatever similar grade the faculty may decide. This would keep the gifted student from being penalized on grade point average by studying with other exceptional students.

3. That we base an enrichment program upon our existing departments, the department heads to be responsible for plans and policy. Occasional department and faculty meetings should be devoted to discussing teaching methods and solving common problems of enrichment.

4. That we consider *in-service training* for teachers of top-ability groups, and the dissemination of information concerning enrichment of gifted students through bulletins, and like means.

5. That the *gifted child be selected* on the basis of intelligence quotient, previous achievement, teacher appraisal, factors of character, personality, and health, and that a student who is gifted in one particular subject only be permitted to take advantages of special training in that particular field.

6. That in all classes we put emphasis to a greater degree upon *creative activities* without cutting down unnecessarily on drill. The committee feels that we now place the emphasis very heavily on drill.

7. That we make better use of *outside resources:* speakers, exhibits, field trips, and so forth.

That we consider a change to a time schedule which would facilitate the use of the above resources. A period at least fifty-five minutes long is recommended.

8. That we employ what is properly called *action research.* This is a high-sounding term meaning simply teachers' experimentation with those

pet ideas and theories which they have always wanted to try but for which they have found neither time nor encouragement.

9. That more planning go into *assemblies* calling for more participation by talented students. A faculty-student committee should work out the plans for making assemblies more profitable.

Class assemblies, especially on the freshman level, should aim at finding and developing talent early.

10. That *school clubs* be required to be creative or cease to exist. Service clubs are recognized to be creative in nature.

11. That our findings concerning the gifted student be made available to the grade schools, and that we encourage them to start locating the gifted on that level.

12. That both teacher and student must be motivated. We recognize that teachers will not achieve outstanding results except in their fields of interest, and then only when they can work several years in one situation.

13. That teachers avoid using the same plans and techniques for high and low groups of students.

14. That we *search for ways* of placing more responsibility upon students who are gifted in talent and leadership.

15. That we continue to examine our curriculum critically, judging each offering on what we feel to be its merits, and not what have traditionally been thought of as its merits. In other words, that we feel free to change our curriculum where our judgment says we should.

SELECTED REFERENCES

Foster, Charles R. *Guidance for Today's Schools,* Chapter 7, "Guidance for Life in School"; Appendix B, "A Specimen College-Day Program." New York: Ginn and Company, 1957.

Jones, Arthur J. *Principles of Guidance,* fourth edition, Chapter 18, "Methods of Educational Guidance in the Senior High School." New York: McGraw-Hill Book Company, 1951.

Ohlsen, Merle M. *Guidance: An Introduction,* Chapter 16, "Vocational and Educational Planning." New York: Harcourt, Brace and Company, 1955.

Recktenwald, Lester Nicholas. *Guidance and Counseling,* Chapter 6, "Information about Education." Washington: The Catholic University of America Press, 1953.

Stoops, Emery, and Gunnar L. Wahlquist. *Principles and Practices in Guidance,* Chapter 4, "Information about Opportunities: Educational and Personal." New York: McGraw-Hill Book Company, 1958.

CHAPTER EIGHT

RELIGIOUS GUIDANCE

True guidance leads man to God, and so is intimately linked to religion. Guidance as it is given today often becomes confused and loses sight of the objective of developing the adjusted and well-rounded individual. This failure is largely due to hesitation in emphasizing spiritual motives and to inability to explain and champion spiritual values and to offer the means so vital in supernatural formation. On the other hand, guidance in Christian schools, free from such handicaps, should not suffer from this confusion. Through religious instruction Christian guidance proposes Christ as the ideal supernatural man and the Christian life as the adjusted, well-rounded life. Through the Mass, the sacraments, and the other means of grace a Catholic program offers the supernatural helps that are necessary and effective for attaining that adjustment and for achieving the proposed goal.

These distinctive elements of complete guidance services harmonize with the purpose of true education. In the words of Pius XI, "The proper and immediate end of Christian education is to cooperate with Divine grace in forming the true and perfect Christian, that is, to form Christ . . . in those regenerated by Baptism. . . . For the true Christian must live a supernatural life in Christ . . . and display it in all his actions. . . . Hence the true Christian, product of Christian education, is the supernatural man who thinks, judges and acts constantly and consistently in accordance with right reason illumined by the supernatural light of the example and teaching of Christ; in other words, to use the current term, the true and finished man of character."[1]

Religious instruction and sacramental guidance, then, must be the primary means in the development of the Christian character. Religion and guidance can be so integrated that these two departments in a school work together almost as a unit. Religious instruction may be looked upon as moral or group guidance; and spiritual direction may be considered to be, as indeed it is, the highest form of counseling. The work of the two programs can be so coordinated that there is no unnecessary duplication of duties and so that the services of one help the work of the other.

The aim of this chapter is to outline the guidance-related responsibilities of those in charge of religious instruction, to suggest some additional methods of encouraging the use of the means of grace so important to guidance in a Catholic school, and to recall some of the principles of religious guidance.

INSTRUCTION IN RELIGION

A sound guidance program will be greatly implemented by teachers who are qualified to teach religion to adolescents. Religion should be given the first place and the greatest attention, especially in the selection of teachers. So much group and individual guidance is involved in the teaching of religion that teacher qualifications should be identical with those of the counselor.[2] Whenever possible, these teachers should be specially trained in such areas as the content, methods, techniques, planning, and supervision of religious instruction.[3]

[1] Pius XI, *Christian Education of Youth*, p. 32. New York: The America Press, 1936.
[2] See pages 58-59.
[3] J. B. Collins, *Teaching Religion* (Milwaukee: Bruce Publishing Company, 1953) gives a clear and detailed treatment. The study of this work should be advised for all teachers of religion.

In studies of the curriculum that it undertakes, the guidance personnel should keep in mind the importance of the formation of correct teacher and student attitudes toward religious instruction. To ensure proper attitudes religion should be given a position of preeminence in the school program. Allotting anything less than equal time and credit to religion engenders the attitude that religion is a mere adjunct of the school program and of minor importance. A proper appreciation of religion will abolish the practice of using religion periods for assemblies or similar school activities. Such substitution tends to minimize the importance of religion and may encourage students to neglect their own religious obligations.

RELIGIOUS INSTRUCTION AND GUIDANCE

The guidance director and the head of the religion department should confer to direct religious instruction and to coordinate it with the guidance program. The head of the religion department may undertake the following duties with the help of his staff:

1 A periodic evaluation of the religion courses of study and an examination of the content and quality of instruction.

2 The gathering of information on new textbooks and materials being developed in answer to the constant demand for functional methods that combine instruction with encouragement to action in the practical living of religion.

3 The supervision of unified instruction on minimum essentials. The head will wisely direct that enrichment activities be employed only after the essentials have been satisfactorily taught. Sometimes the concentration of individual teachers on preferred phases of religion results in the omission of essential matter to the injury of the student.

4 The provision for a uniform testing program which will present a reliable picture of achievement in essentials.[4] Test results will reveal the areas of insufficient instruction which must be rem-

---

[4] Rev. Austin G. Schmidt, S.J., and O. F. Anderhalter, *Religion Test for High Schools,* Forms A, B, C, D (Chicago: Loyola University Press, 1955). Devised to test minimum essentials, these tests have percentile norms facilitating evaluation and comparison with other Catholic students.

edied or supplied. A form of comprehensive religion examination should be given before graduation from high school to make certain that students are adequately equipped with religious knowledge.

5 The establishment of definite objectives and practices in grading for the subject of religion. A just policy concerning religion failures, especially in reference to low-ability students, should be adopted and publicized.

6 The direction of a supplementary program for Catholic students with a deficient background of religious instruction. This deficiency should be determined by a survey of all new students.[5] Arrangements for teacher, textbooks, and time should be made to give a six-week course in the essentials of Catholic doctrine and practice.

7 Acceptance of responsibility for the religious instruction of non-Catholic students. Since such students cannot receive a Catholic education without this important core of religious knowledge, they should be required to attend classes in religion unless an exception is made because of parental objections. Their choice of a Catholic school may be the prelude to the gift of faith.

8 The compilation of lists of non-Catholic students and of Catholic students from non-Catholic parents. Since family background is significant in spiritual development and since some knowledge of the family situation is necessary for counseling, the list should be distributed to members of the faculty. Significant information should be submitted to the pastor. A high percentage of mixed marriages, for example, may call for renewed emphasis on the sacrament of matrimony in both school and parish.

9 A check on the baptism, confirmation, and first Communion status of all students. Notice of those who have not received these sacraments should be sent immediately to the pastors involved. The counselor should cooperate with the parish by urging the student to receive the sacraments and by helping him to prepare to receive them.

[5] See the survey form on page 207.

10 A periodic review of the state of student morality and religious practice. Consultation with members of the faculty and reliable students, questionnaires, and anonymous polls on faithfulness to Mass and the sacraments will reveal the degree of Christian living. The department head should seek means of instilling deeper spirituality among students. Organizations such as the sodality, the Young Christian Workers, missionary organizations, and other groups can be of great assistance. There should be a group dedicated to the spiritual welfare of students and to the performance of tasks connected with religious activities.

11 The preparation of outlines, bulletins, and class plans designed to assure correct morality and attitudes and to remedy recurring spiritual problems. As the occasion warrants, teachers should concentrate simultaneously on uniform material devoted to the current problems of drink, dress, dating, and so forth.

12 The promotion of religious activities and functions, such as visits to the Blessed Sacrament, the recitation of the rosary, and the observance of patronal feast days. If there is a school chaplain or director of religious activities, the religion-department head should work closely with him in these matters.

13 The creation of definite parish consciousness through the religion classes. Loyalty and cooperation of the students in the life of the parish should be stimulated rather than discouraged by the school. The hours for Mass and confession, notices of parish meetings and other parish bulletins should be posted on a bulletin board in the religion classroom.

14 Close cooperation with the director of vocations in fostering vocations to the priesthood and the religious life. If there is no director, the religion-department head should be made responsible for vocation work.

THE ROLE OF THE SACRAMENTS IN GUIDANCE

The sanctifying and sacramental graces which flow from the reception of the sacraments play a singularly effective role in the guidance of youth. The guidance and religion departments of a school should be most concerned about the frequency with which the sacraments are administered and the opportunities for receiving them that are provided. Provision for the administration of the sacraments is the responsibility of the bishop, who in turn delegates authority to the pastor or the principal of the school. The extent to which the ideal of daily Mass, frequent Communion, and regular confession is practiced by students will depend in large measure upon the opportunities offered to them.

Mass and Communion. The opportunity for daily Mass and Communion is as important for the students as for the priests, the brothers or sisters, and the lay staff of a school. The administrator should make every effort to provide a school chapel where the sacrifice of the Mass may be offered daily and the Blessed Sacrament may be reserved for adoration. While daily Mass and Communion should not ordinarily be made compulsory, the practice should be strongly advised and made possible for students. Encouragement should also be given to formation of the habit of making visits to the chapel, which is Christ's classroom in the school. The doctrinal and spiritual reasons for aiding the growth and development of adolescents by these means will be clear to every Catholic guidance worker.

Confession. Equally significant to an effective guidance program is the counseling service of the sacrament of penance. Confession will provide the highest type of professional counseling that can be offered in any school. The confessor deals with some of the most important and basic problems of adolescent adjustment, with failures of soul life and character, and with all the difficulties of reaching spiritual maturity. He may counsel adolescents individually, seek to discover and overcome the causes of sin, and offer his penitents the means of true adjustment for successful living. The sacrament of penance with its sanctifying and sacramental graces gives to the school a model guidance clinic. Students will benefit immeasurably from the ministration of the wise confessor acting as the representative of Christ, who said: "Come to me, all you who labor and are burdened, and I will give you rest" (Matthew 11:28). Further analysis of the relationship of the sacrament of penance to counseling reveals it as a fundamental necessity and an absolute minimum in

Christian guidance. The role of confession in the school program cannot be stressed too much.

The principal should exert every effort to secure the services of confessors, so that students may have ample opportunities for the grace and the guidance which come through the sacrament. Wherever possible, regular times should be provided for confessions, before Mass or classes, during the lunch hour, and before first Fridays and special feasts. On some occasions the time of the religion period may be suitably used for the hearing of confessions in place of the usual classwork.

The priest counselor may find at times that the counseling interview may fittingly conclude with the reception of the sacrament of penance, especially when a moral failure has been discussed. The restoration or increase of sanctifying grace will always be the most effective termination of counseling. In the case of a boy the priest may administer the sacrament in his office at the end of the session or may arrange for another priest to be available in the chapel. Although brothers, sisters, and lay counselors will not be able to provide the same services as a priest, they should nonetheless urge confession as a vital part of counseling service. Counselors of girls should have at hand a schedule of confession hours in the parishes or should try to make special arrangements for a confessor to be available during school hours. Girls should be encouraged to seek from a confessor advice in matters of vocations, temptations, and problems related to the spiritual life. If necessary, the principal should discuss the necessity of greater opportunities for the reception of this sacrament with the bishop, the pastor, and other authorities.

SELECTED REFERENCES

Arnold, Magda B., and John A. Gasson. *The Human Person*, Part 5, "Self-Integration through Religion." New York: Ronald Press Company, 1954.

Cunningham, William F. *The Pivotal Problems of Education*, "Regaining Public Support for Transmitting the Religious Inheritance," pp. 537-50. New York: The Macmillan Company, 1940.

Gilroy, Brother. "The Need for Counseling and Guidance to Develop the Student's Awareness of His Role in the Mystical Body of Christ." *Bulletin National Catholic Educational Association* 51:432-35, August 1954.

Hartshorne, Hugh; Mark A. May; and Frank K. Shuttleworth. *Studies in the Nature of Character.* 3 vols. New York: The Macmillan Company, 1928-1930.

Hull, Ernest R. *The Formation of Character.* St. Louis: B. Herder Book Company, 1943.

Lindworsky, Johannes. *The Training of the Will,* translated by Arpad Steiner and Edward A. Fitzpatrick. Milwaukee: Bruce Publishing Company, 1929.

McCarthy, Raphael C. *Training the Adolescent,* Chapter 13, "The Moral Formation of Youth"; Chapter 14, "The Religious Education of Adolescents." Milwaukee: Bruce Publishing Company, 1934.

McMahon, John T. *Building Character from Within,* Chapter 3, "Build on Natural Virtues." Milwaukee: Bruce Publishing Company, 1940.

Magner, James A. *Mental Health in a Mad World.* Milwaukee: Bruce Publishing Company, 1953.

O'Connor, Paul L. "A Syllabus for Pre-Induction Religious Training." *Bulletin National Catholic Educational Association* 49:325-33, August 1952.

Silverman, Hirsch L. "Moral and Religious Education: A Spiritual Psychology." *Catholic School Journal* 56:269-71, November 1956.

CHAPTER NINE

THE GUIDANCE FOLDER

All the areas of guidance cannot be undertaken unless an adequate amount of information is available in usable form. Information and its recording are worthwhile only if they provide a service and satisfy a need. The purpose of a cumulative record or guidance folder is to supply *what is needed* and *what will be used*. The individual school will gather, sort, and record permanently the information which it considers necessary and useful for specific purposes. Other information may be useful for a time and then should be discarded.

Necessary Data. The following data are recommended as necessary for guidance and counseling.[1]

1 A record of academic ability
2 A record of past achievement and attendance
3 A report of aptitudes and disabilities
4 A profile of personality and character traits
5 A health record
6 An indication of vocational or occupational interests
7 A history of family and religious background

---

[1] Examples of forms contained in a guidance folder are given in Chapter Twelve.

For the continuity of the cumulative record, information for each student should be requested from the school previously attended, whether it be an elementary school or a high school. Whatever data are lacking in the transfer-of-record form should be supplied in the registration form.

Confidential Material. Confidential information secured from any source should not be kept in a cumulative record or guidance folder. A notation "Refer to counselor" or "Contact if necessary" may be placed in a folder if a staff member wishes to maintain some guidance control. School personnel should respect confidences and should not commit confidences to writing. Students should be informed when information is accepted in confidence.

THE GUIDANCE FOLDER

As the high-school life of the student progresses, additional information should be gathered and used by the school personnel. The encouraging of teachers to consult the cumulative record whenever a special problem arises in connection with any student and to cooperate in maintaining this essential source of information is a continuing task of the administrator and the guidance director. Fortunately in our day teachers are trained to consult records whenever they receive new students in the classroom. Nonetheless, constant vigilance to see that teachers use the guidance folder may sometimes be necessary. The manner in which vital guidance material is communicated to the teacher should be looked upon as a test of the efficiency of the guidance department.

Keeping Records Up to Date. The principal should designate a guidance-staff member to supervise the record keeping. The management of records will often depend upon the type of record that is involved. The following practical suggestions will be helpful in keeping current data easily accessible for use:

1 *Scholastic Record.* Subjects and grades are recorded on a permanent card by members of the clerical staff at the end of the grading period.

2 *Personal Data.* Name, address, members of family, and so forth, from the registration or admission form are recorded on a per-

manent record by the clerical staff. The registration form is placed in the guidance folder.

3 *Religious Data.* Religious preference and parish data on baptism, confirmation, and first Communion from the admission form are recorded by the clerical staff.

4 *Health Record.* The card is secured from the elementary school or the school nurse and is kept current by the nurse. Ordinarily the record should be kept in the guidance folder for reference by teachers and counselors.

5 *Ability-Test Record.* IQ, reading, and psychological testing results with date, form, and the name of the test are recorded on the permanent record by the clerical staff as soon as possible after scoring.

6 *Attendance Record.* This record is kept current in a separate file by the attendance officer and is placed on the permanent record by the clerical staff at the end of the year or upon the withdrawal of the student. The attendance card itself may be placed in the guidance folder at the end of the year.

7 *Personality or Character Record.* This record is placed in the guidance folder by the clerical staff at the end of the year or at the termination of the student's attendance.

8 *Counseling Record.* These forms are placed in the guidance folder at the end of the semester by the clerical staff or by the guidance director.

9 *Vocational-occupational History.* Results of testing, reports, questionnaires, and any significant data should be placed in the guidance folder by the guidance director and counselors whenever such information is secured. The vocational plan, follow-up, or dropout study should be placed in the folder with employment-record cards.

10 *Activity Record.* Honors received, positions held, participation in sports and organizations, and pertinent newspaper clippings form worthwhile information for a folder. Such a record may be important for references, employment, and admission to college.

11 *Special.* Significant correspondence, disciplinary matters, unusual home conditions, and other anecdotal material relevant to the

intelligent guidance of a student should be filed in the cumulative record by the staff members. Some of this material may be removed at a later date. If photographs are needed, yearbook photographs may be attached to the guidance folder if others are not available.

The Permanent Record Card. A summary of the essential material to be found in the guidance folder may be arranged on a permanent record card. All the data needed for a sufficiently informative transcript should appear in a readily translatable form. The design of the card should permit neatness in making entries and should be such as to allow subsequent photostating as a transcript. The permanent record card itself should not regularly be kept in the guidance folder, since the loss of this document would seriously handicap the administration of the school. The responsibility for the care and safekeeping of permanent record cards should be assigned to a definite individual of the school staff. Counselors and other personnel are to be encouraged to refer to the permanent record, but they should not be permitted to remove it from the office.

Of their nature all records are more or less permanent; but by common consent "the permanent record" has come to mean the complete record of subjects studied, grades, attendance, test scores, personality ratings, activities, interests, honors, and other similar pieces of information for the entire four years of high school. The permanent record is often printed on both sides of a rather large sheet of paper, folded, and then kept in what is known as a visible file. Two companies that are equipped to print permanent records in a neat and compact manner and that manufacture visible files are Remington-Rand, Inc., 444 North Michigan Avenue, Chicago, and Postindex Company, Jamestown, New York, both of which have branch offices or agents in various cities throughout the country. National School Service, P. O. Box 36, Muskegon Heights, Michigan, carries in stock for immediate shipment a number of records and forms that might be used in Catholic schools.

The permanent record of today contains far more information than the permanent record of fifty years ago. It is to be expected that new developments will render necessary the inclusion of additional information in the future. It is usually considered the principal's responsibility to plan a new and better record form when it seems necessary to do so. Before printing a new record form the principal should by all means study the record forms used by a number of large and progressive schools. One of his problems will be to include the essential information for which colleges will probably call without including more than he plans to gather and without imposing impossible burdens on his clerical staff.

SELECTED REFERENCES

Arbuckle, Dugald S. *Guidance and Counseling in the Classroom,* Chapter 6, "Measurement and Testing." Boston: Allyn and Bacon, 1957.

Crow, Lester D., and Alice Crow. *An Introduction to Guidance; Principles and Practices,* Chapter 9, "The Guidance Folder." New York: American Book Company, 1951.

Harcar, George A., and Regis J. Leonard. "Minimum Guidance Testing Programs for Catholic Secondary Schools." *Catholic Educational Review* 50:394-402, May 1952.

Jones, Arthur J. *Principles of Guidance,* fourth edition, Chapter 6, "Use of School Records in Studying the Individual." New York: McGraw-Hill Book Company, 1951.

McDaniel, Henry B. *Guidance in the Modern School,* Chapter 14, "Applying Individual-Inventory Data to the Instructional Program." New York: Dryden Press, 1956.

Ohlsen, Merle M. *Guidance: An Introduction,* Chapter 10, "Organizing Records and Test Data." New York: Harcourt, Brace and Company, 1955.

O'Neill, John H. "The Cumulative Record as a Guidance Service." *Catholic School Journal* 54:317-19, December 1954.

Recktenwald, Lester Nicholas. *Guidance and Counseling,* Part 2, "Information and Techniques Concerned with the Study of the Individual." Washington: The Catholic University of America Press, 1953.

Smith, Glenn E. *Principles and Practices of the Guidance Program,* Chapter 5, "The Individual Inventory Service." New York: The Macmillan Company, 1951.

Warters, Jane. *Techniques of Counseling,* Chapter 13, "The Cumulative Personnel Record." New York: McGraw-Hill Book Company, 1954.

Willey, Roy DeVerl, and Dean C. Andrew. *Modern Methods and Techniques in Guidance,* Chapter 5, "Gaining Information about the Student." New York: Harper and Brothers, 1955.

CHAPTER TEN

EVALUATION

OF THE GUIDANCE PROGRAM

Measurement and evaluation are today almost universally recognized as essential to education. There is also rather common agreement concerning their purposes and the advantages that can result from them. It is possible, however, that a director of guidance, while busily engaged in compiling records covering the ability, achievement, and personality development of pupils or in appraising the work of his staff, should overlook the desirability of evaluating his own work. A short discussion of the evaluation of the guidance program may therefore be helpful.

ADVANTAGES OF EVALUATING THE PROGRAM

Evaluation is not an end in itself. It should lead to something that is worthwhile. This principle has frequently been overlooked by enthusiasts for measurement. Time and money have sometimes been spent in measuring the intelligence and achievement of pupils, but without any effort to make use of test scores for the accomplishing of some good purpose. The guidance director ought not to think of evaluating his own program unless he knows what good can result from the evaluation. Four advantages may be expected if the evaluation is made intelligently.

Evaluation Clarifies Ideas. The attempt to evaluate the results of the guidance program will force the director of guidance to ask himself exactly what he is attempting to accomplish. Just as a teacher cannot construct a comprehensive test without knowing the content of his subject matter, so the director of guidance cannot evaluate the outcome of his program without knowing what good effects that program is expected to produce.

Before attempting an evaluation the director of guidance will need to look back over all the steps that he took, over all the methods that he introduced, over all the orders that he issued, making a list of all these things as the first step in an attempt to evaluate his program. The making of this list, and still more particularly the effort to devise some means of evaluating the outcomes of his actions, will force the director of guidance to think critically of his program. To take but one example, the director of guidance may have developed a plan for helping incoming freshmen to become adjusted to their new school more quickly and more perfectly. He cannot evaluate this plan unless he sees clearly what evils it is intended to prevent and what good it is intended to accomplish. The attempt to evaluate will inevitably clarify his own ideas.

Evaluation Can Lead to Improved Procedures. The evaluation may indicate that the effects sought are not being achieved or that they are only poorly achieved. The guidance program, for example, may contain provisions for encouraging vocations to the priesthood and the religious life. If very few vocations result, it becomes evident that new procedures ought to be tried, or at least that something should be added to those being used. The same principle applies to any other objective of the guidance program. It may be noted that the improvement of procedures includes the correction of blunders and the discontinuance of unsound methods.

Evaluation Can Lead to Provision for New Needs. In his evaluation of the program the director of guidance will necessarily consider whether all the needs of pupils, homes, the community, and the Church are being met. He has of course studied these needs when setting up his program, but he is forced to study them once more in planning an evaluation. It is at once evident that evaluation must be a continuing process. This is particularly true when significant changes have occurred in neighborhoods or in national life. To take but one example, something new occurred in the lives of young men when military training was made compulsory. The guidance program must take cognizance of the fact that many students will very soon be undergoing training in some branch of the Armed Forces. These students need guidance in connection with the principles and ideals that they should accept, the type of apostolate that they can embrace while in service, and the dangers to faith and morality that they may encounter. Again, when military training becomes compulsory very many students in high school find it difficult to decide whether it is better for them to volunteer and thus interrupt their education or to remain in school and run the risk of being drafted, thus losing the right to choose the branch of service that they prefer. This is another area in which guidance is needed.

The problems created by other social changes may be less acute, but the director of guidance must nonetheless be aware of their existence. Whether there is question of the newer emphasis on the liturgical life of the Church, of greater activity in one's own parish, of cooperation with the bishop in some project for the benefit of the diocese, or of any other movement that may be afoot, a sincere attempt at evaluation will lead to conclusions concerning the extent to which new needs are being met.

Evaluation Can Increase Teacher Cooperation. Each phase of educating the whole man must undergo continuous evaluation to merit its inclusion or retention in the school program. Guidance and counseling services are justified as part of the school program only insofar as they contribute to the achievement of the objectives of Christian education. To some teachers a formal guidance and counseling program may appear to be an unessential and unwarranted addition to the work of an already busy staff. The danger that such an undesirable reaction may occur is far greater if the director of guidance, without making any effort to ascertain what results are being achieved, contents himself with insisting year after year that the program developed by him be carried out. If on the other hand the director of guidance shows a constant willingness to evaluate his own work and to improve procedures on the basis of the evaluation, he can be more confident of receiving the loyal support and co-operation of the school staff. His evaluation, moreover, in addition to providing evidence of desirable outcomes, can also be expected to reveal the existence of student needs for which some provision ought evidently to be made. It is, in short, inconceivable that an intelligent attempt at evaluation should not lead to improved cooperation, unless the entire program has been so stupidly planned that an honest evaluation exposes it as something altogether worthless.

TWO GENERAL TYPES OF EVALUATION

There are two general types of evaluation, each of which can serve a useful purpose. The purposes of the two types of evaluation are by no means identical.

The General Over-all Survey Type. In this type of evaluation the director of guidance aims at studying the entire program in all its aspects. His purpose is to obtain some sort of evidence concerning every detail in the program, or at the very least every major detail. To make the evidence altogether conclusive would in most cases require more time than could well be used, but the findings will at least be suggestive, will settle doubts that may exist concerning certain points, and will indicate the areas within which a more thorough study is desirable.

The Research-Study Type. In this type of evaluation the purpose is to make a very scientific and complete study of some one thing. The director of guidance might feel, for example, that more should be done to improve the reflective thinking of students. He therefore selects this problem as the object of very thorough investigation. He may have a staff member take a special course at a local university. If a member of his staff is working for a graduate degree, he may arrange to have this teacher make the problem the subject of his thesis. Committees are appointed, regular meetings are held at which what has already been accomplished is summarized, groups or individuals are assigned to read the entire literature of some aspect of the problem, and the work is continued until all are satisfied that the problem as originally proposed has been answered as well as it can be answered under existing circumstances.

Under good leadership a group of teachers working on a problem in this manner can accomplish wonderful things for their own self-improvement and for the general betterment of conditions within the school. When this type of evaluation is used, statements of facts proved by evidence take the place of the unsupported expressions of personal opinion which are so often heard at teachers' meetings.

It should be evident that neither of these two types of evaluation should be used exclusively. If the over-all survey type is always used, problems that can be solved only by long and serious study may be neglected. If the research-study type is the only type that is used, all the time that is available is spent on studies of details of the program and the program as a whole, in all its interrelationships, is never appraised.

EVALUATING THE GUIDANCE PROGRAM

First and foremost, the best evaluation of guidance services will come from prayerful thought and the shrewd observation of spiritual-minded men. Next, periodic examination of results accomplished and critical surveys on the part of the school administration will lead to intelligent judgment of the merits of the program. Finally, thoughtfully designed questionnaires submitted to students are an imperative necessity if the true objectives of guidance are to be realized. In this last form of appraisal the responses of graduates and school-leavers are significant to the over-all study.

Observation by Authorities and Others. A trustworthy evaluation of a guidance program may stem from the observation of the bishop of the diocese, of pastors, of the provincial superior of a religious community, and of others concerned with the care of souls. Often the considered judgment of prominent lay people and expressions of opinion by non-Catholic educators and leaders represent impartial and reliable observation, since such evaluations will be founded upon evidence of the Christian life and character of students and graduates, their demonstration of virtue in their daily lives, and their visible concern for and effort to serve the needs of the Church and community. The extent to which students attend Mass, receive the sacraments, and use other means of supernatural life, as well as the degree to which they share in the work of the family, the parish, and the community, will be indices for evaluation. All marks of faithful church membership and community citizenship can be accepted as giving some indication of the effects of Christian guidance. If the lives of students and graduates are edifying, it is at least probable that they were helped by the guidance that they received, and it is certain that nothing essential to good guidance is being neglected. School personnel should also take careful note of the comments of all responsible outside observers and occasionally solicit an evaluation from the most prudent among them.

Examination of Administrators and School Personnel. A thorough evaluation of a guidance and counseling program may be made by a staff member as a part of graduate study or in-service training. Such a study can present conclusions which may be used for the reconstruction and improvement of services.[1]

The school administration, the guidance committee, and the guidance department should undertake a periodic examination of the guidance and counseling program to learn (1) whether the objectives of the program are being attained, (2) whether their duties are being carried out by the staff and whether the services are being utilized by the students, and (3) whether the present program represents overguidance or inadequate services. The work may be simplified by a rating scale covering the objectives, duties, and means on which the evaluator scores each item as excellent, good, fair, or poor. The outline of the guidance program on page 19 or the check lists on pages 233-46 may serve as a basic tool. A form of evaluation for school personnel that will provide a record of the teacher's activities as a group-guidance leader and counselor and of his attitudes toward the guidance program will be found on pages 250-53. Such a form, calling as it does for the formulation of a judgment on the part of the teacher and attaching importance to his criticisms and sugges-

---

[1] Rev. J. J. Neuville, *Survey of Guidance Program at Central Catholic High School, Portland, Oregon.* Unpublished master's dissertation, Gonzaga University, Spokane, 1956.

tions, stimulates his cooperation and his further study of guidance methods and procedures.

Student Evaluation. A complete measurement of the effectiveness of guidance and counseling should take into account the opinions and reactions of the students currently receiving these services. Their judgment concerning the satisfaction of their present needs will frequently reveal the extent to which the program is succeeding or failing. An inventory constructed to gain a student evaluation may be found on pages 246-50.

Studies of the reactions of graduates to the guidance program provide a long-range judgment formed in the light of intervening experience. The fact that some graduates are now parents and hence concerned with the guidance of their children may add to the value of their judgments, and will often result in greater cooperation with school officials. Follow-up studies of those who leave school before graduation and those who do not graduate because of academic failure will also have a place in a complete evaluation of the high-school guidance program.

LIMITATIONS OF EVALUATION

Since many of the most important objectives of guidance and counseling are immeasurable by human and worldly criteria, the final and complete evaluation of what was accomplished will be made only on the day of judgment. The worth of any effort to build a truly Christian character and personality depends upon the extent to which it has assisted the individual to gain eternal life. Eternal life and one's higher or lower place in heaven depend upon the presence of sanctifying grace, upon its amount, and upon the interior virtues of the individual. These are things that cannot be measured, although reasonably safe estimates can sometimes be made, especially in the case of those who are extremely holy or extremely malicious, by observations of overt behavior.

It is a simple matter to determine how many words in a list of one thousand a student can spell correctly, or how many quadratic equations he can solve in thirty minutes. It is far from a simple matter to determine how generously he loves God and his neighbor, and to what extent this love has increased within the past year. While it is not so difficult a matter to obtain by means of observation data enabling us to affirm that an individual is punctual, that he ordinarily tells the truth, that he is willing to cooperate, or that he practices other natural virtues, it is not only difficult but in fact impossible to be certain of the motives because of which he practices these virtues or to be able to predict how well he will practice them if temptation comes. Only God knows the secrets of the heart (Psalm 43:22).

For all these reasons it is a most difficult matter to obtain evidence bearing upon the prime object of guidance and counseling in a Catholic school, which is to help students develop those true and solid Christian virtues that will carry them onward toward sainthood and toward heaven. We must be satisfied with knowing that students do their work faithfully, obey their parents, cause no trouble in the neighborhood, cooperate in a manner that indicates zeal, attend Mass regularly, and frequent the sacraments. It is most certainly well worth our while to do whatever we can to bring about in our school such good overt behavior. We would seem to be safe in assuming that it is prompted, in many cases at least, by a sincere desire to do the holy will of God. Past experience does indeed prove to us that some of our most docile and apparently pious students will before very many years become sources of scandal in the community or even give up their faith completely. It is not our responsibility, nor is it our right, to seek to determine whether such a thing is probable in the case of this individual or of that individual. To make such an effort would be equivalent to becoming guilty of rash judgment. In brief, we must be satisfied to help students behave as they should, use the means of grace, and understand and accept in word and deed truly Christian principles and ideals. It is these things that we can and should evaluate, not the hidden interior virtues, or possibly the insincerity and hypocrisy, that lie behind them.

One further difficulty in evaluation remains. We may succeed in obtaining evidence indicating that student behavior is good, that it makes a good impression on others, and even that it has improved over a period of time. It is another matter altogether to prove that these things are due to the guidance and counseling that students have received. They may be due to any one of very many other causes or to numerous possible combinations of causes, and any trained research worker would say that we are not as yet prepared to set up a controlled experiment leading to certain knowledge of what the true cause is.

The director of guidance ought beyond all doubt to evaluate the effects of his program. The fact that his evaluation suffers from so many limitations, far from discouraging him, should rather increase his determination to continue. The limitations result from the fact that he is endeavoring to evaluate the most precious of all things that a Catholic school seeks to give its students—the supernatural virtues of a true Christian. It is a comparatively simple thing for a classroom teacher to discover by using standardized tests what has been accomplished in a course in algebra, or even in a course in religion if the purpose is to learn how well students have memorized what they were told to memorize. The director of guidance is aiming at results of an altogether different and higher order. The more he feels the limitations of his efforts at evaluation, the more keenly and the more humbly does he realize how completely everything depends upon the grace of God and upon the virtue that flows from Christ into the members of His mystical body; and the more fully, too, does he understand how much whatever he attempts to do depends upon the good example that he sets for students and upon his prayer. It is this mixture in him of the natural and the supernatural, this determination to use the best educational means that he knows and at the same time to place his chief dependence on what is spiritual, that can in the course of time make of him a truly great director of guidance.

SELECTED REFERENCES

Foster, Charles R. *Guidance for Today's Schools,* Chapter 13, "Tests and Evaluation Programs for Guidance." New York: Ginn and Company, 1957.

French, William Marshall, and others. *Behavioral Goals of General Education in High School,* "Form for Evaluating General Education Programs in Terms of Behavioral Outcomes," pp. 218-29. New York: Russell Sage Foundation, 1957.

Hatch, Raymond N., and Buford Stefflre. *Administration of Guidance Services,* Chapter 7, "Evaluation of Guidance Services." Englewood Cliffs: Prentice-Hall, 1958.

Jones, Arthur J. *Principles of Guidance,* fourth edition, Chapter 27, "Present Status and Evaluation of Guidance and Pupil Personnel Work." New York: McGraw-Hill Book Company, 1951.

Kitch, Donald E., and William H. McCreary. *Improving Guidance Programs in Secondary Schools.* Sacramento: California State Department of Education, 1950.

McDaniel, Henry B. *Guidance in the Modern School,* Chapter 16, "Evaluation of the Guidance Program." New York: Dryden Press, 1956.

Ohlsen, Merle M. *Guidance: An Introduction,* Chapter 19, "Evaluating Guidance Services." New York: Harcourt, Brace and Company, 1955.

Recktenwald, Lester Nicholas. *Guidance and Counseling,* Chapter 10, "Evaluation." Washington: The Catholic University of America Press, 1953.

Roeber, Edward C.; Glenn E. Smith; and Clifford E. Erickson. *Organization and Administration of Guidance Services,* Chapter 11, "Evaluating the Guidance Services." New York: McGraw-Hill Book Company, 1955.

Smith, Glenn E. *Principles and Practices of the Guidance Program,* Chapter 11, "Evaluating Guidance Services." New York: The Macmillan Company, 1951.

Stoops, Emery, and Gunnar L. Wahlquist. *Principles and Practices in Guidance,* Chapter 14, "Evaluation of the Guidance Program." New York: McGraw-Hill Book Company, 1958.

Willey, Roy DeVerl. *Guidance in Elementary Education,* Chapter 15, "Evaluation of the Effectiveness of Guidance." New York: Harper and Brothers, 1952.

Willey, Roy DeVerl, and Dean C. Andrew. *Modern Methods and Techniques in Guidance,* Chapter 22, "The Evaluation of the Effectiveness of the Guidance Program." New York: Harper and Brothers, 1955.

Wilson, Frances Morgan. *Procedures in Evaluating a Guidance Program.* New York: Columbia University, 1945.

CHAPTER ELEVEN

THE GROUP-GUIDANCE

BULLETIN

The homeroom is the ideal place for group guidance, for the homeroom provides a homogeneous grouping of students under the person in the school who knows them best, the homeroom teacher. If we consider, however, that most of the homeroom teachers may have received no training in guidance, that they are specialists in many different fields, and that they were educated at various universities, we would almost despair of finding any uniformity in the guidance that they give. Without some device to unify the efforts of the homeroom guidance workers, students would encounter unequal guidance services during their school career even if all teachers possessed the fundamental interest and solicitude in equal degree and were given equal time to prepare their guidance material. An effective means of coordinating the guidance work of the school has been found in the guidance bulletin.

THE ADVANTAGES OF A GUIDANCE BULLETIN

A guidance bulletin prepared by the director of guidance and serving homeroom teachers in much the same manner that textbooks serve the classroom teachers offers many advantages, some of which we may discuss here.

The Determination of the Major Guidance Needs. If the purpose of group guidance is to provide for the needs common to all students, it is essential that someone should know what these needs are, should distinguish between those that are of major importance and those that are of lesser importance, and should decide at what grade level or at what time of the year an attempt to provide for a given need can best be made. Unless homeroom teachers receive some sort of assistance, it is almost certain that some topics will be overemphasized while others are completely neglected. The simplest and most effective means of assisting and directing homeroom teachers is a guidance bulletin.

Unity in Schoolwide Guidance. If all homeroom teachers, or at least all homeroom teachers at a given grade level, are discussing the same guidance topic at the same time, it can be expected that the interest of the student body will be greater and that the response will be better. Moreover, placards, cartoons, and other visual material can the more easily be prepared for display on the school bulletin board, in corridors, and elsewhere throughout the school.

All teachers are helped in their group-guidance efforts by such a bulletin insofar as all students are thereby striving for the same ideals, all have been exposed to the same motives, and all feel the social pressure exerted by the school. A student's respect and regard for the school is perhaps best fostered by the students themselves. It is recognized by psychologists and social workers that a child's misbehavior is very commonly caused by his desire to be applauded and by his need of gaining stature among his fellows. In a school where a good spirit prevails, individuals can best win approval by doing what is right, and hence they have a strong motive for acting as they should. Moreover, good students do not hesitate to let miscreants know what they think of them, and this disapproval is exceedingly powerful when the "good" students include all the best students in the school and not a mere handful of boys and girls who in comparison with disorderly students may appear to be weak, scrupulous, or overly pious. Things have not changed since the days of Cardinal Newman, who declared that the greatest force for good discipline and good behavior on a campus was the spirit of the student body.

If it is true that a good spirit is so desirable, then the school ought to have a comprehensive plan for developing it, and a bulletin helping teachers carry out such a plan is a useful or even an indispensable instrument.

Relieving the Burden of the Teachers. Many teachers urgently need the help that a bulletin gives, and almost all teachers can profit from it. Without a bulletin the group-guidance period can become just another class to teach, just another subject for which to prepare. Guidance material organized into a bulletin provides a handy reference that will aid both experienced and novice teachers. The ideas, quotations, examples, and applications found in the bulletin may be developed and manipulated by the homeroom teacher to meet the specific needs of his own group. The approach to guidance and the treatment of the topic offer the teacher who is inexperienced in formal guidance a uniform and satisfactory method of handling his group-guidance period. As for the teacher who has been convinced of the need for guidance and has already given extensive time and effort to extracurricular guidance, he need not fear that the guidance bulletin will limit his activities or lessen his appeal to his group. Rather, he will find in the guidance bulletin material and ideas that he can incorporate into his own thinking and that will direct and strengthen his own activities.

The Spirit of the School and the Community. The guidance director has made guidance his special field of concentration; he is trained in methods of guidance and he keeps abreast of research and the latest developments in guidance procedures. Moreover, the guidance director has the duty of creating the spirit of the school. He wants to make this school a certain kind of school and he wants to make its students representative of the school in the community. He has not formulated these objectives arbitrarily, but has considered the local community, the wishes of the principal, the ideas of the teachers, and all that he knows about students past and present. Not only can he save his guidance workers much time and work if he prepares material to be used in the group-guidance period, but such material is one of the best means possible of making all the forces of the school work together toward the accomplishing of chosen objectives. The guidance bulletin is to a school what a compass and a rudder are to a ship.

THE CONTENT OF THE BULLETIN

Group guidance, as we have seen, is directed toward meeting the common needs shared by a group of students. Problems of an intimate and personal nature are faced more properly in a private conference or interview. The first step in planning a guidance bulletin is to prepare a list of those common needs which are of such a nature that an attempt to meet them ought by all means to be made.

The Essential Topics of Guidance. The first in importance of the needs common to all students is the formation of a truly Christian character. Hence material on Christ as our model and leader, on the theological and moral virtues, on the means of arriving at perfection, and on the happiness and rewards of a Christian life should be considered essential topics.

Also to be considered essential are applications of the fundamental principles of Christian life to life in school, at home, in association with one's friends and companions, in service to the Church and the nation, and in devotion to all mankind as manifested in international good will and in freedom from racial prejudice.

A third class of essential topics will include problems of a more personal nature, such as how to study, how to succeed, how to make friends, how to develop one's personality, how to choose a vocation and an occupation, and other problems of a similar nature.

In presenting these topics the guidance bulletin should whenever possible employ the means used by the Church in forming character and motivating desirable conduct by basing everything on the life and teachings of Christ and by appealing to the examples of the saints. Short incidents from the lives of the saints may point up the desired habits or virtues, and passages from the liturgical cycle of the church year may propose the example of Christ and set the guidance topic firmly on the word of God. The student is thus put into the mainstream of the thinking and the teaching of the Church.

The Construction of the Guidance Bulletin. It was found at Central Catholic High School that a weekly bulletin presenting one topic could be divided into five parts for use in the ten-minute guidance period on the five days of the week. The guidance material is arranged in outline form and cast in short phrases, so that the home-room teacher can come right to the heart of the topic and adapt its thought to the understanding of his own group. The material itself, although at first glance it might seem to have been taken from the religion textbook or a social-studies unit, was material proper to guidance that had been collected and organized to cover the points considered by the guidance staff to be important for daily school life. It was meant to ensure continuing instruction in and provision for the systematic development of the Christian virtues, often assumed to be constantly in mind during the student's school career but sometimes forgotten or neglected.

The Number of Guidance Units Required. Experience showed that about twenty-five guidance units could be covered in one year. Community projects, such as Brotherhood Week and Junior Achievement Week, and school activities such as examinations, holidays, and the annual retreat break into the traditional thirty-six weeks of school. In addition, an occasional week must be left for guidance proper to one grade level, as, for example, orientation for the freshmen or activities associated with graduation for the seniors. An occasional "free" week also permits each teacher to give guidance that he thinks his group particularly needs or to spend the guidance time in conference with students if he detects no particular group need.

The first twenty-five units, however, did not complete the desired formation nor did they cover all the topics judged essential. When guidance units had been constructed to cover the other important topics, their number had reached fifty. These fifty units gave the director of guidance a choice of units for any one year and was sufficient for a minimum of two years. In actual practice the series of fifty units sufficed for a four-year period. No difficulty was experienced because of the fact that units presented in the lower grades were discussed again in the upper grades. Students' memories are not long, and their problems and concerns differ from year to year. The difficulty encountered because of the repetition of units was not boredom and satiety on the part of the senior student but the danger of superficial understanding on the part of younger students. This minor difficulty was overcome as teachers became more experienced in guidance methods.

Liturgical Material in the Bulletin. It has been said that it is the responsibility of the director of guidance to determine the order in which the fifty units are to be used, and that this order may vary from year to year. For this reason it was found impossible to attach liturgical material to each unit before the time came to use the unit. It was in fact an advantage for the director of guidance to be forced to develop, or to select from material already developed, the liturgical supplement to each unit. The necessity of finding in the feasts of the week an appropriate ideal to accompany the guidance unit resulted in a continual review of the units, helped toward keeping the topic tuned to the current needs of students, and brought an ever-increasing awareness of the truth of God's word. In addition, the weekly preparation of the liturgical material made it possible for the director of guidance to include with the calendar of church feasts a calendar of school events, together with instructions and requests to teachers.

An Example of a Guidance Unit. The following unit is taken from those once used in Central Catholic High School.

GUIDANCE BULLETIN

February ——, 19——

MONDAY

St. Matthias, apostle . . . chosen to succeed Judas as an apostle. You too are selected by God to be an apostle of the faith and the Christian life to the people of Portland. If you are not faithful to that work, another will be selected to take your place. Probably you will receive the same reward as Judas, too.

7:30 p.m. College Night for Seniors and Their Parents. Make a special attempt to persuade your parents to come with you. If there are some very concerned and interested juniors who wish to attend with their parents, please contact Father Saalfeld.

TUESDAY

Mass of the Sunday repeated . . . St. Paul wrote of his many sufferings and of his ability to "take them" in the spirit of the true Christian; he points these out as the greatest glory to God and to himself. Do you know and appreciate that the toughest and most difficult things you do are also the ones that God and you value the most? Of these things you can be proud.—(No senior vocational guidance today.)

Activity period: **Panel Discussion on College Education** . . . for junior class. Fr. Hooyboer (University of Portland), Fr. Kelley (Seattle University), Fr. Gubbins (Gonzaga University). Will the teachers of juniors at third period please attend with classes.

WEDNESDAY

St. Gabriel of Our Lady of the Seven Dolors . . . died at the age of 24 after having done a lifetime (a long one!) of suffering and penance. His self-denial can be a real example and challenge to high-school boys.

THURSDAY

Mass of the Sunday repeated . . . The Gospel speaks of the seed sown in the field. Analogy: Some of the seed of truth sown in the classroom falls on good soil in good minds; some hear the truth but do nothing about it (no homework, application, etc.); some falls on the ears but is quickly choked out by indifference, inattention, or refusal to work. Which classification do you belong to?

FIRST FRIDAY

We have never been completely satisfied or happy about the number of Central students who use the first Friday for more sleep instead of attending Mass and receiving Communion when we specifically make it possible. *A boy who can attend Mass and receive Communion and does not is a poorly performing Christian; he is not a good student of Central Catholic.* Surely in the mind of God this is worse than skipping a class or assignment. If they do not attend on first Friday now, it is unlikely they will later.

Character-Personality Record . . . May I ask the freshman, sophomore, and junior religion, English, and social-studies teachers to begin work on the compiling of this record of students.

The attached guidance material may be used in reference to the record and the rating of a student as: 1. assumes responsibilities; 2. usually dependable; 3. dependable in some areas; 4. unreliable.

Responsibility

Objectives: to direct the thinking of students to understand the true meaning and scope of responsibility

to have them examine their lives to determine their personal responsibilities

to encourage them to better fulfillment of these duties which lead most rapidly to a well developed character

to suggest specific action in accepting responsibility

Definition: a duty or an accountability for physical, mental, moral, or spiritual action

MONDAY

What responsibilities do I now have? (students can list them for each other)

A. *to myself . . . care of*   *where?* . . .

my soul	at home
my mind	at church
my body	at school
my ideals	at play
my reputation	at work
my emotions	in social groups

for example:

1. being a good Christian in the use of the means of grace and in the imitation of Christ
2. being a reasonably good student according to my ability: getting a passing grade and a *one* for effort
3. assuring good care of health, exercise, rest, recreation, and cleanliness
4. setting and achieving goals for myself that are worthy and high
5. taking care to protect my good name by decent conduct and work
6. developing an even temperament and confident self-control
7. using my money and time as best I can; developing common sense and good judgment; discovering my hidden talents and perfecting my abilities

TUESDAY

B. *to others . . . in same areas as above*
being interested in the soul welfare of others
being a means of grace for someone else; a source of good example
respecting their minds by being truthful
attention to the needs of others, performing a corporal work of mercy;
   avoiding physical harm to another
helping someone else to learn a lesson or to solve a problem
encouraging others to high ideals and good standards of life
   e.g. the influence of Catholic students on others in the city
      the harm that comes from smirching the reputation of others
         by bad example or actions
      the good that arises from any distinction you bring to a Cath-
         olic school
      honestly forgiving injuries, paying just debts, returning bor-
         rowed articles, care of property
      avoiding the causing of emotional damage, such as losing
         temper or control, unreasonable teasing, carrying a chip
         on one's shoulder
      NOTE: *I am my brother's keeper*
      Do you now have any responsibility to the girl you will
         marry, the children you will have, or the parish in
         which you will live?

WEDNESDAY

What responsibilities do I now overlook?
   Recall the surprise of those who said: "Lord, when did we see you
      sick, in hunger, in prison, etc.?"
   Remember the reply: "As long as you did it to one of these, the least
      of my brethren . . ."
What responsibilities can I handle from now on? What am I ready to
   assume?
   as a member of a family, of a church
   as a student and as a Christian
   as a citizen
   as one confirmed and baptized
   as a temple of the Holy Ghost and a tabernacle of Christ in the
      Eucharist

What is the proper order of responsibilities? Which came first and why?

    to myself . . . What doth it profit a man if he gain the whole world . . .

        Seek first the kingdom of heaven . . .

    to others . . . Social responsibility

        If a man give his life for another . . .

THURSDAY

What is the proper motive for assuming and fulfilling responsibility?

    Not for our own glory but for the honor of His name

    for the happiness of others and for ourselves

    for the welfare of one's community

What are the virtues involved in the development of responsibility?

    justice . . . giving everyone, including self, his due

    charity . . . love of God; love of neighbor as thyself

Other questions: What is my responsibility to the future of school, church, country?

    What is the result of assuming responsibilities and fulfilling them?

FRIDAY

How much responsibility can I *safely* handle at this age?

    Each boy or girl wants to be completely independent . . . free of all control . . .

    but rarely wants to accept the obligations that go with freedom

    They must know that independence means *less* freedom and *more* duties for which they are bound in conscience and accountable to God

    When they have learned and proved that they can handle securely these responsibilities, then they are mature

Guiding rule: As I handle my present responsibilities and fulfill them well, I will be given more and put on my own

Guiding grace: As each new responsibility is given, as each new duty arises, the grace of vocation and state in life is supplied by God

What can I do this week to prove my development of the virtue of responsibility?

THE USE OF THE BULLETIN

A guidance bulletin, regardless of the wealth of its material and the perfection of its form, will not of itself guarantee that all students will receive the guidance they need and that the desired spirit of the school will be attained. The effectiveness of the bulletin depends upon the convictions and the attitudes of homeroom teachers concerning guidance and their consequent use of the bulletin. It is the responsibility of the guidance director to build up positive, constructive attitudes among his group-guidance teachers and to ensure their fullhearted support. Without the cooperation of the homeroom teachers and the staff any guidance program, group or individual, may look good on paper and be worth just that much.

Four things can contribute to the successful use of the bulletin. These are support from the administration, the development of proper attitudes on the part of teachers, the preparation of homeroom teachers for the work, and the cooperative planning of the bulletin by the director and his staff.

The Support of the Administration. The unflinching support of the administrative officers of the school is of the greatest help in persuading teachers of the value and importance of the guidance program and of their obligation to use the bulletin faithfully and intelligently. The principal first of all, the superior if the school is under the control of a religious congregation, the superintendent of schools if he is active in such matters, and all those who have any authority over teachers must make it very clear that they approve of the bulletin and that they desire teachers to make use of it. In addition to giving the director of guidance and his bulletin their moral support, the principal and other members of the administration must protect the guidance period from various encroachments that can only too easily occur. The guidance period must be a time for group guidance, not a time for gathering records of one kind or another or for transacting school business. Unless the administration is firm on this point, the guidance bulletin will soon be set aside and forgotten, or at best used so irregularly as to be of little real help. The administration must encourage teachers to sincere effort in their group-guidance activities by showing regard for the importance of guidance time, by issuing occasional directives in notices or during faculty meetings, and by showing knowledge and appreciation of the progress that is being made.

The Development of Proper Attitudes. Most teachers hold quite decided opinions about the nature and purposes of education and about what their own field of specialization contributes to the whole, yet they bow to the judgment and experience of the administrator in matters affecting the entire school. If they are certain that the bulletin has the blessing of the authorities, they are more willing to re-examine their opinions on guidance and how it should be organized. It may still be necessary, however, for the director of guidance to correct certain undesirable attitudes or to encourage the growth and further development of certain desirable ones.

In particular, the guidance director may have to disabuse some teachers of the notion that guidance is satisfactorily accomplished in the religion class or the social-studies course. Religion teachers especially may feel that they are giving all the facts and principles that a student needs to become a good citizen and that the guidance bulletin contains only a superficial treatment of the obligations of the Catholic citizen. The director of guidance must recognize the fact that good teachers of religion are not satisfied with requiring students to learn by heart the facts and principles found in textbooks, but aim primarily at helping students translate facts and principles into action. He must also admit that what has to be done in ten minutes is necessarily superficial when compared with what can be done in fifty or sixty minutes. He can remind teachers of religion, however, of certain other facts: that the bulletin provides for calling to the attention of students the very things that are taught in the religion class, that it does this regularly and for all four years, that it causes numerous teachers to reinforce what is taught by the religion teachers, and that a teacher of religion would be untrue to his own principles were he to endeavor to muzzle all other teachers in the building and to forbid anybody but himself to speak of spiritual things to students.

Other teachers, while they recognize the value of a plan for teaching the basic qualities necessary for a good citizen, may feel that guidance materials the use of which is made mandatory for every teacher limit a teacher's efforts in guiding his students. The guidance director must convince these teachers that the guidance material permits wide variation in its use and in no way reduces any teacher's freedom to step forward and guide students whenever the opportunity presents itself.

Most teachers, realizing that purposive guidance is necessary to supplement the educational program and that uniformity in guidance topics is desirable throughout the school, welcome the positive assistance in preparing and presenting material that the guidance bulletin offers. They appreciate the information and the practical suggestions they receive through the bulletin. Young teachers especially rely on the guidance bulletin. Even experienced teachers are grateful for the saving in time and energy that the bulletin means to them. All teachers, however, must be convinced of the soundness of basic guidance principles represented by the bulletin before they can use it intelligently and enthusiastically.

Orientation in the Use of the Bulletin. The guidance director must also be certain that the homeroom teacher is aware of the importance of his adapting the material of the guidance bulletin to the specific needs and abilities of his group. When the teacher realizes that the material placed in his hands gives the basic idea to be used in the guidance of the week and the direction that guidance is to take, and that the material is presented in general terms for use with students of different ages and at different stages of development, he has no qualms about selecting and concentrating on what fits his group. The question is not how to cover all the material in a brief session, but what of it to use to get a basic idea across to his group. The teacher's task is not to create perfect virtue, but to expose the student to an ideal and foster his gradual growth to perfection. It is therefore evident that not all teachers will use the bulletin in the same way.

The teacher must do some thinking in preparing to use the guidance bulletin with his class. Some have reported that they use the material in their own morning meditation and find that this is an excellent preparation. There could be no better way so long as the needs of the group are kept uppermost in mind. Other teachers have asked for the bulletin a week in advance in order to have adequate time to go through it and plan the week's activities.

A staff meeting at the beginning of the year or a faculty meeting devoted to the various possibilities in using the guidance bulletin has been found of great help to individual teachers and to the guidance program. A brief review of the purposes of group guidance and the setup of the guidance bulletin may be followed by a discussion of questions of procedure. It must be clear to teachers that a slavish following of the text of the unit is not good guidance. The teacher will probably explain or add to what is there, but he should feel obligated to present the topic that is developed in the bulletin for school use. If he feels that his group has a particular need, he should make this known to the guidance director. It may be decided that the whole school would profit from the discussion of a topic designed to meet that need; otherwise the teacher may construct his own unit for use during the occasional "free" week that is purposely left open for such needs or for personal conferences with students.

In preparing the guidance material for his group the homeroom teacher should determine his method of presenting it to the group. He may simply talk to his students or he may provoke discussion by asking questions. When there is question of information to be given, the lecture method is usually better. Some topics may require observations made by the students and resolutions to action which gain strength by being expressed in words. Panel discussions, committee reports, and other such devices are good insofar as they make the topic of vital interest to the student, but the idea of an "assignment" should not be connected in the student's mind with the guidance period.

The Cooperative Planning of the Future Bulletin. The general discussion of ways of using the bulletin stimulates interest in the bulletin and leads to more serious attempts to understand the guidance needs of the students. One of the best means of guaranteeing effective and uniform guidance is a staff meeting held toward the end of the year for the express purpose of planning the following year's guidance units. The aim should not be to rewrite the units in their entirety. Such a task would be altogether too great if undertaken every year, and the units as they exist represent a large amount of careful work. The planning should rather have to do with the order in which units are to be taken, with effective methods of presenting units, and with methods of enriching certain units. Teacherᶜ will have many experiences to share and many suggestions to make. Such a meeting not only makes the individual teacher a more responsible member of the guidance staff, but it also keeps the guidance director in intimate contact with the everyday guidance needs of the students. It gives him insight into the special abilities for guidance of his teachers. Because of what he learns during the meeting he may ask some to prepare a new unit for the guidance bulletin or to become counselors.

Meetings in which the director of guidance and the guidance workers come to be of one mind and heart always contribute to the effectiveness of the guidance program. Although their primary purpose is the formation of a well-knit staff of group-guidance workers, they are also a most excellent way of gaining more thorough insight into guidance needs and means of meeting them. As the guidance director and the homeroom teachers come together more as co-workers than as teacher and pupil, there can be a freer interchange of directions and recommendations. Brief notes to the teacher on the weekly bulletin, requests for comments, and reports on the results of some topics all work for better guidance.

It is difficult to judge the strength of a guidance program and to assign reasons or place responsibility for its success. As a guidance program weaves itself into the very fabric of school life and as the teachers become "guidance conscious," it becomes more and more difficult to think of the educational program without its guidance activities, for guidance is what perfects the education of the Christian citizen.

SELECTED REFERENCES

Saalfeld, Lawrence J. *Group Guidance Units for Catholic High Schools*. Chicago: Loyola University Press, 1957.

Schroeder, John. "Tell the Public about Your School." *Catholic School Journal* 55:107-09, April 1955.

CHAPTER TWELVE

RECORD FORMS, CHECK LISTS,

AND ORIENTATION MATERIAL

Frequent reference has been made in the preceding chapters to various records, questionnaires, and check lists. Every school will have at least a limited number of such printed forms designed for the general purpose of obtaining, preserving, or conveying information that pertains to students or that is intended to help students. While the purpose of these forms is always, ultimately, to provide help or service to the student, their nature and the extent to which they survey phases of student life will depend upon the degree to which the school, and especially the guidance personnel, need and wish to use the information.

Since it is the responsibility of a guidance department to supply the administration with data necessary for the proper management of the school and to provide personnel with the tools for the intelligent direction of students, a discussion of some appropriate forms and questionnaires is presented in this chapter. A school just beginning to organize or to expand its guidance services may either use some of these forms as they are or as guides in constructing those which best serve its own needs.

The development of a satisfactory form often requires some experimentation and trial before a final decision is made. Not all widely used record forms are necessarily the best, and many questionnaires could be better arranged in order to reveal more clearly the desired information. Sufficient spacing for writing answers to questions, the proper grouping of items, legible type, and a suitable size for the form are important for the quick sifting and use of the data secured through the form. Any form that is to become part of the permanent record of a student must be thoughtfully constructed to lend itself to easy storage or microfilming. Needless to say, it should be filled in with care and accuracy. Nothing is ever gained by the accumulation of misinformation.

While public schools quite often use, and are satisfied with, the printed forms required or recommended by state or city authorities, private schools tend to develop forms that meet their own individual needs or preferences. When there is question of a detailed and comprehensive form such as a cumulative record, it will rather seldom be found that two schools wish to include exactly the same items and to arrange them in the same order. Even a comparatively simple form such as an attendance record will vary from school to school because of variations in the length and divisions of the school year. Larger schools operating on generous budgets will as a rule be found to use printed forms specially designed to meet their own needs. A principal who has just been given charge of a school, if he is aggressive or a perfectionist, may be expected to develop new forms and to seek to improve old ones. For these reasons most printed forms are planned and designed by the individual school for its own use. Forms printed in large quantities and carried in stock by supply houses are of course far more economical; but the number of supply houses producing such forms appears to be small, for the obvious reason that the market for stock forms is limited.[1]

[1] National School Service, P. O. Box 36, Muskegon Heights, Michigan, was at the time of this writing carrying in stock the following forms: Admission, Discharge and Promotion Card; Attendance and Scholarship Record (2A, for schools operating on a four-week period; 2B, for schools operating on a six-week period); Census Record; Class Card (a record of attendance and scholarship); Class Schedule; Office Record (place and date of birth, data on parents, attendance, scholarship, disciplinary action); Permanent High School Record; Physical Record; Pupil's Record Card; Pupil's Report Card (to be sent to parents); and Transfer Card.

Permission is hereby granted to schools to print for their own use any form or questionnaire found in this book. Those who reproduce the check lists for appraising the guidance program found on pages 233-46 are indebted to the California State Department of Education, which refrained from copyrighting the check lists and thus made them of the public domain.

It should be noted that the aim of the author and publisher has not been to space forms and questionnaires as they should be spaced for practical use. To have done so would in some cases have been impossible in a book of this size. Whoever wishes to use one of our forms or questionnaires, either by reproducing it on a duplicating machine or by having it printed, must necessarily make a typewritten copy of it. When making this copy, or when discussing the matter with his printer, he should decide upon the spacing which in his judgment will best serve his purposes.

FOR STUDENTS ENTERING SCHOOL

Registration Form. New students registering in a school invariably fill out a registration form. This form provides space for giving the name; the home address and telephone number; the date and place of birth; the name, occupation, and place of business of father or guardian; the name of mother; and the name of the school last attended. Other information that the student may be asked to give includes his religion; his parish; whether he has been baptized, made his first Communion, and been confirmed; the number of older and younger brothers and sisters; the extent to which he works to support himself; and the activities in which he plans to participate. For the information of the student the form may list the tuition fee per semester and special fees for which the student may become liable. Space may be provided for transfers from other high schools to list the subjects they have already taken and the credits and grades they have earned. This is sometimes desirable when it is known from experience that delays may occur in obtaining transfers of credit. In such cases information given by the student himself, although not official, is the only basis on which decisions concerning placement and the choice of courses can be made.

Request for Elementary-School Record. Students enrolling in freshman class of Catholic high schools can ordinarily present certificates of graduation from elementary school and report cards showing their marks in eighth grade. The more elaborate transcripts of credit that high schools are accustomed to provide when their graduates wish to enter college are not as a rule prepared by elementary schools for the benefit of high-school principals.

It is highly desirable that the information concerning students gathered during the eight years of elementary school should be made available to high schools. While the elementary school may not test and study students as thoroughly and scientifically as is done in high school, this shortcoming, if it actually exists, is offset at least to some extent because children spend twice as many years in elementary school and thus become quite well known to teachers and other school personnel. The elementary school should be happy to use this intimate knowledge of its graduates for their own benefit and should have a practical working arrangement with the high schools in the area.

No longer can high schools accept the once general practice of merely requiring an elementary-school diploma as sufficient for admission and placement in high school. The widely different educational patterns and the increasing reliability of elementary-school testing make the transfer of data much more essential and the coordination of testing programs more necessary, particularly in our Catholic elementary and high schools. As the elementary school becomes less terminal for students, it becomes more important to transfer more complete records to the high school at which the child continues his education.

If the elementary school follows the procedure of transferring the entire cumulative record folder to the high school, a separate record must be kept of such minimum data as identification of the child, standardized-test results, evidence of the completion of requirements, and the name of the high school to which records have been sent. A second method to be considered is the use of photostatic equipment to reproduce records of which copies are to be sent to the high school requesting them. The third method, to be preferred to all others, is for the elementary school to transfer only that information which is requested and which satisfies the needs of the high school.

Two forms of such requests are given here, with the understanding that any form must lend itself to modifications that meet the special needs or conditions that so often exist among schools. Some may find the first form more suitable for requesting records from Catholic elementary schools because of the reference made to the religious life of the pupil.

REQUEST FOR ELEMENTARY-SCHOOL RECORDS

To .... School   From .... School

.... Address   .... Address

.... City   .... City

.... (intends to enroll) (has enrolled) in our .... grade.
pupil's name

Please send: ☐ official transcript ☐ cumulative record folder ☐ health record

☐ Please complete and return the information requested on this form.

last name	first	middle

street address	city	zone

month of birth	day	year	telephone

parish

Mental-Test Results:

IQ	name of test	date tested

Achievement Tests:

Arithmetic

grade level	name of test	date tested

Reading

grade level	name of test	date tested

Language

grade level	name of test	date tested

Study skills ....
                    grade level   name of test   date tested

Battery median ....

                                                ☐ excellent

Check your estimate of pupil's academic success in high school: ☐ average

                                                ☐ poor

Health Record:

General condition ....

Handicaps: vision .... hearing ....

           speech .... other ....

Personality Traits (rate as 1 for low; 2, below average; 3, average; 4, above average; 5, high):

Industry	....	Emotional stability	....
Responsibility	....	Concern for others	....
Honesty	....	Manners	....
Leadership	....	Appearance	....

Religious life (indicate any specific conditions meriting our attention or describe as irregular, scrupulous, possible vocation, and so forth):

Other significant information: ....

Date .... Signature ....

REQUEST FOR ELEMENTARY-SCHOOL RECORDS

To .... School   From .... School

.... Address   .... Address

.... City   .... City

.... (intends to enroll) (has enrolled) in our .... grade.

☐ Please send pupil's official transcript of credits and health-record card.

☐ Please send pupil's cumulative record folder.

    If these records are not available, please complete and return to us the information requested below.

Date .... Name .... Position ....

Place available test results in the left-hand column. If test results are not available, give your estimates in the right-hand column. Rate personality traits as 1, 2, 3, 4, or 5, 1 being low and 5 being superior.

Mental-Test Results

IQ ....

Name of test ....

Date tested ....

Estimate of Mental Ability

.... Superior

.... Above average

.... Average

.... Below average

.... Low

Reading-Test Results

Grade level achieved ....

Name of test ....

Date tested ....

Estimate of Reading Ability

.... Superior

.... Above average

.... Average

.... Below average

.... Low

Arithmetic-Test Results

Grade level achieved ....

Name of test ....

Date tested ....

Estimate of Arithmetic Ability

.... Superior

.... Above average

.... Average

.... Below average

.... Low

Personality Traits

.... Industry

.... Responsibility

.... Honesty

.... Leadership

.... Emotional stability

.... Concern for others

.... Manners

.... Appearance

(Check Yes or No)

Yes .... No .... Was pupil's attendance satisfactory?

Yes .... No .... Any significant health or physical disabilities? (Explain on back.)

Yes .... No .... Any significant home conditions which affect school performance? (Explain on back.)

Yes .... No .... Any significant behavior or personality problems? (Explain on back.)

Yes .... No .... Any religious habits or attitudes requiring attention? (Explain on back.)

Yes .... No .... Did pupil make any special contributions to your school? (Explain on back.)

Yes .... No .... Is there anything special that our school can do to help your former pupil? (Explain on back.)

New-Student Questionnaire. The following questionnaire covers many of the points concerning which information could prove helpful to counselors. Some well-informed faculty member should be present while it is being answered by groups of students. He should read to students the introductory instructions and then tell them to come quietly to the desk should they wish to ask a question.

NEW-STUDENT QUESTIONNAIRE

Your counselor and others will be working for your complete adjustment and development in high school. They must have certain information about you as an individual. Please complete this questionnaire accurately and honestly.

Name .... Date ....

Age .... Date of birth .... Place of birth ....

Address .... Telephone ....

Your Family

Father's name .... Occupation ....

Religion .... Where employed ....

Education .... Nationality ....

Mother's name _____ Occupation _____

   Religion _____ Where employed _____

   Education _____ Nationality _____

If either parent is deceased, how old were you at the time of death? _____

If parents are divorced or separated, how old were you at the time? _____

Number of older brothers _____; of younger brothers _____; of older sisters _____; of younger sisters _____

Does anyone else live in your home? _____

Your Religion

Parish _____ How long have you lived there? _____

Have you been baptized? _____ made your first Communion? _____ been confirmed? _____

Is religion an important factor in the life of your family? _____ Give your reason for answering yes or no. _____

If there are family prayers, frequent Communion, rosary, meal prayers, or devotions, state which. _____

Are you or your family active in the parish? _____

Do you belong to parish clubs? _____ Which clubs? _____

If there is a difference in your parents' religion, has it caused any difficulty? _____ How for you? _____

Have you thought of a religious vocation? _____

Has anyone ever spoken to you about a religious vocation? _____
   Who? _____

What are your religious problems? _____

Your Home

What language is spoken at home? _____

Is there sickness in your home always? _____ often? _____ occasionally? _____ never? _____

Is the way in which your parents treat you very strict? _____ moderately strict? _____ easygoing? _____

How many nights a week do you go out? .... How many a month? ....

Is a definite time set for you to be in? .... What time? ....

Do you have responsibilities at home? .... What? ....

Do you work to support yourself? .... , to help support the family? .... ,
How many hours a week? .... , Where? ....

Do you have an allowance? .... How much a week? ....

Do you or your parents entertain frequently? .... , occasionally? .... ,
never? ....

How many hours a day do you spend watching TV? .... What is your
favorite program? ....

What magazines do you read? ....

Is your home life happy always? .... , usually? .... , occasionally? .... ,
never? ....

Why is your home life as happy or as unhappy as you say it is? ....

What worries you about your home? ....

Your Leisure Time

Do you have some real friends of your own age? .... , older? .... ,
younger? ....

Are most of your friends boys? .... , girls? .... , from this school? ....

Are you going steady? .... Do you care to dance? ....

Do you drive? .... Your own car? ....

What sports do you play? .... Where? ....

What is your special interest, hobby, talent, leisure-time activity? ....

Vocational Interests

Have you decided your life vocation or occupation? .... What would you
like to be or do? .... Why? ....

Do you want to go to college? .... Which school? ....

What do you want to study in college? ....

Have you sought guidance from anyone on your future? .... From
whom? ....

Do you have someone with whom you can talk things over confidentially? ....

Your Education

What schools have you attended? .... Years ....

.... Years ....

.... Years ....

Are you here because both you and your parents desire it? .... , because you alone want to be here? .... , because someone is making you come here? .... , because you don't care where you go to school? ....

What subjects do you like best? ....

What subjects do you like least? ....

Have you ever failed or repeated a grade or subject? .... Which? ....

What are your problems in school? ....

Do you feel your teachers are reasonable in their demands and in their treatment of you? .... Why? ....

Is your school life happy? .... Why? ....

Do you worry over schoolwork? .... Why? ....

Do you regard yourself in school as successful? .... , fair? .... , low? .... , failing? ....

How many hours a day do you study at home? .... Where? ....

Is the thing that interferes most with your study TV? .... , radio? .... , outside work? .... , friends? .... , the telephone? .... , your family? ....

If anything else interferes with your study, what is it? ....

Is there someone at home who can help you with schoolwork? .... Who? ....

What do you like about your present teachers? ....

What do you want to get from your high-school education? ....

Your Special Needs

If there are any special problems or needs for which you want help from your counselor and teachers, are these problems: religious? .... , mental? .... , social? .... , physical? .... , other? ....

Special comments: ....

Can you suggest any improvement in this questionnaire? ....

If so, what? ....

Vocational-Interest Form for Freshmen. As a means of assisting students to arrive at a reliable choice of their vocation or occupation by the end of high school, it is advisable to begin a record of their interests early in their high-school career. The autobiographical outline given here as the initial step can be followed by the sophomore vocational-interest form on page 217 and can be evaluated further in the light of the vocational-preference tests (Kuder, Strong, and so forth) that may be given in the junior and senior years.

MY AUTOBIOGRAPHY OUTLINE

Name ....

Date and place of my birth ....

My earliest recollections of life at home ....

The subjects and activities in which I did best in elementary school ....

The subjects I disliked the most ....

My interests and hobbies ....

My work experience ....

My favorite reading material ....

My vocational ambitions ....

What I intend to do when I graduate from high school ....

Religious-Instruction Survey. Quite frequently new students, whether they are incoming freshmen or transfer students from other high schools, do not have the same background of religious instruction. The extent of instruction by parents will differ greatly, and may often be entirely lacking; and the nature of instruction in religion in both Catholic elementary and Catholic high schools varies considerably. The Catholic high school must discover the content of the previous religious instruction of its new students and plan an adequate program to assure a well-rounded education in Catholic belief and practice. Students ignorant of their faith should not be allowed to wait until the sequence of courses brings them to a study of things that they urgently need to know, such as the sacraments or the implications of the sixth commandment. The following form will bring to light the needs of new students.

RELIGIOUS-INSTRUCTION SURVEY

Name _____ Date _____

(Circle or check the correct answers)

Your present class: Freshman, Sophomore, Junior, Senior

Number of years in a Catholic grade school: 1 2 3 4 5 6 7 8

Number of years already spent in a Catholic high school: 1 2 3 4

When you did not attend a Catholic school, did you have the opportunity to receive religious instruction in religious vacation schools? yes _____, no _____ .

Did you go to Sunday School? yes _____, no _____ . Regularly? yes _____, no _____ .

Did you go to public-school released-time classes? yes _____, no _____ .

In what parts of your faith do you need or want instruction or further knowledge in order to be considered a good Catholic? The Mass _____ Confession _____ Communion _____ Prayers _____ Doctrine _____ Sixth Commandment _____

List any other _____

Do you feel that you have had sufficient religious knowledge and instruction for your age? yes _____, no _____ . Are you a convert? yes _____, no _____ .

Freshman Orientation. Something must always be done to introduce freshman students to their new school. Schools that can afford to do so often print a student's handbook containing information and good advice. Other schools have a selected faculty member address the new freshmen in a group meeting. Material such as the following, modified of course to fit the school using it, can be issued in mimeograph or offset form.

HINTS FOR FRESHMEN

Welcome to _____ School!

The faculty extends a hearty welcome to you. We are happy to have you with us. We want your stay at _____ School to be a profitable and enjoyable one. The following suggestions are intended to help you get along better during your stay with us. Please read them carefully.

It's Your School

We say "your school" because it does not belong solely to the faculty, no matter how the deed to the property is written. This school belongs, at least to some extent, to you and all the other Catholics of this city whose generosity made its existence possible. The members of the staff have been trained in many colleges and universities and have dedicated their lives to the art of educating youth. Now they are commissioned to serve you, and have been directed by the bishop, by your parents, and by the other Catholics of the city to use this building for providing your education.

Take a look about the place and notice the neat appearance of the building. You wouldn't think that students like yourself have been using the place for so many years. But this building can't keep up its neat appearance by itself. You must pitch in and help keep it that way.

Look upon this school as your school. Look upon it as the school that your own children may one day attend. You want it to be in good shape for them too. Yes, it will have to serve the Catholics of your city for many years to come. So in justice to our Catholic parents and ourselves, let us help in every way we can to maintain a school of which we can continue to be proud.

Your Help Needed

Your teachers are intent on giving you the finest high-school education that can be had. But no matter how earnestly your teachers try, they cannot give you that kind of education unless you work with them. You know how important teamwork is on the athletic field. It's a "must" for a good team. Without it a very good team can become just an ordinary team. The same is true in your schoolwork. Work with your teachers. They want to work with you. That is their one reason for being where they are.

You've Got a Big Job Cut Out for Yourself

You owe it to God, your parents, and yourself to do your best in school. It isn't fair if you go at this job halfheartedly. No one will ever make a success of himself if he does not give all he has. That is true in every phase of life. See how many stars or athletes fade out because they never work hard enough.

They have the ability to be great stars but they never force themselves to do tough jobs. Your studies might be tough at times too. But don't give up because the work sometimes gets difficult. Your job right now in life is to do your schoolwork. So how about tackling your job with all you've got!

Your Attendance

It is mighty important for you to be at school regularly. Ask some of those who know. Specifically, ask those who failed in subjects because of irregular attendance. They will tell you that it's really hard to catch up in algebra, Latin, English, or history once you get behind. So don't play sick. Playing sick is always a very risky business.

Know How To Study

Adopt a system for study, so that you will not go at this important job in a haphazard fashion. The person who is not afraid to work, who knows how to organize lessons, and who spends a couple of hours in study each day is building a solid foundation for a successful and happy future.

Here are a few suggestions for study. Your teachers will help you as the year goes along.

1. Be prompt. Learn to begin work without losing five or ten minutes looking around to see what the other fellow is doing. Get out your books and pitch in right away. Immediate action is half the battle won!

2. Be busy. Do not do a problem or translate a sentence and then fall back into a daydream. Work consistently! You will be surprised how much you can accomplish during a study period if you get down to real work.

3. Be independent. Do your own work. Do not depend on the other person for the answers. You will be sorry when exams come around if you have received much of your work from a classmate.

4. Be sure of your subject. Do not be satisfied with anything less than perfection. Get the *right* answer, not *any* answer. Check your work! If you think you know the matter, then test yourself with certain questions.

Study at Home

The school requires two hours of home study. Try to find a quiet place to do your homework at night. If you haven't a room of your own, use the next-quietest place in the house. Turn off the radio while studying. You cannot listen to the radio or watch TV and at the same time concentrate on what you are doing in such a way that you are working effectively.

Let Your Friends Study Too

Experience shows that you cannot go out on weekday nights and still expect to keep up in schoolwork. Save the shows for Friday, Saturday, or Sunday.

Cut down the other outside activities that take you away from home at night. Do not be going over to your friend's house so often in the evening. It interferes with your homework, and he wants to do his homework too.

Your Classmates

You are going to meet many boys and girls here whom you did not know previously. In grade school you were acquainted with everyone in school. Now it will seem like starting all over again. It is good for you to meet new boys and girls of your own age from all parts of the city. They will be your friends when you get older. Learn to work with your classmates as well as with your teachers. Some never make a success in school because they never make any effort to get along with their fellow students and teachers.

Pick Your Friends Wisely

It is frequently said that "you are known by the friends you choose." If you are always in the company of those who have bad reputations, you will be judged accordingly. Choose those whom you admire for their fine character and those whom your parents will be glad to welcome into your home.

You Are Always on Display

Always remember that you are a student of a Catholic high school. Never forget it! You are put on the spot, so to speak, because a lot of Catholics and non-Catholics are going to be watching you. They are going to judge the school by your conduct. People rightly judge a school by its students, and your school is no exception. So be on your guard. Do not give your school and fellow students a bad name by your conduct.

Help Protect Our Good Name

Every Catholic school wants to pride itself in its good name. During the past years our students have built up a good name for this Catholic institution. Now you are one of those who must protect that name. Just one unfortunate incident can tear down our fine reputation, and the work of earnest students, zealous teachers, and interested parents can be wholly undone.

Streetcars and Buses

Some people of your age like to cut up on streetcars and buses. They like to show off a bit, especially if "she" happens to be on that bus. Do not be a baboon! People who meet you everyday, and others too, know what school you attend. They expect more from you because you come from a Catholic school. Another reason is that these people might become interested in the Catholic Church because of their admiration for the good conduct of a boy or girl from a Catholic school.

That does not mean that you must be what they call a "sissy." No, you can still have your fun, but let it be in such a way that it will not reflect badly upon your Catholic education. Be a Catholic gentleman or lady always and no matter where you are. It will pay off.

Be a Good Sport

Football, basketball, and baseball games can be occasions for great glory for your school, but at the same time they can be highly dangerous as far as the name of _____ School is concerned. While the team is on the field or the floor performing according to the best standards of sportsmanship, it could be that certain "clowns" in the stands can be undoing the whole thing. Do not be one of those clowns.

This school has a good reputation for sportsmanship in her athletic games with other schools. How about helping us keep that good reputation?

Do not boo any team or official. That simply is not tolerated. When you travel with the team to a game away from home, you will be doing a big favor to the team if you always show good sportsmanship. You will not do anything to help the team by proudly displaying the school's emblem on your jacket or coat if at the same time you give the school a black eye by your conduct at the game or after the game. When visiting teams come to our school they are our guests. Treat them as such.

Desks and Other School Property

Be careful with the desks and other furniture in the building. Your mother would not enjoy having us scratch our initials on her nice tea table, would she? Neither would we enjoy seeing your initials scratched on school property. Remember that a heavy fine and penalty, including possible expulsion from school, may be given to any boy or girl who defaces school property. That includes the toilets, too.

The Hallways

Do not show off your speed in the hallways. They are narrow and become crowded during a change of class. To avoid congestion keep to the right when walking to your next class. You have only four minutes between class periods, so you cannot stop in the hallways for a little visit with your friends. Save that for the noon hour or after school. Avoid all pushing and shoving.

Your Locker

Keep your lockers clean. From time to time they will be inspected. Do not tinker with another person's locker. Anyone found attempting to open another locker will be sent to the prefect of discipline. He will handle your case, and it will not be in a gentle manner.

The Jug

Our penal institute, commonly referred to as the "jug," is reserved for all who beg to differ with any of the rules of the school. You can stay away from this torture chamber by being on time for your classes, by handing in your homework regularly, and in general by keeping out of trouble.

Lost Books and Other Articles

These can be reclaimed in the activity room. Be sure to write in ink your name and the number of your registration room in each textbook when you buy it. Otherwise there isn't much chance of recovering misplaced books.

Your Counselor

In a few weeks you will be assigned a counselor. He will act as your personal friend and adviser during the year. You are free to talk over any matter with him. If things are going badly at school or home and you need a little help, why not see him? He will try to help you in every way possible.

Let's Get Serious about This Matter

We are anxious to help you become a good Catholic citizen. Here are a couple of suggestions on how you can help yourself develop spiritually while at _____ School.

1. Receive the sacraments regularly. If you want a sure-fire rule for success, not only in this life but in the next, it is this: Go to confession and Communion every week. We are proud that many students do receive Holy Communion every week during the school year. Why don't you do the same?

2. Confessions are heard daily at _____ o'clock [during the lunch hour] in the chapel. On the Thursday preceding a first Friday and on special days confessions are heard throughout the day.

3. On a first Friday school begins forty minutes later than usual. You are expected to attend Mass and receive Communion in your own parish church. If you cannot do so and still get to school on time, then why not attend Mass and receive Communion at school? Mass is at _____ o'clock and you can get your breakfast afterwards in the cafeteria.

4. Develop the habit of visiting the chapel during your years at _____ _____ School. Noon hour is the most popular time with the boys and girls. Some of our graduates made it an everyday practice during their four years to visit the chapel before and after their lunch at noon. How about it? Can you do the same? Mass is offered each school day at _____ o'clock to ask God's blessing on the efforts of that day. If you have troubles at school, home, or elsewhere, there is no better time than the Mass to change them into a source of blessing and help from Christ the King.

Form for the Selection of a Counselor. Students should fill out the following form in duplicate, so that one copy may be given to the counselor and the other kept by the director of guidance.

SELECTION OF COUNSELOR

Name of student _____

Address _____

Telephone _____ Parish _____

Counselor, first choice _____

Counselor, second choice _____

SCHEDULE

Period	Subject	Room No.
1		
2		
3		
4		
5		
6		
7		

Check as you wish: I have no preferences for a counselor _____ ; I should like to see my counselor as soon as possible _____ ; I can come after school for counseling _____ .

FOR STUDENTS WHILE IN HIGH SCHOOL

The Permanent Record

The most comprehensive and the most important of all the single records that a school keeps of its students is the permanent record, which as a very minimum will contain a record of subjects taken, credits earned, and grades received, and which ordinarily contains a record of attendance, the IQ and standardized-test scores, honors earned, offices held, personality ratings, interests, hobbies, and other things that the school considers worth recording. Schools that can afford to do so commonly use so-called "visible record" equipment, by means of which the record of any individual student can be located and consulted in an instant.[2] The better permanent records are too large to be conveniently reproduced here. Each school, as a rule, develops its own permanent record, for no two schools seem to want exactly the same things in their permanent record or to want them arranged in the same way.

Character-Personality Record. We reproduce on page 215 a character-personality record (or better, rating scale) that has been successfully used. This rating scale provides space for ratings by four teachers in each of the four years of high school. A program of rating as time-consuming as this should not be undertaken without the observance of certain precautions, of which the first and most important is this, that some intelligent person or persons should make use of the ratings for the benefit of the individual student. It is all too easy for a principal or a director of guidance to insist on the administration of tests and the use of rating scales, and then to bury the results in records that are never helpfully consulted, never really used. It is also necessary, or at least highly desirable, that some experienced person of good judgment should study the various ratings for the purpose of discussing with teachers problems associated with the making of character and personality ratings. It is exceedingly difficult to pass judgment on character as opposed to mere overt behavior, which may be the result of diametrically opposed motives and indicate states of mind that are altogether different. As Scripture says, "Man seeth those things that appear; but the Lord beholdeth the heart" (1 Kings 16:7). There should be group conferences for the benefit of those who are asked to make ratings. The various traits should be clearly defined; the need for adequate evi-

---

[2] Two companies that carry equipment for visible records are Postindex Company, Jamestown, New York, and Remington-Rand, Inc., 444 North Michigan Avenue, Chicago, Illinois, both of which have branch offices or agents in numerous cities. Both companies are prepared to set up and print record forms that fit their equipment, and their printed forms are neater and more serviceable than what the ordinary printer can easily produce.

CHARACTER—PERSONALITY RECORD

NAME

TEACHER NAME

Category	Descriptor	Freshman	Sophomore	Junior	Senior
SCHOLASTIC ABILITY (promise)	exceptional				
	above average				
	average				
	poor				
INDUSTRY (initiative)	seeks additional work				
	prepares assigned work				
	needs occasional prodding				
	needs constant pressure				
	seldom applies himself				
INFLUENCE (leadership)	strongly contributing				
	contributing				
	retiring but cooperative				
	passive				
	negative				
CONCERN FOR OTHERS (cooperation)	genuine consideration				
	somewhat socially concerned				
	self centered				
	indifferent				
	anti-social				
RESPONSIBILTY (reliability)	assumes responsibilities				
	usually dependable				
	dependable in some areas				
	unreliable				
INTEGRITY (honesty)	completely trustworthy				
	usually trustworthy				
	questionable				
MANNERS (courtesy)	highly developed				
	usually good				
	frequently discourteous				
	generally poor manners				
APPEARANCE	well-groomed				
	neat				
	careless				
	untidy				
EMOTIONAL STABILITY (maturity)	exceptionally stable				
	well-balanced				
	usually mature				
	worries excessively				
	excitable				
	unresponsive				
	undeveloped				

dence should be stressed; great variations between the ratings given by one teacher and those given by another should be noted and the reasons studied; trends from year to year should be observed; suggestions for ways of encouraging students to improve weak traits should be made.

Spiritual Inventory and Program. At the beginning of each year students may be asked to fill out the following form. The purpose is twofold: to lead students to give thought to their own spiritual condition and to provide the director of guidance, the counselors, and the teachers of religion with information concerning general conditions in the school. Students should then be required to plan a practical program for better attention to their religious duties. Students may be told, when the inventory is being filled out, that carelessness during vacation indicates a childish need of supervision. They should not sign their names to this inventory.

SPIRITUAL INVENTORY AND PROGRAM

There were thirteen Sundays and one holyday since the close of school. List the number of times during this period that you went to Mass, Communion, and confession: Mass _____ times; Communion _____ times; confession _____ times.

Give yourself a rating as to your saying of morning and evening prayers and your performance of other religious duties by placing a check mark after one of the following ratings: above average _____ ; average _____ ; unsatisfactory _____ .

Put a check mark after those things at which you need to work for your better development as a good Catholic: attendance at Mass _____ ; frequent Communion _____ ; frequent confession to overcome bad habits _____ ; regularity in daily prayer _____ ; watching bad language _____ ; more strength in regard to purity _____ ; showing respect to parents and superiors _____ ; more care in regard to reading _____ .

Put a check mark after the things that you intend to make part of your spiritual program for the year: attending Mass in the chapel daily _____ , three times a week _____ , twice a week _____ , once a week _____ ; receiving Communion _____ times a week, _____ times a month; visiting the Blessed Sacrament in the chapel daily _____ ; saying the rosary daily _____ ; making some acts of charity daily _____ ; trying to break a bad habit _____ .

Additional: _____

Sophomore Vocational-Interest Form. As stated on pages 113-14 it is advisable to ask students about their vocational interests in both freshman and sophomore years in order to encourage them to think about this most important matter. There is reference to vocational interests in the New-Student Questionnaire, pages 202-06. The following form can be used as a follow-up in sophomore year. The same form, or a similar one, may be used in junior year, where special attention is of course given to vocational guidance.

SOPHOMORE VOCATIONAL-INTEREST FORM

Name .... Date ....

List the vocations or occupations of which you thought when in elementary school: ....

List the ones you thought about as a freshman: ....
....

What do you now think you would like to do for a lifework? ....

Why does this work appeal to you? ....

What interest do you have in the priesthood or religious life?...................

Educational Plan or Forecast. Toward the end of the year, or toward the end of the semester in high schools offering courses only one semester in length, students should discuss with their counselors their educational plan for the coming year or semester. In the case of entering freshmen this must be done when they register or during Freshman Week. It is advantageous to have a record covering all four years and showing, not only the student's choices, but also the grades that he made. The subjects are entered at the time of forecasting; the grades must of course be entered later. This makes it possible for the counselor to encourage the student to make wise choices by showing the wisdom or the apparent lack of wisdom of previous choices. The counselor also has an excellent opportunity to discuss the necessity of a proper selection of subject matter as a means of preparing for the vocation of which the student is thinking. In schools with few or no electives forecasting may consist in planning for successful work in the subjects to be taken.

STUDENT EDUCATIONAL PLAN OR FORECAST

Name _____ Telephone _____

Address _____ Parish _____

Vocational Preferences _____

FRESHMAN, 19___		SOPHOMORE, 19___	
Subjects	*Grades*	*Subjects*	*Grades*
....	....	....	....
....	....	....	....
....	....	....	....
....	....	....	....
....	....	....	....

JUNIOR, 19___		SENIOR, 19___	
Subjects	*Grades*	*Subjects*	*Grades*
....	....	....	....
....	....	....	....
....	....	....	....
....	....	....	....
....	....	....	....

Reasons for Failing. Guidance personnel are often consulted by parents in regard to the unsatisfactory progress of an individual student as part of the review of the over-all development of the student. If teachers are not available for a conference that is to be held with parents or guardians, they should be asked to fill out the following form and file it in the guidance office. Even if there is to be no conference with parents, teachers may be asked as a matter of routine to fill out the report for every student who has failed in a course taught by them. These reports will prove of very great help to counselors, deans, and the principal. The fact that the filling out of these reports throws a rather heavy burden on teachers must not be overlooked. It is by all means best if teachers can be led to accept the task themselves when plans are being discussed in a staff meeting. A principal or director of guidance who forces too much unpleasant work on teachers may find that he loses more by injuring the morale of his teachers than he gains by accumulating additional records for his files, especially as records made under such conditions may be lacking in reliability.

REASONS FOR FAILING

Your student _____ has received a failing mark in _____ . To help in determining the real cause of failure, please put a check mark before the reasons that seem to you to be responsible for it. Add, if feasible, other reasons and details that may be appropriate to the case.

_____ lack of necessary foundation
_____ IQ too low for course
_____ poor start
_____ illness
_____ extracurricular activities
_____ outside work
_____ neglect of written work
_____ fear of failure
_____ physical defects
_____ poor study habits
_____ failure to follow instructions
_____ too easily distracted
_____ bad home conditions

_____ general dislike of school
_____ failure to complete assignments
_____ irregular attendance
_____ outside interests
_____ social life
_____ laziness
_____ feeling of inferiority
_____ lack of application
_____ dislike of subject
_____ lack of attention during explanations
_____ poor reading ability

(Signed) _____
(Date) _____

Remarks:

It will be observed that none of the reasons for failing that are mentioned in the preceding form have anything to do with the teacher or with the teacher's methods of presenting his subject. It frequently happens that teachers are too exacting, that their explanations are not clear, that they fail to give individual help when help is needed, that they conceive prejudices against certain pupils, that they are unable to maintain classroom discipline, or that they have other weaknesses which make success difficult for students. Reasons for failure may also be found in the principal's office if the principal is an easygoing individual who does not insist on discipline and achievement and who is unwilling to back up his teachers. Students who would fail elsewhere do not always fail in schools with principals of vision and under teachers who are masters of their craft. The director of guidance may wish to add to "Reasons for Failing" a few questions inviting the teacher to examine his own conscience. The reasons for failing as given here should not be interpreted as meaning that the entire reason for failure is always found in the student. If a student, for example, is actually guilty of lack of attention, the cause should be investigated. Underlying causes are more important than the behavior that results from them.

Counselor Guide and Record Form. Few forms that the director of guidance may develop are more important than a form for keeping a record of interviews between counselors and students. A form such as the one given here will ensure systematic and more thorough counseling, since it provides both a guide to counseling areas and a place to record data that would otherwise be forgotten. The counselor needs during the interview a reminder of the things about which he should inquire, and likewise he needs in a later interview a record of what he did or learned in earlier interviews. It is altogether too easy to forget the specific problems or plans that were discussed some months or even years before, especially when a counselor confers with a large number of students each year. A guidance director will always urge counselors to make note of significant data on the form, and to do so in sufficient detail, for this action tends to guarantee intelligent counseling and assures the counselee that the knowledge of the facts in his case are fresh in the memory of his counselor. The counselor who is doing a really thorough job of individual guidance will in many instances use the reverse side of the form to present the complete profile of such things as home problems, difficulties in study, personality conflicts, and the like.

When nothing worthy of comment develops in the counseling session, the counselor may simply enter a check mark before "physical," "social," and other headings to indicate that the area was discussed and that the student had an opportunity of talking on the subject. All the recording can be done in notes briefly entered at the appropriate point, following the principles given on pages 74-75. The director of guidance, who must have some means of checking on the frequency and progress of the counseling program, will call for the interview records at regular intervals. He should then place the record in the student's cumulative file, where the counselor and other staff members may find it in case of another interview or further discussion of a certain problem.

This form may be ruled off in sections on a single page and prepared for duplication by inserting the stencil sideways in a wide-carriage typewriter with elite type. If this method does not allow sufficient space for the items and comments, reduction and printing by use of the offset process will prove feasible as well as quite inexpensive. The typed material reduced to the size of an 8½ x 11 page presents a neat form that may be prepared in pads with carbon paper if additional copies are needed.

COUNSELOR GUIDE AND RECORD FORM

------------------------------   -----------   ----------   ----------------------------------
     counselee   year   date   counselor

Physical

General Health
- ☐ excellent
- ☐ normal
- ☐ poor

Care of Health
- ☐ excessive concern
- ☐ normal
- ☐ lack of concern

Rest
- ☐ sufficient
- ☐ insufficient

Diet
- ☐ adequate
- ☐ inadequate

Exercise
- ☐ excessive
- ☐ sufficient
- ☐ insufficient

Handicaps
- ☐ sight
- ☐ hearing
- ☐ speech
- ☐ other

Comment:

Social

Home Life
- ☐ happy
- ☐ indifferent
- ☐ unhappy
- ☐ special problems

Home Guidance
- ☐ overly protective
- ☐ adequate
- ☐ inadequate

Home Finances
- ☐ abundant
- ☐ adequate
- ☐ inadequate
- ☐ student employed

Activities
- ☐ hobbies
- ☐ sports
- ☐ spectator only
- ☐ parties

Dating
- ☐ going steady
- ☐ occasionally dates
- ☐ never dates

Companions
- ☐ many
- ☐ few
- ☐ only one
  (give names if significant)

Comment:

Moral

Responsibility
- ☐ complete
- ☐ average
- ☐ unreliable

Personality
- ☐ extrovert
- ☐ balanced
- ☐ introvert

Emotional Control
- ☐ mature
- ☐ satisfactory
- ☐ unpredictable

Attitudes
- ☐ desirable
- ☐ indifferent
- ☐ defiant

Comment:

Spiritual

Practice of Religion
- ☐ daily
- ☐ discussed
- ☐ did not discuss

Plan for Growth
- ☐ serious
- ☐ routine
- ☐ haphazard
- ☐ none

Attitude to Religion
- ☐ positive
- ☐ indifferent
- ☐ negative

Participation in Parish Life
- ☐ active
- ☐ periodic
- ☐ inactive
- ☐ list activities

Comment (do not violate conscience or confidence):

Educational

Use of Ability
- ☐ to capacity
- ☐ average
- ☐ unsatisfactory

Finds Schoolwork
- ☐ excessive
- ☐ difficult
- ☐ challenging
- ☐ easy

Teacher Relationship
- ☐ friendly
- ☐ respectful
- ☐ tolerant
- ☐ contemptuous

Educational Plans
- ☐ definite
- ☐ hazy
- ☐ confused
- ☐ Catholic college

Comment (note special problems existing and plans for further education):

Vocational-Occupational

Choice of Lifework
- ☐ definite
- ☐ uncertain
- ☐ confused
- ☐ special

Priesthood or Religious Life
- ☐ considering
- ☐ rejected
- ☐ never considered
- ☐ decided

Capabilities
- ☐ unusual
- ☐ average
- ☐ none

Opportunities
- ☐ plentiful
- ☐ normal
- ☐ limited

Means To Attain Goal
- ☐ attainable
- ☐ impossible
- ☐ knows them
- ☐ does not know them

Interest or Desire
- ☐ deep
- ☐ average
- ☐ insufficient

Comment (note any definite decisions, unusual capabilities or opportunities, or plans made by the counselee):

Special Problems:

Recommendations:

Students Seeking Employment during High School. Three forms are needed when students ask the help of the school in obtaining employment. These three forms are entitled Employment Wanted, Employment Referral Card, and Employment Record.

If he has had any previous work experience, he gives the names of the companies and of the individuals who may be used as references. The student applies for help by filling out an employment-wanted form.

The vocational counselor, having decided upon a company where it is possible that the student might be given a job, gives the student an employment referral card which is to be presented to the prospective employer. The reverse side of this card calls for information which the prospective employer is asked to give the school. Since it is better that this information be kept secret from the student, the employer is asked to return the card by mail. Courtesy requires that a stamped and self-addressed envelope should be provided, which the student can give to the prospective employer when he presents the referral card.

If the student is successful in finding a position, he is given an employment record form which he is to fill out at once and give to his counselor. If a school wishes to know where students are working and the hours and wages at which they work, all employed students may be asked to fill out the employment record card. An excellent job-opportunity list can be made for future years in this manner. The three forms follow.

EMPLOYMENT WANTED

Name _____ Telephone _____

Address _____ Parish _____

Work Experience	*Supervisor*
_____	_____
_____	_____
_____	_____

Work Preference

_____

_____

(Notify the Placement Office when you secure a job.)

EMPLOYMENT REFERRAL CARD

To _____

Firm _____

Address _____

This will introduce _____ who is an applicant for the position of _____ .

(Signed) _____

Vocational Counselor

_____ School

Date _____

(*reverse side*)

To assist us in preparing students for employment, please check the following. Kindly return this card by mail.

Hired: Yes _____ ; no _____ ; may be hired lated _____ .

Interview was excellent _____ ; good _____ ; fair _____ ; poor _____ .

Comment: _____

Written application was excellent _____ ; good _____ ; fair _____ ; poor _____ .

Attitude was excellent _____ ; good _____ ; fair _____ ; poor _____ .

Qualifications are excellent _____ ; good _____ ; fair _____ ; poor _____ .

(Signed) _____

EMPLOYMENT RECORD

Name _____ Telephone _____

Address _____ Parish _____

Employer	*Type of work*	*Hours*	*Wage*
_____	_____	_____	_____
_____	_____	_____	_____

(Notify the Placement Office when you leave a job.)

Guidance for Seniors. The following Post-High-School Plan can be used to impel students to determine upon their future course of action and to make plans concerning it. The guidance director or the person in charge of senior guidance may then tabulate, to be used in connection with curriculum studies, the number and percentage of those going to college, to work, or to military service. He will know which students need last-minute assistance or counseling to correct obvious mistakes in plans or decisions. When employers wish to employ a graduate, the placement office will have available a listing of students who may be contacted.

POST-HIGH-SCHOOL PLAN

Name _____ Telephone _____

Address _____ Parish _____

Do you intend to go to college? yes _____ , no _____ , undecided _____ .

Name of college _____ undecided _____

Proposed vocational or occupational choice _____

Proposed major in college _____

Do you have the necessary funds? yes _____ , no _____ .
From what source? _____

If you need aid to go to college, explain what aid _____

Are you going into the service? yes _____ , no _____ ; when? _____ which branch? _____ .

Are you in the reserve now? yes _____ , no _____ ; which branch? _____

Are you going to work full-time? _____ , part-time? _____ ; where? _____

Do you wish further occupational testing? yes _____ , no _____ .

Are you looking for permanent employment? yes _____ , no _____ ; what kind? _____

To enable school personnel to inform you about a job or other opportunities, give the name of someone with whom you expect to be always in contact and whose address you think is permanent.

Name _____ Address _____

High-School-College Conference. We spoke on pages 129-31 of the advantages of conferences between students, their parents, and the representatives of colleges. In preparation for such a conference students should fill out the following Student Data Sheet. Some school official adds information about the student's academic ability. There is provision for memoranda by the college representative.

STUDENT DATA SHEET

To the student

Fill out a copy of this form for each of the colleges you wish to contact.

Name _____ Telephone _____

Address _____ Parish _____

Name of parent or guardian _____

High school you are now attending _____

College choices: first _____, second _____,
third _____

Your vocational interests: First _____ Second _____

To the high-school official

Check at least one of the following indexes of probable college success, and all four if you can conveniently do so.

Prediction of college success: high _____, average _____, low _____.

Grade-point average _____.

IQ: above 120 _____, 110-20 _____, 105-09 _____, 100-04 _____, below
100 _____.

Scholarship: in upper 10 per cent of class _____, above average _____, average _____, low _____.

For the college representative

Scholarship: satisfactory _____, not satisfactory _____, doubtful _____,
evidence lacking _____.

Send catalog _____. Also send _____

Refer to:

In advance of the conferences with college representatives students should be given as many copies as necessary of the following Student Study of Individual College. They should preferably make their study from college catalogs and literature before the date of the conference. This work may well be part of an assignment in the unit on education in the sociology class. If this plan is not feasible, students can fill out a few of the answers before the conference, others during the interview, and still others after the interview is over. They should give a copy of their study to their counselor or to the director of guidance.

STUDENT STUDY OF INDIVIDUAL COLLEGE

Name _____ Telephone _____

Address _____ Parish _____

Name of college _____ Location _____

Population of town _____ . Number of students _____ , of faculty _____ .

Who may apply for admission? _____

When and how is application for admission made? _____

In what course do you expect to enroll? _____

What high-school credits are required for enrollment in this course? _____

What grade-point average is required for admission? _____

What is your grade-point average? _____

What degree will you receive when you complete your course? _____

For what work or positions will this course qualify you? _____

What are the costs per year in dollars for tuition _____ , fixed fees (health service, laboratory, library, activities, etc.) _____ , board and room _____ , books and supplies _____ , transportation, including vacation _____ , incidental costs _____ . Estimated total cost per year _____ .

Can you pay this without working at college? yes _____ , no _____ .

If you expect work, where and how will you look for a job? _____

Why does this particular college interest you? _____

FOR DROPOUTS AND GRADUATES

Dropout Information. The following form can be used for obtaining information from students who voluntarily or involuntarily drop out of school. Longer questionnaires and lists of reasons for dropping out are given in a plan for a dropout study in the *National Association of Secondary School Principals Bulletin,* March 1953, pages 77 ff. and February 1954, pages 33 ff. Included are questionnaires for students who left school in previous years. It is important that this information be reviewed for purposes of curriculum study and then placed in the student's cumulative record.

DROPOUT INFORMATION

Name _____ Date _____

Address _____ Parish _____

School from which admitted _____

Reason or reasons for leaving school _____

Courses which have been of greatest help to you in high school _____

Who has been the greatest help to you in high school? _____

Future educational plans _____

Future employment plan _____

What could have made you stay in school until graduation? _____

Do you feel secure in the faith and its practice? yes _____, no _____, uncertain _____ .

(Pupil data to be supplied by Guidance Department.)

IQ _____ ; age at leaving _____ . Year: freshman _____ , sophomore _____ , junior _____ , senior _____ .

Total credits earned _____ . Attendance: good _____ , average _____ , poor _____ .

Scholastic average: freshman _____ , sophomore _____ , junior _____ , senior _____ .

Comment:

Follow-up Study of Graduates. Graduates owe a debt of gratitude to the school that has educated them, oftentimes without charging them for their education and almost invariably at less than cost. It is right that graduates should in turn help their old school when they become able to do so. This is the first reason for maintaining an up-to-date mailing list of alumni and for knowing which ones are best able to assist the school. So far as the director of guidance is concerned, his reason for wishing to know what graduates are doing is that such knowledge helps him in appraising the guidance services being rendered and in making suggestions for curriculum revision. Something is evidently wrong if attempts are made to prepare students for certain occupations and if it is found that few if any students enter those occupations or that those who do enter them prove unsuccessful.

Members of the senior class and other students are often able to give information about graduates of the preceding year, but this method of gathering information is slow and uncertain and the information tends to be incomplete and often inaccurate. The best way to keep a mailing list up to date and to obtain information is to send questionnaires by first-class mail and to include business-reply cards or stamped envelopes for replies. This method is of course costly, and someone must decide whether the good that is accomplished justifies the outlay. If the director of guidance is thinking of questionnairing graduates, he should consider the possibility of combining forces with the director of the alumni association or with the principal, if the latter is the one who keeps in touch with alumni. This is not always easy to do, even when both individuals are as cooperative as men can be, since both can be expected to desire information of a different kind, to want it at different seasons of the year, and to wish to keep it in files of their own.

Information concerning graduates may continue to be gathered for twenty-five years or more, and hence it is quite difficult to devise any form for recording it. The best method is probably to use a card system. The following selections from a follow-up of graduates are not intended to suggest how such a record should be kept, but rather to indicate how the information can throw light on problems connected with the curriculum, with educational planning, and with guidance.

NAME	1954	1955	1956	1957
Adler, Charles	Portland U.	Portland U.	Portland U.	Portland U.
Bastasch, Jane	Marylhurst	Business school	Stenographer	Secretary
Bean, James	Santa Clara	Santa Clara	Coast Guard	Coast Guard
Bishop, Michael	Seminary	Franz Bakery	Franz Bakery	Salesman
Bolton, Betty	Clerk, Howe's	Clerk, Howe's	Married	Married

FOR APPRAISALS OF SERVICES

Evaluation of High-School-College Conference. After the high-school-college conference (see pages 129-31) the following College-Conference Evaluation Sheet may be used to obtain expressions of opinion from the representatives of the colleges.

COLLEGE-CONFERENCE EVALUATION SHEET

For the representative of .... College (University)

The method used by us to give students information about higher institutions and to help in student recruitment is excellent .... , reasonably satisfactory .... , unsatisfactory ....

Comment:

The best time for such a program is before December .... , January .... , February .... , March .... , April ....

Comment:

Arrangements should be made for longer sessions .... , sessions of the same length .... , shorter sessions .... , more time for individual conferences .... , time for the work during the school day ....

Suggestions:

The presence of parents is desirable at the group meetings .... , during individual conferences with students .... , at no time ....

The information on prospective students given to representatives of colleges is sufficient .... , insufficient ....

What other specific information does your college desire?

Additional suggestions or comments:

(Please leave your evaluation in our office.)

Check Lists for Appraising the Guidance Program. The following check lists are designed to provide a means of appraising the program as a whole and in various aspects.[3] Their chief value lies in the fact that they present a rather complete statement of what it is thought that guidance should do. They may be taken up for discussion at staff meetings for the purpose of seeing where improvements can be made. Such discussions should lead to conclusions concerning the greater or less importance of certain points. In some cases the group may decide that a school should refrain from doing something which a check list represents as desirable.

A Catholic school will be slow to approve without qualifications the statement that "The counselor accepts the student as he reveals himself, without expressing values on anything the student says." This principle accepts as universally valid the theories of those who advocate nondirective counseling. Whatever may be said about counseling methods with adults, at the high-school level failure to express disapproval of a morally wrong opinion voiced by a student is so apt to be interpreted as tacit approval that few Catholics would sanction such a procedure. It is true that a counselor who is a perfect master of nondirective techniques will be able to avoid creating false impressions and to lead counselees to accept the correct values in which he himself believes, but it is dangerous to assume that all high-school counselors have been so well trained. While a counselor should avoid showing horror or disgust when a student expresses an unorthodox opinion on such subjects as sex, obedience, social service, or the obligations of divine worship, he should not fail to instruct the student in the truth. The scientific evidence pointing to the fact that a counselor does harm rather than good by affirming, tactfully of course, the true values is far from being conclusive. It must also be kept in mind that students in Catholic schools understand rather well that a divinely promulgated moral code exists and that they expect their teachers to defend this code.

[3] These check lists may be found in *Improving Guidance Programs in Secondary Schools*, by Donald E. Kitch and William H. McCreary, *Bulletin of the California State Department of Education* 19:13-56, December 1950. The authors and the California Department of Education made this material available to all by refraining from copyrighting it.

CHECK LIST FOR APPRAISING ADMINISTRATION
OF A GUIDANCE PROGRAM

Consider each item carefully. Then check it in the appropriate column: (1) Our program is strong in this respect. (2) Our program is fair in this respect but needs improvement. (3) Our program is very weak in this respect.

Aspect of the Program	Strong (1)	Fair (2)	Weak (3)
1. Does the administration provide adequate leadership in developing the guidance program?			
2. Are the resources of the faculty utilized by delegating appropriate guidance duties to various members?			
3. Is the support of the community enlisted in the development of the guidance program through contacts with organizations which influence public opinion and might serve as resource groups?			
4. Are staff members encouraged to increase their understanding and competency through in-service training in guidance and other means?			
5. Does each counselor have a private office for counseling and the necessary facilities, clerical help, telephone service, etc., for carrying on his duties?			
6. Is a reasonable counselor-student ratio maintained or being developed as new staff members are employed?			
7. Does every student have opportunity for a periodic interview with a counselor and for further interviews as needed?			
8. Is the practice avoided of assigning to counselors duties which may be detrimental to their professional relationships with students?			
9. Are the needs of the guidance program specifically considered in making up the school budget?			

10. Has a qualified person been given direct responsibility for the operation of the guidance program?

11. Has a guidance committee been established to serve as an advisory and coordinating body in matters involving guidance policies and practices?

12. Have members of the guidance staff worked out together a satisfactory statement of their respective functions and responsibilities?

13. Have classroom teachers been adequately oriented to their roles in the guidance program?

14. Has effective liaison been established between the school guidance program and referral sources in the community, including any services provided by county or city school departments?

15. Have good working relationships been established between the guidance staff and staff members working in the areas of health, child welfare and attendance, special education, and related fields?

CHECK LIST FOR APPRAISING THE ORIENTATION PROGRAM

Consider each item carefully. Then check it in the appropriate column: (1) Our program is strong in this respect. (2) Our program is fair in this respect but needs improvement. (3) Our program is very weak in this respect.

Aspect of the Program	Strong (1)	Fair (2)	Weak (3)
1. Does the school have a planned, regularly conducted program of orientation activities for new classes coming from feeder schools?			
2. Does the school have such a program for students who transfer in at the beginning of or during the year?			

3. Have students, teachers, counselors, administrators, and parents been consulted in the planning of the program? ....

4. Is the program planned in terms of the transfer problems that students are likely to consider important rather than altogether in terms of what the teachers and administrators consider important? ....

5. Have representatives of the sending schools, the county or city office guidance staff, and other interested parties been involved in planning the orientation activities? ....

6. Does the orientation program provide for the following:
   a. Conferences with parents? ....
   b. The preparation, use, and transfer of cumulative records on all new students? ....
   c. Planned visits to sending schools by staff members? ....
   d. Recognition of incoming students with special learning problems? ....
   e. Visits to the new campus by prospective students? ....
   f. Student handbooks or other devices for giving new students information concerning the school and its program? ....
   g. Activities to provide new students with an opportunity to get acquainted with each other and with students who have been in the school before? ....

7. Are the orientation activities a part of a planned program of coordinating the educational philosophies, the teaching practices, the curriculum content, and the guidance services of the sending and receiving schools? ....

CHECK LIST FOR APPRAISING THE
GROUP GUIDANCE PROGRAM

Consider each item carefully. Then check it in the appropriate column: (1) Our program is strong in this respect. (2) Our program is fair in this respect but needs improvement. (3) Our program is very weak in this respect.

Aspect of the Program	Strong (1)	Fair (2)	Weak (3)
1. Does the school have a planned program of group guidance activities in connection with a home room system, a basic course program, required courses, or special classes of a guidance nature?	....	....	....
2. Is the group guidance program planned to provide needed learning experiences for all students?	....	....	....
3. Are studies of the adjustment problems important to students made periodically . . . ?	....	....	....
4. Are the units included in group guidance placed on grade levels appropriate to the physical, social, and emotional maturation of students?	....	....	....
5. Are group guidance activities planned in such a way as to prepare students for making decisions . . . in connection with their school programs?	....	....	....
6. Are the following topics covered by one or more units included in the curriculum as a part of the group guidance program:			
a. Orientation to the school?	....	....	....
b. Effective study habits and use of the library?	....	....	....
c. Self-appraisal and self-understanding?	....	....	....
d. Educational and occupational planning?	....	....	....
e. Effective human relationships?	....	....	....
f. Applying for a job?	....	....	....
g. Use of leisure time?	....	....	....
h. Good mental and physical health practices?	....	....	....

7. Do teachers of group guidance activities generally have the personal traits and training necessary to effective teaching in this area?

8. Are group guidance teachers provided with necessary materials and teaching aids?

9. Is a planned program of in-service training carried on for group guidance teachers?

10. Are special activities such as Career Conferences, College Days, Work Days, and special assemblies carried on at appropriate intervals as a part of the group guidance program?

11. Is the cocurricular program of the school used as a part of the group guidance program?

CHECK LIST FOR APPRAISING PROCEDURES FOR STUDYING INDIVIDUAL DIFFERENCES

Consider each item carefully. Then check it in the appropriate column: (1) Our program is strong in this respect. (2) Our program is fair in this respect but needs improvement. (3) Our program is very weak in this respect.

Aspect of the Program	Strong (1)	Fair (2)	Weak (3)
1. Does the school have a planned program for securing and filing data on the individual characteristics of all students?			
2. Is the information secured sufficiently complete to provide teachers, counselors, and administrators with the data they need about individual students?			
3. Are student questionnaires and other forms used to collect information for the cumulative records?			
4. Are clerks used to relieve teachers and counselors of a major share of the clerical work involved in maintaining the cumulative records?			

5. Are the records kept where they are easily accessible . . . ?

6. Is the information accumulated about individual students regularly interpreted to the students themselves through individual counseling?

7. Is the information accumulated about students regularly used by teachers in adjusting their classroom activities to the needs and characteristics of individual students?

8. Is the information accumulated about students regularly used in connection with the school's program for evaluating and improving its curriculum?

9. Do members of the school staff . . . exercise proper caution in making use of test results?

10. Does the school's program for securing information . . . place undue stress on . . . tests and neglect . . . observation, student questionnaires, the recording of data secured through interviews with students and parents, etc.?

11. Is the ability of staff members to evaluate, interpret, and use information about students systematically improved through regular in-service training activities?

CHECK LIST FOR APPRAISING INFORMATION SERVICE

Consider each item carefully. Then check it in the appropriate column: (1) Our program is strong in this respect. (2) Our program is fair in this respect but needs improvement. (3) Our program is very weak in this respect.

Aspect of the Program	Strong (1)	Fair (2)	Weak (3)
1. Does the school maintain an adequate collection of school and college catalogs and other types of information about educational and training opportunities?			

2. Does the collection cover opportunities such as junior colleges, vocational and trade schools, adult and evening schools, and apprenticeship programs?

3. Does the school have a collection of books, pamphlets, and other materials on a wide range of occupations, which is kept up to date?

4. Is the collection of occupational information easily available to counselors, teachers, and students?

5. Are the educational and occupational information materials used in connection with planned group activities which enable all students to become familiar with them and their uses?

6. Are members of the school staff assigned specific responsibilities for keeping the materials up to date and in usable condition?

7. Do the teachers regularly provide their classes with occupational information related to their respective subject-matter fields?

8. Are individual students assisted to work out their educational-vocational plans through interviews with a trained counselor?

CHECK LIST FOR APPRAISING
COUNSELING SERVICE

Consider each item carefully. Then check it in the appropriate column: (1) Our program is strong in this respect. (2) Our program is fair in this respect but needs improvement. (3) Our program is very weak in this respect.

Aspect of the Program	Strong (1)	Fair (2)	Weak (3)
1. Do members of the staff regard counseling as a specific activity which involves certain definite knowledges and skills?			

2. Are counselors selected on the basis of the personal traits, experience, and training which equip them to counsel individuals effectively? ....

3. Are counselors used as resource persons by other members of the staff? ....

4. Do members of the counseling staff participate in the school's curriculum development program? ....

5. Are counselors who do not possess desirable knowledges and skills encouraged to become more competent through professional study and work experience? ....

6. Do counselors accept the following basic principles as fundamental to their work with individual students? ....

   a. The counselor is concerned with the complete adjustment pattern of the individual. ....

   b. Individual differences in abilities and interests and variations in the social and economic resources available to individuals are of basic importance. ....

   c. Counseling is directed toward the development within the individual of the ability to make his own decisions in an increasingly mature and effective fashion. ....

   d. The counselor is responsible for assisting the individual to implement the decisions which he makes. ....

   e. The student's voluntary acceptance of the counseling relationship is essential to effective counseling. ....

   f. The counselor observes strict ethical standards in his relationship with his counselees. ....

7. Do counselors use the following procedures in counseling students? ....

   a. The counselor prepares for each interview by carefully studying all the data pertinent to the case. ....

b. The interview is organized purposefully, but flexibility is maintained to adjust to any emerging problem of the student. ....

c. The student is encouraged to express himself freely. ....

d. The counselor avoids domination of the interview or of the student. ....

e. The counselor accepts the student as he reveals himself, without expressing values on anything the student says. ....

f. The counselor keeps a written record of the interview. ....

g. The counselor maintains an objective attitude toward the student and his problems. ....

h. The counselor is mindful at all times that a student's decisions must be emotionally as well as intellectually acceptable to the student. ....

i. The counselor aims at assisting students in becoming increasingly self-reliant. ....

j. The counselor makes the student aware of their joint responsibilities in the counseling relationship. ....

k. In helping the student carry out his counseling decisions, the counselor does not assume the role of a supervisor or administrator in his relations with teachers or students. ....

l. The counselor recognizes problems which are beyond his counseling skill or can most appropriately be handled by others and refers such problems to an appropriate resource if available. ....

m. The counselor maintains high ethical standards regarding confidential information. ....

n. The counselor enlists the cooperation of parents, teachers, administrators, and community resources in assisting the student with his problems. He is careful, however, to retain the confidence of the student in making such contacts.

o. Cooperative study of individual student problems is facilitated through such means as case conferences.

p. The counselor makes provision for follow-up of each student counseled.

CHECK LIST FOR APPRAISING PLACEMENT SERVICES

Consider each item carefully. Then check it in the appropriate column: (1) Our program is strong in this respect. (2) Our program is fair in this respect but needs improvement. (3) Our program is very weak in this respect.

Aspect of the Program	Strong (1)	Fair (2)	Weak (3)
1. Does the school provide an organized placement service that is adequate in terms of the needs of its students?			
2. Is assistance provided for all students who need help in working out educational placements?			
3. Is assistance provided for all students who need help in securing part-time employment?			
4. Is assistance provided for all drop-outs and graduates who need help in securing full-time jobs?			
5. Are all students kept fully informed as to the placement services provided by the school?			
6. Are all members of the school staff fully informed as to the school's placement services and problems?			
7. Are former students encouraged to make use of the school's placement services?			
8. Does the school have a central placement desk or office?			

9. Are the placement activities of different staff members coordinated in such a manner that periodic reports on all school placements are available to the staff and the general public?

10. Are efforts made to maintain frequent and regular contacts with potential employers of students, drop-outs and graduates?

11. Are public employment services and other community resources used to good advantage in developing school placement services?

CHECK LIST FOR APPRAISING
FOLLOW-UP PROGRAM

Consider each item carefully. Then check it in the appropriate column: (1) Our program is strong in this respect. (2) Our program is fair in this respect but needs improvement. (3) Our program is very weak in this respect.

Aspect of the Program	Strong (1)	Fair (2)	Weak (3)
1. Does the school conduct periodic studies of all school-leavers including both drop-outs and graduates?			
2. Are students who drop out of school interviewed as they leave in order to secure information concerning their reasons for leaving and their plans?			
3. Is information about former students that is secured by school staff members in informal contacts with former students, parents, and employers used to good advantage?			
4. Is the information secured through follow-up studies used in evaluating the school's administrative practices? Its curriculum? Its guidance program?			
5. Are follow-up study data used in orienting students to the problems and experiences they will face upon leaving school?			

6. Is information concerning former students used in appropriate ways in connection with the school's community relations program? ....

CHECK LIST FOR APPRAISING
GUIDANCE-CURRICULUM RELATIONSHIPS

Consider each item carefully. Then check it in the appropriate column: (1) Our program is strong in this respect. (2) Our program is fair in this respect but needs improvement. (3) Our program is very weak in this respect.

Aspect of the Program	Strong (1)	Fair (2)	Weak (3)
1. Are studies made of the problems that young people feel to be important to them? Is this information used in the development of learning activities based upon such problems?	....	....	....
2. Is the guidance staff expected to analyze, organize, and present to the staff data on the individual characteristics of students for the purpose of assisting in the evaluation and improvement of the school's curriculum?	....	....	....
3. Are students who would benefit by special curricular adaptations to individual handicaps or special abilities identified and reported to the staff?	....	....	....
4. Do teachers plan the content of their courses and their classroom activities with regard for available information concerning the problems, interests, and abilities of students?	....	....	....
5. Is information concerning former students and their experiences after leaving the school collected and used in evaluating the curriculum?	....	....	....
6. Have units or courses been added to the curriculum recently as a result of studies of student characteristics and needs?	....	....	....

7. Have units or courses been dropped from the curriculum as the result of such studies?

8. Have changes been made in the curriculum as the result of studies of the community?

9. Does the curriculum provide an opportunity for students to make progress toward their individual goals and objectives?

10. Have the administrative, curricular, and instructional practices of the school been examined from the standpoint of good mental health practices?

CHECK LIST FOR APPRAISING GUIDANCE-COMMUNITY RELATIONSHIPS

Consider each item carefully. Then check it in the appropriate column: (1) Our program is strong in this respect. (2) Our program is fair in this respect but needs improvement. (3) Our program is very weak in this respect.

Aspect of the Program	Strong (1)	Fair (2)	Weak (3)
1. Is the school staff encouraged to become familiar with the different types of neighborhoods and homes from which students come?			
2. Does the orientation program for new teachers include an opportunity to observe the different types of neighborhoods and homes served by the school?			
3. Does the staff recognize the different socioeconomic, racial, and religious groups from which students come and make an attempt to gain familiarity with the special adjustment problems of young people from these groups?			
4. Does the staff have some familiarity with the economic structure of the community, its important businesses and industries,			

and the kinds of occupations followed by its citizens?

5. Are studies of important aspects of community life made periodically in order to better fit the program of the school to the needs of the community?

6. Does the guidance staff have a listing of all services provided to young people by community agencies and organizations?

7. Have referral procedures been worked out so that individual young people may obtain services from which they might benefit?

8. Does the community coordinate its services to youth through some type of coordinating or community council?

9. If such an organization exists, does the school staff know about and participate in its program?

10. Does the community have a plan for gradually strengthening its program of services for young people?

Student Appraisal of Guidance Services. On page 176 the suggestion was made that students should be asked to evaluate the guidance services rendered them. The following form may be used for that purpose.

GUIDANCE INVENTORY FOR STUDENTS

Do not sign your name unless you desire to do so. Answer the questions by putting a check mark in the proper place or in your own words when asked to express an opinion. Use the margins or the reverse side of the sheet for comments that you may wish to make.

Name .... Date ....

Year: freshman ...., sophomore ...., junior ...., senior ....

General Information

How many years have you attended this school? one ...., two ...., three ...., four ....

Has your counselor interviewed you at least once a year? yes ...., no ....

If not, in which year were you not interviewed? first _____ , second _____ , third _____ , fourth _____ .

If you were not interviewed, did you have any other contact with a counselor in class or out of class? yes _____ , no _____ .

Studies

Were studies a difficulty for you always? _____ , sometimes? _____ , never? _____ .

If you did have difficulties with your studies, did you know that you could get guidance in study habits? yes _____ , no _____ .

If and when you failed, were you counseled by your teacher? _____ , the prefect of studies? _____ , a counselor? _____ , no one? _____ .

In difficulties with studies or of other kinds, did you voluntarily ask someone for help? yes _____ , no _____ .

In forecasting (choosing the courses to take) have you regularly sought the guidance of your teacher? _____ , the prefect of studies? _____ , your counselor? _____ , someone else? _____ , no one? _____ .

Did you know that a counselor had been appointed for you? yes _____ , no _____ .

Have you sought help from your counselor frequently? _____ , occasionally? _____ , never? _____ .

Have you been satisfied with the guidance of your counselor or registration-room teacher always? _____ , sometimes? _____ , never? _____ .

If not, state why you thought the assistance insufficient. _____

Do you think that guidance in your studies by the entire school staff has been adequate? yes _____ , no _____ .

If not, state what is lacking and what might be done to improve school guidance in studies. _____

Home Life

Is your home life happy all the time? _____ , most of the time? _____ , sometimes? _____ , never? _____ .

Did you know that, if there were difficulties at home, you could get help through school guidance, your religion classes, or your counselor? yes _____ , no _____ .

In your home problems have you sought help from your counselor or from someone else in the school? yes _____ , no _____ , did not need help _____ .

Did you find this help and guidance satisfactory? yes _____ , no _____ , did not need help _____ .

Religious Problems and Practices

Have you maintained or acquired regularity in your religious duties during your high-school years? yes _____ , no _____ .

Have you improved in regularity and received the sacraments more frequently since you came to high school? yes _____ , no _____ .

Has school guidance helped you keep up or improve your practice of religion to a great extent? _____ , to some extent? _____ , not at all? _____ .

If you were helped at all, were you helped most by your counselor? _____ , your registration-room teacher? _____ , the religion class? _____ , the retreat? _____ , none of these? _____ .

If you were helped most by someone else, state by whom. _____

Do you think that school guidance could and should do more to help toward the practice of religion? yes _____ , no _____ .

If your answer is yes, what would you suggest for more guidance? _____

In regard to good morals, particularly honesty and purity, do you think school guidance has been adequate? yes _____ , no _____ .

If you have been helped to keep good morals, were you helped most by your counselor? _____ , your registration-room teacher? _____ , the religion class? _____ , the retreat? _____ , none of these? _____ .

If you were helped most by someone else, state by whom. _____

What suggestion would you offer for more guidance in morals? _____

Has the opportunity for going to confession at school helped you to regularity in receiving this sacrament? yes _____ , no _____ .

Do you think that going to confession at school has made you careless about going to confession in your parish during vacation or at other times? yes _____ , no _____ .

Has school guidance assisted you to greater awareness of the value of religion and of the importance of the best development of your soul life? yes _____ , no _____ .

Choice of Vocation

Do you intend to follow as your vocation the priestly life? _____ , the religious life? _____ , the married life? _____ , single life in the world? _____ . Are you undecided? yes _____ , no _____ .

As regards your occupation or profession, have you made a definite and final decision? _____ , only a tentative decision? _____ , no decision? _____ .

In thinking about your vocation or occupation were you helped most by your parents? _____ , your counselor? _____ , registration-room guidance? _____ , career talks? _____ , some other person or thing? _____ .

If you were helped most by some other person or thing, tell by whom or by what. _____

In making your decisions have you sought out a source of guidance at the school? yes _____ , no _____ .

Did you attend the career conferences regularly? _____ , only occasionally? _____ , never? _____ .

Did you find your teachers and classes a help in making a vocational and occupational decision? yes _____ , no _____ .

Have you discussed your decisions with your counselor? yes _____ , no _____ .

If you have not as yet reached a decision, are you nevertheless satisfied with the guidance of your counselor? yes _____ , no _____ .

If not satisfied, do you think that your counselor lacked interest in you and your problems? yes _____ , no _____ .

If not satisfied, do you think your counselor failed to give you the necessary information? yes _____ , no _____ .

In regard to vocations to the priesthood and the religious life, do you think the school gives too much attention? _____ , the right amount of attention? _____ , not enough attention? _____ .

Do you think that guidance to the priesthood and the religious life is over-stressed by your parents? _____ , by your counselor? _____ , in the registration room? _____ , in religion classes? _____ , during retreat? _____ .

Do you think that guidance to the priesthood and the religious life is neglected by your parents? _____ , by your counselor? _____ , in the registration room? _____ , in religion classes? _____ , during retreat? _____ .

Have you ever been personally asked if you have a possible vocation to the priesthood or religious life? yes _____ , no _____ .

Do you think that marriage as a vocation is overstressed by your parents? _____ , by your counselor? _____ , in the registration room? _____ , in religion classes? _____ , during retreat? _____ .

Do you think that marriage as a vocation is not sufficiently emphasized by your parents? _____ , by your counselor? _____ , in the registration room? _____ , in religion classes? _____ , during retreat? _____ .

Are you satisfied with the amount of information on vocations and occupations available to you at school? yes _____ , no _____ .

What suggestions would you offer for improved vocational and occupational guidance at school? _____

Teacher Appraisal of Guidance and Guidance Services. This final questionnaire or check list is intended to obtain from teachers an expression of opinion concerning their own preparation for guidance work, a statement as to what they do, a criticism of the existing program, and suggestions for its improvement.

GUIDANCE INVENTORY FOR SCHOOL PERSONNEL

Do not sign your name unless you desire to do so. Answer the questions by checking the right word or expression, or in your own words when asked to express an opinion.

Preparation

Have you had any college courses preparing you for guidance work? yes _____ , no _____ .

If your answer was yes, what courses? _____

Do you read any current guidance literature? yes _____ , no _____ .

If your answer was yes, what? _____

Do you feel there is any utility in such reading? yes _____ , no _____ .

Do you feel that your professional background is adequate preparation for the guidance required of you as a teacher, counselor, or staff member? yes _____ , no _____ .

As a Teacher

Do you consult the cumulative records of your students frequently? _____ , occasionally? _____ , never? _____ .

Do you make it an objective to tell students of the vocational and occupational opportunities associated with the subject you are teaching frequently? .... , occasionally? .... , never? ....

Do you make it a point to refer personality or behavior problems to the guidance department or the counselor frequently? .... , occasionally? .... , never? ....

If you have referred problems to the guidance department or the counselor, have you been satisfied by the response on the part of the student always? .... , sometimes? .... , rarely? .... , never? ....

If you have not been satisfied, do you feel that the lack of response was due to failure of the counselor to interview the student? .... , to misguided counseling? .... , to failure of the student to cooperate? ....

Do you readily assume guidance responsibilities in regard to your students, particularly in the case of failures, always? .... , usually? .... , occasionally? .... , never? ....

Do you feel that enough is being done to help failing students by the prefects of students? .... , by counselors? .... , by yourself? ....

Do you feel that sufficient effort is being made for the development of the gifted student by the prefects of studies? .... , by counselors? .... , by regular teachers? .... , by those responsible for the curriculum? .... , by yourself? ....

As regards behavior problems, do you feel that whatever correction or improvement could be expected is being achieved by deans of discipline, counselors, and others? yes .... , no ....

Summarize your criticisms of teacher guidance in this school, and add your suggestions for the improvement of the work. ....

As a Group-Guidance Leader

Do you feel that the registration-room or homeroom guidance period is an effective means of group guidance? yes .... , no ....

Do you think that registration-room or homeroom guidance gives a Christian tone to the day? yes .... , no ....

Do you think that group guidance should be given in some other way? yes .... , no .... If your answer was yes, in what way? ....

Do you regularly use the full time allotted for guidance work? yes .... , no ....

Do students take part in the guidance period by questions, discussions, or reports? yes _____ , no _____ .

Do you think the ten-minute period is too short to be effective? yes _____ , no _____ .

Do you think one full period of guidance each week would be more effective? yes _____ , no _____ .

Do you look upon your religion classes as guidance work? yes _____ , no _____ .

Do you use regularly the guidance bulletin provided for the registration-room teacher? yes _____ , no _____ .

Do you feel that the material contained in the bulletin could be used elsewhere in the school with equal or greater effectiveness? yes _____ , no _____ .

If you have failed to use the guidance bulletin, is it because it is too long? _____ , it is too detailed? _____ , it is not suited to students? _____ , there are too many interruptions to make the bulletin effective? _____ , because of other reasons? _____ .

As regards the response of students to the bulletin, is interest generally shown? _____ . Does the bulletin often provoke discussion? _____ . Is lack of interest usually evident? _____ .

If you think the present group-guidance program can be improved, please offer your suggestions. _____

As a Counselor

Is the percentage of your counselees whom you interview at least once a year 100? _____ , 75? _____ , 50? _____ , 25 or less? _____ .

Do you ordinarily consult the cumulative records before interviewing a counselee? yes _____ , no _____ .

Is the average time you spend on an interview 40 minutes? _____ , 30 minutes? _____ , 20 minutes? _____ , less than 20 minutes? _____ .

If you do not see all counselees at least once a year, is the reason too many counselees? _____ , a heavy teaching load? _____ , extraclass responsibilities at school? _____ , outside school work and duties? _____ , other reasons? _____ .

Is the usual reaction of students in interviews responsive? _____ , noncommunicative? _____ , suspicious? _____ , indifferent? _____ , other? _____ .

Do you think that your counseling is most effective in the field of home problems? .... , personality problems? .... , study difficulties? .... , moral problems? .... , vocational problems? .... , other problems? ....

Do you ask each counselee about the possibility of his having a religious vocation or inquire if he has considered it? yes .... , no ....

If not, what prompts you not to ask? ....

Do you make out a report for each interview and deliver it to the department? yes .... , no ....

If you do not make out a report for each interview, is your failure due to lack of time? .... , the difficulty of saying just what you think should be said? .... , the confidential nature of interviews? .... , the feeling that the record will serve no useful purpose? .... , other reasons? ....

If there are any areas or features of counseling, such as study habits, sex problems, social life, vocational guidance, and so forth, in which you feel an inadequacy or a lack of necessary information, state what they are. ....

Summarize your criticisms of the counseling program and add your suggestions for the improvement of this work. ....

INDEX